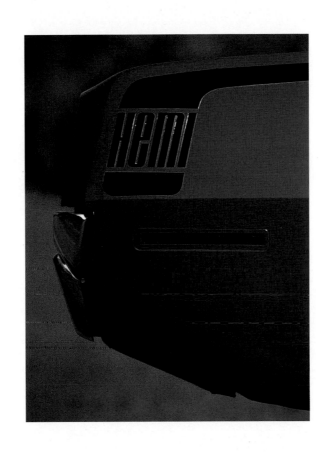

MUSCLE CARS

Mike Mueller, Dan Lyons, Jason Scott, and Robert Genat

BARNES & NOBLE

NEW YORK

This edition published by Barnes & Noble, Inc., by arrangement with MBI Publishing Company

2006 Barnes & Noble Books

M 10 9 8 7 6 5 4 3 2 1

ISBN-13: 978-0-7607-8171-5
ISBN-10: 0-7607-8171-0

Pontiac Muscle Cars © Mike Mueller, 1994
The Muscle Car © Dan Lyons & Jason Scott, 2002
Hemi Muscle Cars © Robert Genat, 1999
Chevy Muscle Cars © Mike Mueller, 1994

Printed in China

On the cover: Perhaps Detroit's most popular muscle car, Chevrolet's Super Sport Chevelle reached the pinnacle in SS 454 form for 1970. In base trim, the SS 454 featured the 360 horsepower LS5 454 cubic inch big-block. The king of the hill, however, was the LS6, which pumped out 450 horsepower worth of mid-sized muscle.

On the frontispiece: These "hockey stick" stripes appear on the rear quarter panels of this 1970 'Cuda and don't leave anything to the imagination. In no uncertain terms, they shout to the world that the 'Cuda is powered by Chrysler's most formidable engine – the Hemi. The relatively compact E-bodied 'Cuda, created to challenge the Mustang and Camaro, is the fastest of the Hemi-powered street cars.

On the title page: Plymouth's introduction of the Road Runner in 1968 was big news. The finely trimmed GTX was still available, and it featured the same hood as the Road Runner with side-facing nonfunctional scoops.

On the back cover: There is no mistaking the one-of-a-kind profile of the 1970 Plymouth Superbird. With it's elongated front fascia and huge rear wing, it dominated NASCAR stock car racing during the 1970 season. It was so dominant that it was banned the following year. The street version never caught the public's attention and sales stagnated. Today, it is one of the rarest and most sought after Hemi muscle cars ever built.

CONTENTS

The Muscle Car

Chevy Muscle Cars

Hemi Muscle Cars

Pontiac Muscle Cars

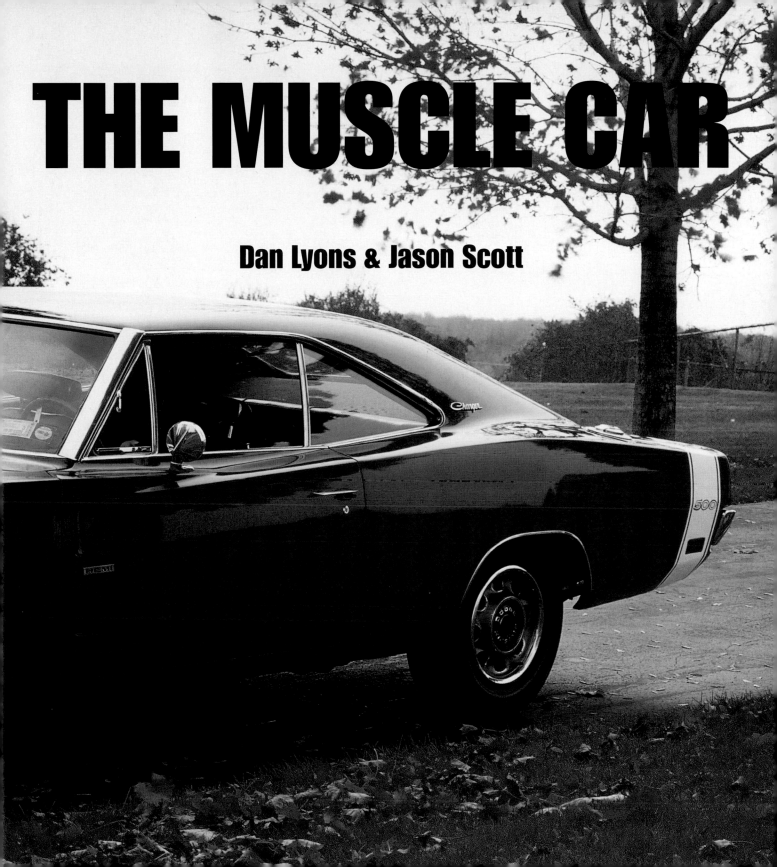

THE MUSCLE CAR

Dan Lyons & Jason Scott

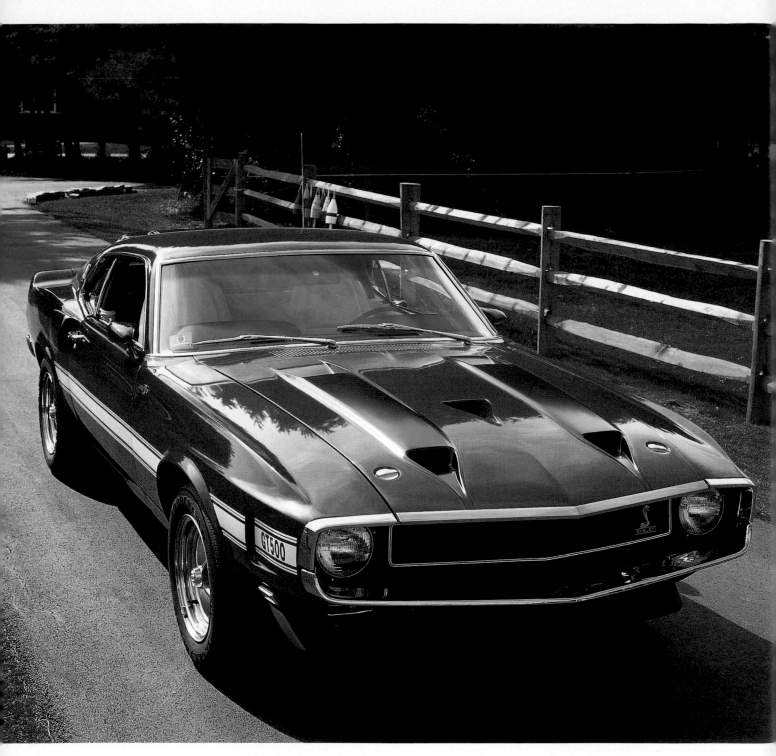

INTRODUCTION

American musclecars were once plentiful and abundant, like many of the world's once-great creatures. But it's been 30 years since most of the vintage musclecars were produced, and while they're hardly extinct now, they are an endangered species. Time, traffic accidents, rising fuel costs, and even governmental legislation are all working against our beloved musclecars.

Layed out on the pages that follow are some of the most intriguing musclecars ever produced. But the intention of this book isn't to be the definitive work on "the ultimate musclecars of all time"—that's a subject far too debatable for the various GM, Ford, Mopar, and AMC fans to find much agreement on. Instead, what this book was designed to do is to help preserve the memory of some of the cars that shaped automotive history, that altered how we thought about our cars, and that changed people's lives.

Like any "best of" list, we were forced to make some hard decisions about which cars to include, about which cars were "milestone" material. A car didn't have to be ultra-rare to be worthy of inclusion; nor did it have to be ultrapopular. Most of the vehicles you'll find on the following pages are from somewhere in between those two extremes. Some may have been almost entirely overlooked in comparison to other offerings at the time, but each has its own special characteristics or traits that earned it milestone status.

Cars such as the 1964 Pontiac GTO and the 1965 Mustang are obvious choices for any milestone compilation. The 1971 Plymouth Road Runner, however, is far less obvious yet played an important role in the evolution of the musclecar. And the 1969 AMC AMX made the cut because it helped (if only for a while) save an entire car company from an untimely demise.

This book is about the dedication and against-all-odds spirit that put some of the roughest, toughest musclecars in the hands of enthusiastic buyers who appreciated brute force over creature comforts.

Ultimately, we hope you enjoy reading about these memorable musclecars as much as we enjoyed reliving old memories and putting them down in photos and words for you.

—Dan Lyons
—Jason Scott

The 1970 Shelby GT-500 was the last of a great breed of musclecar. Fitted with a 335-horsepower 428-ci V-8, this wickedly fast musclecar was one of the fastest of the era.

CHAPTER 1

General Motors

Charge of the High-Performance Brigade

There's a saying that you should "lead, follow, or get out of the way." At the beginning of the 1960s, the Pontiac Motor Division of General Motors was a follower, both in the showrooms and on race tracks. Pontiacs were excellent vehicles, to be sure, but they weren't particularly exceptional.

When John Z. DeLorean was placed in the division's highest post, as general manager, he began a rapid transformation that would put Pontiac in a leadership position and leave its sister divisions and other manufacturers scrambling to catch up.

DeLorean was quick to realize that the booming youth market wasn't satisfied with the cars that had pleased their parents during the previous decade. These younger buyers wanted smaller, sportier cars with contemporary styling. And they wanted better performance—especially the male buyers.

A young advertising executive assigned to Pontiac's account, Jim Wangers, pointed out to DeLorean that all the company had to do to attract the young, male buyers was to do for them what they had been doing on their own for years: swapping big-car engines into smaller cars to achieve a better power-to-weight ratio.

Wangers pitched a concept to DeLorean that called for installing Pontiac's 389 V-8 into the midsize LeMans/Tempest. Wangers called the car the "GTO," after the famous Ferrari of the same name. The project required little investment—after all, the company already made all the components except the emblems—and DeLorean gave it an immediate green light. And in doing so, Pontiac created the musclecar.

When the GTO debuted in the fall of 1963 as a 1964 model, it was—as Wangers had predicted—an immediate success. Combining the potent 389 (which came standard with 325 horses, but could be had with 348 with a trick-looking trio of two-barrel carbs) with the LeMans' handsome good looks was

Musclecar enthusiasts generally credit Pontiac's 1964 as the first musclecar. It was the first mass-produced car to follow the old hot rodder's practice: stuff a big engine into a small car and go win some races.

just the thing to get a young man's heart racing—especially when you factored in such hot-rodding mainstays as red-stripe tires, a Hurst shifter, dual exhaust, and other performance parts.

And by pricing the GTO affordably, Pontiac convinced many buyers that it was easier to buy a finished GTO off the showroom floor than to invest comparable dollars, *plus* a lot of time and effort, into building up their own older car.

The GTO was, quite simply, the right car, with the right stuff, for the right price, at the right time. But Pontiac knew how quickly buyers' interests change.

As exciting and successful as the original GTO was, it wasn't for everyone—nor was it an all-around success for Pontiac, which realized relatively little profit from the often stripped-down cars. And while part of the appeal of the original GTO was its bare-bones, not-included-unless-it-improves-performance nature, a few years later, when buyers of those original models got around to trading them in for new models, most had progressed to a point in life where creature comforts and image were at least as important as performance.

Not to worry—Pontiac was still ahead of the game. In 1969 it introduced a special GTO named "the Judge," which bolstered the car's image with attention-grabbing paint and graphic treatments. Though the Judge wasn't an immediate success, it made an indelible mark on the buying public's mind. A stripped-down musclecar no longer captured the younger driver's imagination. Now buyers wanted to take the wheel of a vehicle all onlookers would recognize as something special.

Four years later, in 1973, Pontiac would again foreshadow performance cars of the future when it redeveloped the musclecar to meet the particular challenges and needs of the day. Refining the popular Firebird line, Pontiac introduced the Super Duty Firebirds, engineered to perform on low-octane, low-lead fuels in order to meet federally mandated emissions requirements. Meanwhile, the cars' handling and braking were improved to broaden the overall performance "envelope." The Super Duty Firebirds—still plenty powerful—were much more politically and environmentally correct than any musclecar before

them, and set the course that all successors would have to follow.

No other manufacturer was as adaptable—let alone as insightful—as Pontiac at building muscle-cars. And no other manufacturer had as much impact on shaping the musclecar era.

1964 Pontiac GTO

In 1962, cars such as the Chevrolet Impala SS 409, Chrysler 300, and Ford Galaxie 500 all offered big V-8s in a two-door sedan. But those cars were not big sellers because they appealed to a maturing market. Although this group was still interested in high performance, they had other priorities on their mind, including house payments, raising kids, and being a responsible spouse. These buyers would sit in the SS 409 for a moment of dreaming—then drive away in the plain-Jane Impala.

America's youth market, however, was booming thanks to a postwar population bulge that began reaching driving age in the early 1960s. Devoid of adult responsibilities, younger buyers were free to pursue whatever struck their fancy. For teenage and

1964 Pontiac GTO

Specifications

Body	Base Price	Units Built
Coupe	$2,852	7,384
Hdtp.	$2,963	18,422
Conv.	$3,081	6,644
Total		*32,450*

Engine

Std.	325-hp 389-ci 4-bbl. V-8
Opt.	348-hp 389-ci 6-bbl. V-8

1/4-mile (typical)

ET	15.5 secs.
Speed	91 mph

The GTO's "big engine" was a 389 Pontiac V-8 equipped with a trio of two-barrel Rochester carbs. With a hot cam and dual exhaust, the engine put out 348 horsepower! Most stock 1964 GTOs were fast enough to turn quarter-mile times in the high 14- or low 15-second range.

The GTO was reasonably well appointed with performance equipment inside and out. Externally, it had dual exhaust, red-stripe tires, and the mark of distinctiion—GTO emblems.

twenty-something American males, that meant one thing: performance.

This crowd, who had grown up during the days of hot rodding, knew that as fast as the full-size muscle machines were, smaller, lighter cars with the same engines would deliver better performance. And more than a few kids took it upon themselves to create those kinds of cars.

Fortunately, Detroit wasn't asleep at the wheel. The automakers took note of the small car/big engine movement that was growing in popularity, and it responded. Pontiac was first out of the gate, due to the tireless efforts of marketing exec Jim Wangers and support from the very top of Pontiac's food chain, president John Z. DeLorean. Wangers sold DeLorean on the concept of dropping the full-size Pontiac's high-output 389 into the midsize Tempest, and throwing in the usual assortment of performance amenities young buyers were likely to want or add— a floor-shifted four-speed manual transmission (or optional automatic), dual exhaust, twin-scooped hood, and other assorted goodies.

The swap was straightforward from a manufacturing standpoint, given that the 389 featured the same external dimensions as the 326 that was readily available in the Tempest. And as the young hot rodders knew, shedding weight was as effective as adding power when it came to acceleration contests.

Wangers and DeLorean settled on the name "GTO," which they pilfered from the race-winning Ferrari of the day, the "Grand Tourismo Omologato" — Italian-speak for a car approved by the FIA sanctioning body for Grand Touring competition.

Of course, Pontiac's GTO wasn't exactly designed to compete with its Ferrari namesake— though one popular magazine of the day did arrange just such a shootout and picked the Pontiac as the better bang for the buck. But where the Pontiac really shone was in stoplight-to-stoplight match-ups. And by virtue of its better power-to-weight ratio, the mid-size Pontiac was more than a match for nearly any production vehicle to date, except perhaps top-optioned Corvettes.

Even in the hands of amateur drivers, the GTO was capable of low-15-second quarter-mile trips right off the showroom floor. And with minimal tuning and preparation effort, 14-second dashes were doable—all for a price that was well within the grasp of any red-blooded American boy or girl.

The GTO's combination of price, performance, and dynamite styling proved irresistible with the buying public: 32,450 GTOs were sold in 1964. Far more important than its end-of-year tally, however, was the GTO's impact on the automotive industry and performance enthusiasts. It ushered in the musclecar era and kicked off a horsepower war that would last for nearly a decade.

In the end, the 1964 GTO became the benchmark against which all later musclecars would be compared. And that's an admirable position to be in—especially when you're as well equipped as the GTO to take on all challengers.

1970 Pontiac GTO Judge

Performance-car enthusiasts were a fickle bunch. In 1963, Pontiac introduced its GTO to rave reviews and unprecedented acceptance. The car's combination of high-performance engine, attractive midsize styling, and moderate price was exactly right for the times.

But while auto manufacturers can produce and sell thousands of low-priced cars, those aren't the cars that make for outstanding profits. Pontiac realized this earlier than most manufacturers, and so by 1969, Pontiac was working hard to reinvent the musclecar.

Ironically, this higher-profit musclecar grew out of a lower-priced little brother to the GTO, code-named "the E.T.," which was intended to compete with Plymouth's budget-priced Road Runner. As the project progressed, however, one change after another pushed the car out of the bargain basement.

Pontiac's general manager, John DeLorean, insisted that the model be a GTO, and that no GTO would come with anything less than a 400-ci engine, so the E.T.'s 350 was axed. The E.T.'s planned LeMans chrome front bumper also went back to the parts shelves, in favor of the GTO's heavier, costlier Endura rubber-coated snout. Likewise, the stripped interior—complete with rubber floormats—was deemed too sparse, so a GTO's interior supplanted

Judge interiors were comfortable places to pass sentence on other musclecars. Aside from usual GTO items, like the wood wheel and woodgrain applique, special items like the Hurst T-handle shifter made the Judge even more inviting.

1970 Pontiac GTO Judge

Specifications

Body

	Base Price	Units Built
Hdtp.	$3,604	3,629
Conv.	$3,829	168
Total		*3,797*

Engine

Std	366-hp 400-ci 4-bbl. V-8, (Ram Air III)
Opt.	370-hp 400-ci 4-bbl. V-8 (Ram Air IV)
	360-hp 455-ci 4-bbl. V-8 (455 H.O.)

1/4-mile (typical)

E.T.	14.4 secs.
Speed	98 mph

When Pontiac showed off the new Judge package in 1969, it reinvented the musclecar and gave enthusiasts a glimpse of the future image of high performance. The body was revised and adapted to the new 1970 sheet metal, as this 1970 Judge shows.

Though largely a styling package, the Judge's base engine was the Ram Air III 400 with 366 horsepower. Optional engines included the 370-horse Ram Air IV and the 360-horse 455.

it. By the time the changes were done, the E.T. had moved considerably upscale—and had even been renamed after a popular segment on a TV sitcom of the time: The Judge.

The initial 2,000 GTO Judges were equipped nearly identically, right down to the paint scheme: a bright-orange hue named, oddly, Carousel Red, plus bold red, yellow, and blue striping and decals. Not only was the engine not a 350, it wasn't even a base GTO's 400. The base Judge engine was the Ram Air III 400 with 366 horsepower. The only optional engine was the Ram Air IV 400, which was (under-) rated at 370 horsepower. The mill featured large, round-port cylinder heads, free-flowing cast-iron exhaust manifolds, a high-rise, two-piece aluminum intake manifold, and a large Rochester QuadraJet four-barrel carburetor.

The 1973–1974 Super Duty Firebirds had superb styling, respectable acceleration, exceptional handling, competent braking, and luxurious comfort. In essence, Pontiac yet again redefined the musclecar. The 455-ci four-barrel V-8 had a mellowed 8.0:1 compression ratio and produced 250 net horsepower at 4,000 rpm, but it was still fast.

Pontiac ultimately sold just under 7,000 Judge-equipped GTOs in 1969. Despite that disappointing unit production, the Judge returned in 1970, featuring updated sheet metal, graphics, and engines, as did "lesser" GTO models. The revised 1970 nose did away with the attractive, but complex and trouble-prone hidden headlamps of 1968–69, and used a split grille that was almost indistinguishable from the new-for-1970 Firebird beak. The new fenders, door skins, and quarter panels sported sharp creasing for a tough, chiseled look. On Judge models, the side striping was changed from 1969's long nose-to-C-pillar decals to simple "eyebrows" that were applied to the fender and quarter-panel creases over the wheel openings.

Underhood, Judge options—like those of a standard GTO—expanded with the addition of two 455-ci engines, now that GM Corporate had lifted its 400-inch engine limit for midsize car lines. Both the base 455 and the H.O. (high-output) version offered a considerable torque boost over the 400s. But the top engine for racers was still the Ram Air IV 400, which retained its laughable 370-horsepower rating. Of course, the big news in engines was about the one that got away: the Ram Air V. With massive tunnel-port heads and a completely revised bottom end, the RA-V 400 was reportedly good for over 500 horsepower with just a set of headers and a tune-up. Alas, the RA-V was only built in limited quantities for testing purposes, though a few are rumored to have escaped through GM's Service Parts Operations crate motor engine program.

Despite the Ram Air and H.O. engines, the GTO Judge was hardly a match for the Hemi Mopars, the Cobra-Jet Fords, or even GM's own LS-6 Chevelle, Stage I Buicks, and W-30 Olds 4-4-2. Still, thanks to its outstanding styling, Pontiac's GTO Judge succeeded in reinventing the musclecar, by ushering in an era when image was as important as performance.

1974 Pontiac Super Duty Firebirds

By all accounts, Pontiac had no business producing the 1973 and 1974 Super Duty Firebirds. The musclecar market was all but dead (thanks to the insurance industry, OPEC, and good ol' Uncle Sam), and GM's engineering team faced an uphill battle to convert an aging line of powertrains and vehicles for the new, government-mandated reduced-emissions output and more stringent safety standards.

Quite simply, Pontiac didn't have the brainpower to spare on creating a low-volume, gas-guzzling, emissions-belching performance machine. Moreover, the 455-ci Super Duty engine alone called for dozens of new components designed specifically for it. But Pontiac knew that musclecars weren't really dead; they weren't even dying. They were evolving. And just as it had created the musclecar nearly a decade before, Pontiac was determined to re-create it for a new era.

Interestingly enough, the Super Duty was quite aptly named, for it wasn't so much a powerhouse engine—sure, the SD-455 made 310 horsepower (down to 290 for 1974)—but rather it was engineered specifically for durability.

From its beefy four-bolt main bearing caps (on all five bulkheads), through its high-strength cast crankshaft and forged-steel connecting rods, up to its incredible, free-flowing cylinder heads, the Super Duty 455 was built from the ground up to

1974 Pontiac Super Duty Firebird

Specifications

Model	Base Price	Units Built
Formula	$4,334*	58
Trans-Am	$5,024*	943
Total		1,001

Engine

290-hp 455-ci 4-bbl. V-8

1/4-mile (typical)

ET	14.8 secs.
Speed	96 mph

*model base price plus SD-455 engine option

both produce and withstand twice its standard power output. With careful modifications and select parts replacements, the Super Duty could be massaged to generate measurably more power than it came with from the factory.

Fortunately for most buyers, what the Super Duty Firebirds came with from the factory was plenty exciting already. OK, maybe 310—or even the later 290—horsepower doesn't sound that impressive, but compared to other cars of its day, it was positively excessive. Offerings from Ford, Chrysler, and even other GM divisions boasted of power outputs that were only half to two-thirds the power of the SD-455.

More important, however, the Super Duty Firebirds proved their worth on the streets and tracks. Able to cruise down the quarter-mile in the 14-second bracket, Super Duty Firebirds were able to run with the best musclecars—in factory trim or otherwise.

Yet climbing inside a Super Duty Firebird was—as with any Firebird—a delightful experience for the senses matched by few other musclecars. The bucket seats provided a comfortable, supportive position from which to grasp the sports steering wheel and the floor-mounted shifter—controlling either a Turbo Hydramatic 400 automatic or a close-ratio Muncie four-speed manual transmission. A raft of gauges in the engine-turned instrument panel allowed you to remain well informed about the health of the vehicle—and to whatever jeopardy you might choose to subject your license.

Whether Pontiac's engineers knew it or not, with the Super Duty Firebirds the company was showing the world that performance could coincide with safety, environmental responsibility, and even economy. The Super Duty Firebirds were, at once, the last hurrah for the musclecar era that was, and the first of a new breed of modern musclecars that were yet to be.

CHEVROLET: A REPUTATION BUILT ON HIGH PERFORMANCE

Chevrolet had a lot going for it during the musclecar era. It had the Chevelle, Camaro, Chevy II/Nova, and, of course, the Corvette. It had such exceptional engines as the L78 396 and L72 427 big-blocks plus a host of potent small-blocks, highlighted by the LT-1 350. It certainly had the marketing to let the public know about its cars. And then there was that little issue of price: as General Motors' "entry-level" division, Chevrolets were priced to sell—even the high-performance models and options. The beauty

The Super Duty 455 engine was a transitional engine, and it demonstrated that traditional musclecar engines could be updated with then-modern technology to produce excellent power and reduced emissions.

The 1974 Super Duty Trans-Am featured one of the most comfortable and functional muscle car interiors. High back bucket seats featured solid foam with integral springs. The Rally Gauge cluster contained speedometer, engine temperature, oil pressure, voltmeter gauges, and rally clock.

of the system, for Chevrolet, was that it sold a lot of vehicles, and the more it sold, the less it could charge for them.

Chevy had something else going for it, too: history. The company's namesake, Louis Chevrolet, was a well-known racer (of Buicks) when the company was founded and Chevrolet made sure the company was very active in motorsports. By the 1950s, that involvement had grown to include NASCAR stock car racing and extensive drag racing activities. And in 1955, Chevrolet took performance to the streets with its revolutionary "small-block" V-8, a relatively lightweight and compact 265-ci powerhouse that put out as much as 190 horsepower, in special-order trim. Just two years later, the engine had evolved to 283 cubic inches and 283 horsepower when equipped with a Rochester Fuel Injection system.

The Chevy small-block V-8 became an instant hit with hot rodders. This popularity attracted the attention and efforts of such aftermarket performance parts manufacturers, as Edelbrock, Holley, Offenhauser, and others, which produced a wide array of components to improve the engine's power, durability, and appearance. Little did anyone know at the time that 50 years later, the basic small-block Chevrolet engine would not only still exist, it would be the most popular performance engine with the largest assortment of aftermarket equipment of any engine available.

In the 1960s, Chevrolet introduced the Super Sport Impala. With power coming from an overgrown, 409-ci version of Chevy's "W" motor (an unrelated precursor to the Mark IV big-blocks) putting out as much as 430 horsepower in 1963, the Impala SS was a formidable competitor on drag strips and boulevards all across America.

But Chevrolet's first "musclecar" didn't come until 1964, when the midsize Chevelle SS debuted. With a 327-ci small-block under the hood, the Chevelle SS was at a disadvantage in horsepower and torque when compared to cars such as the GTO. Chevy corrected this deficiency in 1965 with a limited run of 201 Chevelle Super Sports equipped with the Corvette's L-78 396.

Despite less power than some of its rivals, Super Sport Chevelles sold to countless thousands of power-hungry Americans throughout the 1960s and early 1970s. Add to that the sales of Camaros, Corvettes, Impalas, Biscaynes, El Caminos, Chevy IIs, and Novas and it's easy to understand how high-performance Chevys made such a strong showing on the streets and at the race track. And thanks to sneaky methods of producing "unavailable" options under the guise of "Central Office Production Orders," or COPOs, Chevy produced some of the hottest, most outlandish vehicles ever unleashed on the American public.

But by 1971, the musclecar wars were all but over, having subsided just as quickly as they began. And while Chevy had survived the wars on the streets and race tracks, no manufacturer was able to withstand the onslaught of the federal government

1962 Chevrolet Impala SS

Specifications

Body	Base Price	Units Built
Coupe	$2,722.80*	
Conv.	$2,972.80*	
Total		99,311

Engine	
Std.	135-hp 235-ci 1-bbl. I-6
Opt.	170-hp 283-ci 2-bbl. V-8
	250-hp 327-ci 4-bbl. V-8
	300-hp 327-ci 4-bbl. V-8
	380-hp 409-ci 4-bbl. V-8
	409-hp 409-ci 4-bbl. V-8

1/4-mile (typical)

E.T.	14.7 secs.
Speed	96 mph

* model base price plus SS equipment option
† includes 15,019 cars equipped with 409-ci engine

The Impala SS 409 "W" engine was so inspiring that songs were written about it and races were won with it. The renowned V-8 was available with as much as 425 horsepower with dual four-barrel carbs.

The 1961–1964 Impala SS interior was comfortable and sporty, though hardly luxurious by today's standards. This 1963 model featured all-vinyl bucket seats, which weren't widely available.

and the insurance industry. Chevy continued to put up a good fight, with cars such as the Chevelle SS, Nova SS, Z28 Camaro, and the Corvette. But the Z28, 454 Corvette, and Chevelle SS all disappeared at the end of 1974 as Chevrolet quietly conceded defeat. It would be nearly 10 years before Chevrolet would again find itself in the business of building musclecars. But that's a story for another day. . . .

1962 Chevrolet Impala SS 409

Despite explosive performance improvements, 1950s automobiles are generally remembered more for their styling than whatever powerplant lay beneath their dramatic hoodlines.

By the dawn of the 1960s, however, the exciting designs of the 1950s had given way to longer, wider, and lower body styles that gave cars the appearance of being sleeker and faster. Of course, for the majority

of cars built in the early 1960s, that appearance was just that—an appearance. Under the hood, the early 1960s cars were generally powered by updated versions of the same engines that powered their 1950s ancestors, but which seldom provided the levels of performance their body designs implied.

Chevrolet's Impala Super Sport changed all that.

With the choice of an economical 327 small-block or thundering 409-ci version of the "W-motor" V-8—with as much as 425 horsepower!—the Impala SS was well equipped to prove it not only looked fast but was fast.

Though the SS package included improvements to the suspension and braking systems, plus various interior and exterior accoutrements, it was the lineup of W-motor engines that made the Impala SS legendary.

Introduced in 1958, the first W-motor displaced 348 cubic inches and pumped out 315 horsepower—more than enough to propel the two-ton Chevys of the day down the quarter-mile in 15 seconds at nearly 100 miles per hour. Attesting to the engine's exceptional design was the fact that it developed its power with only a single four-barrel carburetor, a relatively modest hydraulic camshaft, and few performance-tuned components. A welcome byproduct of the W-motor's mild-mannered engineering was its rock-solid reliability.

The 1962 Impala was available with the 409-ci W-motor that had debuted midyear in 1961. With twin Carter four-barrels sitting atop a dual-plane aluminum intake manifold, plus a high-lift, long-duration camshaft, high-domed pistons to increase compression, and unique free-flowing exhaust manifolds, the top-option 409 was capable of revving to 6,200 rpm. When put to the test on the drag strip, showroom-stock SS 409 Impalas could trip the timers in just over 15 seconds. With traditional drag racing preparation—induction and exhaust improvements

While Chevrolet's first high-performance engine was the 1955 265 "small-block," the 1962 Impala Super Sport was the company's first sedan to be packaged and marketed based on its performance merits.

and tires with more "bite"—runs in the 14-second range awaited. Chevrolet illustrated the performance possibilities by producing a limited number of lightweight 409 Impalas for competition in the NHRA's (National Hot Rod Association) Factory Experimental, or F/X, classes. With various aluminum body panels and brackets, and *sans* unnecessary items including sound deadener, radio, and heater equipment, the lightweight 1962 Impalas were exceptionally fast. And they were the predecessors of the famous 1963 Z11 Impalas, which featured even more radical weight-saving measures and a higher-output version of the 409 enlarged to 427 cubic inches—the NHRA's seven-liter limitation.

As impressive as the 1962 Impala SS 409s were, they were only marginally successful in dealers' showrooms, accounting for just 15,019 of the 1,424,008 Impalas built that year—a figure some historians attribute to the car's mismatched attributes. On the one hand, its Super Sport equipment appealed to performance enthusiasts, most of whom were among the booming youth market. On the other hand, the car's size and styling were decidedly more conservative, which made the car an easier sell to more mature buyers. Taken individually, either attribute had what was needed to attract its intended audience, but combining the options only succeeded in alienating both markets: the older buyers weren't generally interested in the performance (nor expense) of the Super Sport package, while the younger buyers were less than impressed by the body.

But the Impala SS 409 wasn't about production figures, it was about performance figures. And to that end, the model was a bona fide success, demonstrating beyond a doubt Chevrolet's ability to produce a car capable of dominating the competition both on the street and on the track.

1967 Chevelle Super Sport

The horsepower wars were well under way by the fall of 1966, as the 1967 models debuted in showrooms across the country. Would-be buyers flocked to dealerships to see the new models: Chevy's Camaro, Pontiac's Firebird, Ford's redesigned Mustang, Plymouth's Barracuda, and others.

While those models each garnered their share of sales, the traffic they drew to showrooms was perhaps equally important, because many of those shoppers wound up purchasing other models. All too often a buyer would come into the dealership lusting after one of the exciting new models, but drive home in an established model.

One of the most popular up-sells for Chevy dealers was to move customers from the 2+2 Camaro into the more practically sized Chevelle. And for buyers drawn in by Camaro's promises of power and performance, one look at a Super Sport Chevelle was enough to close the deal.

To the victor goes the spoils, and for those buyers whose victory was a 1967 Chevelle SS, the spoils included a 396-ci big-block V-8 with a minimum of 325 horsepower and a manual transmission. More adventurous buyers could select a 350-horse 396, or the top-dog 375-horse L78 396. The engines differed in terms of cylinder heads, camshafts, induction systems, pistons, crankshafts, connecting rods, and myriad smaller components.

The 325- and 350-horse 396s were inexpensive performance engines that thrived on street driving. Thanks to a hydraulic cam, cast-aluminum pistons, cast-iron intake, and Rochester QuadraJet four-barrel carburetor, the entry-level and midlevel 396s were virtually bulletproof yet powerful enough to hold their own when battling Hemi Mopars, Cobra Jet Fords, and Ram Air Pontiacs.

RPO L78—the 375-horse 396—on the other hand, was literally a purebred racing engine, based directly on the 1965 Corvette's 425-horse L78 396. The bottom end of the L78 featured a forged steel crankshaft, forged connecting rods, high-compression forged aluminum pistons, and four-bolt main bearing caps to keep everything securely in place through high-rpm (6,000 redline) activity. Farther up in the block, a solid-lifter, high-lift cam activated

Beginning in 1966, Chevy's SS-396 Chevelle brought affordable musclecar performance to the masses. The two-door hardtop went for $2,776 and the convertible was priced at $2,962. It was refined and improved as evidenced by this 1967 model.

The heart of the SS-396 Chevelle was the 396-ci Mark IV "big-block" V-8, which was available in three performance levels: 325, 350 (shown), and 375 horsepower.

Chevelle SS interiors were businesslike but comfortable with such options as vinyl-covered bucket seats, a wood steering wheel, a console, and more. The standard transmission was a fully synchronized three-speed manual transmission made by Borg-Warner.

1967 Chevrolet Chevelle SS-396

Specifications

Body	Base Price	Units Built
Hdtp.	$2,825	
Conv.	$3,033	
Total		63,006*

Engine

Std.	325-hp 396-ci 4-bbl. V-8 (L35)
Opt.	350-hp 396-ci 4-bbl. V-8 (L34)
	375-hp 396-ci 4-bbl. V-8 (L78)

1/4-mile (typical)

E.T.	14.8 secs.
Speed	99 mph

no exact breakdown of hardtops or convertibles exists; however, it is estimated that a maximum of 29,937 SS convertibles were built

oversize pushrods to open massive, 2.19-inch intake valves. Air and fuel flowed to those valves through a 780-cfm (cubic feet per minute) Holley four-barrel, a high-rise aluminum intake, and mammoth, nonrestrictive, rectangular intake ports instead of the smaller, oval ports in the garden-variety heads.

On race tracks, L78 Chevelles could run the quarter-mile in 14 seconds all day long, while the lower-powered 396s made for slightly slower 15-second runs. But it was on the street where the Super Sport Chevelles earned the distinction of being the ultimate musclecar for the masses: they were powerful, attractive, and most important, affordable. In 1967 alone, 63,006 Super Sport–equipped Chevelles were sold, bringing the total SS Chevelle population to 293,250 since their debut in 1964.

Chevelle remained a force to be reckoned with for the rest of the musclecar era, adding to its legendary models the 427-powered 1969 COPO Chevelles and the awesome 450-horsepower LS6 454 model of 1970.

While there were and would be more powerful and more unique Chevelles, none were any more important than the 1967 models, which redefined the musclecar.

1967 Chevrolet Camaro Z28

Chevrolet moved quickly when it saw the runaway success of Ford's Mustang. Within two years, it was able to finish its own "pony car," which had been code-named "Panther" until the eve of its introduction, when the name was abruptly changed to "Camaro."

Camaro was designed from the outset to suit a wide range of buyers, from those interested in an economical-but-stylish sporty car, to drag racers and even sports car racers. With two body styles—coupe and convertible—and roughly a dozen engines (nearly any of which could be had with a variety of transmissions), a Camaro could be ordered in a mind-boggling array of configurations. And there were scores of additional options from which to choose, allowing buyers to further personalize their Camaros.

While the SS package got all the press and attention as the "performance" options for Camaro, a little-publicized and unassuming option quietly established Camaro's reputation as a world-class competitor in the Sports Car Club of America (SCCA) Trans-Am racing series.

RPO Z28, which Chevrolet labeled as a "Special Performance Package," was the company's secret weapon to compete with Carroll Shelby's GT Mustangs for the manufacturers' championship. While racers would undoubtedly make their own specific modifications, Chevrolet provided a very complete—and *capable*—performance package, right from the factory.

The Z28 Camaro's high-winding 302-inch small-block engine is often cited as the option's principal feature; yet the car's suspension,

Z28-equipped Camaros received a special race-ready 302 small-block with a 4-inch bore and 3-inch stroke, which featured an 11.0:1 compression ratio that produced 290 horsepower. A special aluminum intake manifold, a Holley 800-cfm carburetor, a solid-lifter camshaft, forged crankshaft, forged pistons, premium connecting rods, an oil pan windage tray, and dual-exhaust were the essential go-fast goodies.

1967 Chevrolet Camaro Z28
Specifications

Body	Base Price	Units Built
Coupe	$2,930.10	602
Conv.	$3,167.10	1*
Total		602

Engine

290-hp 302-ci 4-bbl. V-8

1/4-mile (typical)

E.T.	15.1 secs.
Speed	95 mph

* one Z28 convertible is believed to have been built for a GM executive; it is not counted among the "official" production figure

Chevrolet rolled out its long-awaited Mustang fighter, the Camaro, in 1967. A few months after its release, the company quietly added an RPO Z28 option that turned the car into one of the finest-handling musclecars of its day. The list of high-performance equipment is long and distinguished—front disc brakes, dual exhaust, multi-leaf rear springs, and a plethora of others.

steering, and braking system improvements were of far more significance.

Z28-equipped Camaros received higher-rate coil springs up front and beefier leaf spring packs in the rear. Re-valved shocks complemented the new springs and helped minimize unwanted body movement, as did a larger-diameter front stabilizer bar. A unique "torque arm" that was connected to the right side of the rear axle housing helped control axle "wind-up" and wheel hop under hard acceleration, while a special, fast-ratio steering box made it easier to point the front wheels in the needed direction. Putting it all to the road were 15x6-inch steel Rally wheels wearing lower-profile, wider tires. This setup provided more traction and less sidewall deflection, which allowed for more predictable handling, especially during rapid transitions.

Racers know that good braking abilities are every bit as important as having a powerhouse engine, and so did Chevrolet. Every Z28 that left the factory had front disc brakes and revised rear drum brakes. Better brakes allowed racers to drive deeper into the corners, and then use the brakes harder to shed speed to safely navigate the turn.

As important as these other features were to the Z28's on-track success, the engine stands out as one of the top-performing small-blocks in musclecar history. Ironically, the engine was one of the primary reasons RPO Z28 was so easily overlooked by buyers. At only 302 cubic inches of displacement, the engine was perceived as a puny small-block in a big-block world. Few buyers chose to believe that the engine could be powerful, especially when a trio of 396-ci big-blocks were available in the SS models—for less money.

Chevrolet developed the 302 to meet the SCCA's strict 5-liter displacement rules for the Trans-Am series. The company had small-blocks that displaced 283, 327, and 350 inches, but nothing (at the time) in the 5-liter range. But it did have the makings of a 5-liter engine, if it creatively matched components. By mating a 3-inch-stroke crankshaft from a 283 with the 4-inch bores of a 327 or 350 cylinder block, the resulting engine would produce 302 cubic inches—just under the 305-cube maximum. As a bonus, the short stroke allowed the engine to rev to the moon

with a reasonable degree of durability, which was nearly perfect for racing use. A high-lift, long-duration camshaft, high-compression forged aluminum pistons, and free-flowing heads and induction system made for 290 horsepower and 290 foot-pounds of torque. More important, the engine was an ideal starting point for a true racing engine.

Not that the Z28 wasn't race-worthy right out of the box. In fact, the Z28 was so racy in stock form that Chevy was worried about letting inexperienced drivers get their hands on one. To prevent that, Chevrolet intentionally overlooked the Z28 option in its advertising and promotional materials, and even priced the option to minimize the chance that curious shoppers would select it.

Conversely, Chevrolet did what it could to ensure that racers were well informed of the Z28's many virtues. The presentations were good enough to rack up 602 sales of Z28s in 1967, several of which went to Roger Penske's racing team for driver Mark Donahue to pilot. And pilot them Donahue did—to within an inch of nabbing the manufacturers' championship, ultimately losing to the Mustang.

The original Z28 built a reputation that has helped the Camaro withstand the test of time, surviving from those early days through more than three decades, thrilling and satisfying drivers all the while—achievements certainly deserving of milestone status.

1967 Corvette Sting Ray

The 1967 Corvette is not the car Chevrolet had in mind. The all-new third-generation Corvette was due to be released as a 1967 model, which would have cut the "midyear" Corvette's reign to just four years—1963 through 1966. But when Zora Duntov insisted the new car go back to engineering to improve its quality before launch, Chevy had to extend the Sting Ray an extra year.

It's pure irony that the resulting 1967 Corvette would be deemed by most enthusiasts to be the best of the breed.

With no time to retool, Chevy was forced to make only minor changes to the 1966 model for another year of service. Externally, stylists removed

Corvette interiors were hardly standard musclecar fare. Rich materials, such as a real teakwood steering wheel and a stylish, twin-cockpit layout, set it apart from most of the inexpensive competition.

all extraneous trim, retaining only the crossed-flags emblem at the front of the car and the "Sting Ray" emblem on the rear. Inside, similar cleanup efforts made the cockpit a more inviting place to spend time, thanks to revised bucket seats, a relocated parking brake lever, and other tweaks.

But what really made the 1967 Corvette so much more fun were the changes under the hood: in addition to a pair of 327-ci "small-blocks"—rated at 300 and 350 horsepower—were four versions of the 427 big-block.

With the 350-horse small-block, the 1967 Corvette was a fabulous sports car, nimble and light, able to slice through corners and stop on a dime, yet with ample power to outrun even many big-blocks.

To most Corvette lovers, the 427 big-block 1967 coupe is the finest of the breed. Big-blocks such as this 390-horse 427—or the three other 427s, including the mighty 430 L88—made the Corvette a fire-breather. Though the body was cleaned up for 1967, options such as the Stinger hood and sidepipes provided a tasteful, muscular image.

Even from the rear, the Corvette was high style. Note the center-mounted back-up lamp, and the racing-style flip-up gas cap under the crossed-flags emblem.

1967 Chevrolet Corvette

Specifications

	Base Price	Units Built
	$4,388.75	8,504
	$4,240.75	14,436
		22,940

Engine

	300-hp 327-ci 4-bbl. V-8
	350-hp 350-ci 4-bbl. V-8
	390-hp 427-ci 4-bbl. V-8
	400-hp 427-ci 3x2-bbl. V-8
	430-hp 427-ci 3x2-bbl. V-8
	435-hp 427-ci 4-bbl. V-8

¼-mile (typical)

	15.0 secs.
	93 mph

Still, some buyers were willing to sacrifice a little corner-cutting capability for the 427's big-block displacement and raw horsepower. For $200 and change, you could get the RPO L36 with its 390 horsepower. Another $105 put 10 more horses under your right foot. But if you really wanted serious horsepower at your disposal, a misleading choice was yours to make: Should you spend $437 for RPO L71, with its top-rated 435 horsepower and impressive-looking triple-deuce induction system, or fork over $947 to get . . . 5 *less* horsepower? If you opted to save yourself $500 because you wanted those "extra" 5 horses, you fell right into Chevy's trap. The company really didn't want people buying RPO L88.

RPO L88 was, for all intents and purposes, a race car in street car clothing. Developing an estimated 550 horsepower, the engine was so radical that it barely idled, didn't produce enough vacuum to feed power brakes, and didn't develop peak power until well beyond a normally streetable engine speed.

Rather than tempt incapable drivers (and probably risk wrongful-death lawsuits) Chevy purposely under-rated the L88 427 to trick buyers who were looking for the highest horsepower engine into getting the more streetable L71 engine. The company wanted to give racers access to this brutal machine, but didn't want amateur speed freaks driving more car than they could handle

In a bang-for-the-buck competition, though, the 390-horse L36 was the clear leader, and a solid foundation for a formidable street or track warrior. Not surprisingly, it was the best-selling big-block option, making up nearly one-fifth of total production for the year, with more than 3,800 copies rolling off dealers' lots, and right into the history books.

1970 Chevrolet Chevelle SS 454

Large-displacement engines had always defined the musclecar, and at no time was there more displacement than in 1970.

If the musclecar wars leading up to that year could be characterized as casual name-calling, then the escalation in 1970 could only be characterized as a knock-down, drag-out, winner-take-all street fight. And one of the hardest hitters was the redesigned 1970 Chevelle SS with the optional 454-ci Mark IV big-block V-8.

While the 1970 Chevelle SS 454 did feature a redesigned body that was heralded for its clean lines, it was its radical powertrain that commanded so much attention and instantly earned the respect of any challengers.

Mind you, the Chevelle SS had already developed a reputation as one of the toughest machines on the street, thanks to the 396-ci Mark IV engines that debuted in 1965. And in 1969, Chevy quietly upped the ante with a 427-ci Corvette variant of the Mark IV, though it made the car available only to those in-the-know under a Central Office Production Order, rather than the traditional Regular Production Order system.

But the SS 454 was a whole new animal. In base LS-5 trim, buyers got the full SS treatment, but with "only" 360 horsepower. An optional LS-6 configuration upped the horses to 450. And the fact that it was

The 1970 Chevelle SS is considered the pinnacle of Chevy's musclecar era. For 1970, five V-8 engines were available for the Chevelle SS—one 350-horsepower 396, two 375-horsepower 396 engines (L78 and L89), one 360-horsepower 454, and one 450-horsepower 454 LS-6.

being made widely available to the public bordered on sheer lunacy. (With this much juice off the show-room floor, it's small wonder the insurance industry began to take notice.)

The 454 was so astounding that, despite being engineered as a cost-effective, low-performance powerplant, the engine still developed an honest 360 horsepower—more than most high-performance engines. Yet, the LS-5 made its power without a trick part, or any fancy preparation. It relied on a cast-iron crankshaft, a passenger-car block with stan-dard two-bolt main bearing caps, cast pistons, a mild

The legendary LS-6 454 Mark IV "big-block" Chevy V-8 developed 450 horsepower, featured a 11.25:1 compression ratio, and had a long-duration solid lifter cam.

Like the exterior, the 1970 Chevelle interior was all new, and perhaps the most accommodating of any musclecar. The dash contained a large analog tachometer, speedometer, and clock. Fuel, amp, and temperature gauges accompanied the mammoth three gauges.

1970 Chevrolet Chevelle LS-6

Specifications

Body

Body	Base Price	Units Built
Coupe	$3,485.75*	
Conv.	$3,738.75*	
Total		4,475

Engine

Std.	360-hp 454-ci 4-bbl. V-8 (LS5)
Opt.	450-hp 454-ci 4-bbl. V-8 (LS6)

1/4-mile (typical)

E.T.	13.9 secs.
Speed	102 mph

includes model base plus SS-454 (LS5) equipment, plus LS6 option price

camshaft, and low-performance oval-port cylinder heads. All were durable, low-cost parts, which helped keep the RPO Z15 SS package to a reasonable $503.45, including the LS-5, the F41 suspension system, disc brakes, and a host of interior and exterior styling touches.

The LS-6, however, was the favorite among the press, enthusiasts, and would-be buyers. For all intents and purposes, the LS-6 was a large-displacement version of the L-78 396. Chevy fitted the LS-6 with its finest high-performance pieces, such as a forged crankshaft and rods, forged aluminum 11.25:1 pistons, large-port heads, and a low-rise aluminum manifold (which was actually dictated by the Corvette's minimal hood clearance).

The second-generation Camaro was introduced with much fanfare in 1970. The fastback two-door coupe incorporated European styling trends and provided improved handling through a redesigned suspension. The track was pushed out 1.5 inches in front and 1/2 inch in back. Chevy eventually offered the F41 performance handling package that included heavy-duty shocks, a larger-diameter front anti-sway bar, and a rear anti-sway bar.

The Z28 housed what many consider to be the best small-block V-8 GM ever produced—the 350-ci LT-1 engine. Based on the Corvette engine, it featured a forged steel crankshaft, drop-forged steel connecting rods, and forged aluminum pistons.

Officially, the LS-6 developed 450 horsepower. But it was hardly a secret that manufacturers often under-rated engines in the hope that doing so would result in the car being misclassified into a lower-than-appropriate racing class. Under-rating also became a great way to win favor (or at least try to) with the insurance industry, which began cracking down on performance cars at the end of the 1960s. Independent dyno tests of stock LS-6 454s equipped with headers typically showed numbers in the neighborhood of 550 horsepower.

Ironically, the LS-6's power was, in some ways, its own worst enemy. With 500 foot-pounds of wrenching torque, the tires didn't have a prayer of maintaining traction. But that was actually a good thing. If the tires could have harnessed the LS-6's power, failures of the transmission, U-joints, and rear axle assembly would have been far more prevalent than they already were, plus would have cost Chevy a fortune in warranty repairs.

Even when the 454's torque wasn't breaking parts it was creating problems. For instance, buyers who opted for the four-speed manual transmission had to contend with shifter linkage that jammed under hard acceleration as the engine's torque caused the engine and transmission assembly to rock sideways, wedging the linkage up against the floor pan. Obviously, those who opted for the shift-for-itself Turbo 400 automatic had no such worries.

When the rest of the car was modified to properly harness the 454's power, the car ran like a tiger. An LS-6 454 Chevelle could handily dash through a quarter-mile in under 13 seconds with slicks and a good tune-up. Adding headers and swapping the low-rise intake for a more efficient high-rise unit would bump power measurably. And if you put the Chevelle on a diet (they had grown pretty hefty), quarter-mile elapsed times (E.T.s) in the 12-second range were possible at speeds well above 100 miles per hour.

For many enthusiasts, there is no greater musclecar than the 1970 LS-6 Chevelle SS 454. And certainly none is more iconic of the era of excessive power and outstanding styling.

1970 Chevrolet Camaro Z28

General Motors had established a tradition of redesigning vehicle bodies every two years. On the in-between years, it usually introduced reengineered drive trains and made other mechanical improvements. This not only kept the product line fresh and exciting to buyers each fall, it also spread out the engineering workload for GM.

But Chevrolet flip-flopped that schedule with the 1970 Camaro.

It should be understood that there was little reason to redesign the Camaro for 1970. After all, the model was only three years old, and it had been restyled for 1969 with a more aggressive appearance, requiring the redesign of every body panel except the hood and the roof. And the new look was a rousing success, judging by the record 243,085 units produced for the production run—which, by the way, was extended abruptly when the United Auto Workers went on strike, delaying the launch of the all-new 1970 model.

Likewise, the Camaro powertrains were hardly lacking. In 1969 buyers could choose from among 12 different engines: there were two six-cylinders, five small-block V-8s, and five big-blocks. Additionally, there were eight different transmissions, and an array of rear-axle gear ratios.

Chevrolet had learned that a completely new Mustang was due in 1971, when it had planned to release a redesigned Camaro. Launching a new Camaro at the same time as a new Mustang would have splintered the market: both would be "all-new," thus neither would have a clear advantage. Armed with this knowledge, Chevy decided to get the jump on its rival and release the new Camaro a year early.

The new Camaro was elegantly styled with a decidedly European look. With its long hood and short, fastbacklike rear, the 1970 F-body was reminiscent of various Jaguars, Alfa-Romeos, and Lancias. The car was long, low, and sleek, just like any good sports car should be.

Under this fresh sheet metal was a new, world-class suspension system that gave Camaro outstanding handling abilities. Large-diameter, vented front disc brakes were made standard equipment to ensure that every Camaro had braking power to match. And that was just the base model; Z28 suspension, steering, and braking systems were highly tuned for improved handling and stability at racing speeds.

On first glance, the 1970 Camaro's engine line-up appeared to take a step backward, retreating to only one six-cylinder (the 250-inch straight six), two sizes of small-blocks (307 and 350 cubes), and the

To improve rear downforce, a spoiler was attached to the deck lid; this Z28 features the "late"-style three-piece spoiler.

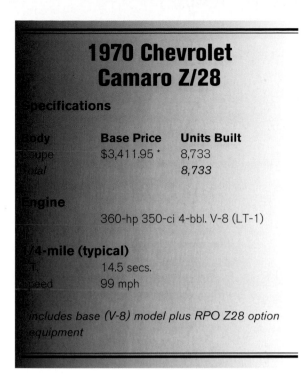

1970 Chevrolet Camaro Z/28

Specifications

Body	Base Price	Units Built
Coupe	$3,411.95 *	8,733
Total		8,733

Engine

360-hp 350-ci 4-bbl. V-8 (LT-1)

1/4-mile (typical)

E.T.	14.5 secs.
Speed	99 mph

*includes base (V-8) model plus RPO Z28 option equipment

396. Gone were the beastly 427s of 1969, and the new 454-ci big-block was notably absent from the order form. The 5-liter 302 that had been such a critical part of the Z28's introduction three years ealier was also gone.

Thanks to a rules change at the SCCA, Trans-Am competitors could now utilize 5.7-liter engines, which allowed Chevy to replace the 302 with its larger-displacement 350, in the form of the new 360-horsepower LT-1. The extra cubes provided a significant torque increase—an 80-foot-pounds jump to 370—over the twitchy 302 that had preceded it. The heartier torque curve even allowed for a welcome addition to the Z28 option list: an automatic transmission.

With its new looks, new underpinnings, and new drive train, the 1970 Camaro Z28 was, quite simply, the best Z yet, and possibly the best Z28 ever. And though the Z28 wasn't able to clinch a third straight manufacturers' championship in the Trans-Am series, it nonetheless raised the bar for all future sporty cars.

OLDSMOBILE: AN IMPECCABLE BLEND OF MUSCLE AND LUXURY

Musclecars weren't the only things racing in the 1960s. It was also the time of the "space race" between the United States and the Soviet Union.

The space race captured the attention and imagination of the world, including the marketing and engineering teams at Oldsmobile. Olds created a new logo that bore more than a passing resemblance to a rocket at liftoff. Carrying the spacecraft theme underhood, the company slapped the "Rocket" name on its high-performance engines. More important, Olds engines were given more thrust than NASA's Atlas rockets, which made it even easier to put space between your Olds and the competition. Yet unlike NASA's rocket, Oldsmobile's Rockets were tailored for comfort while others were built solely for speed.

True to Oldsmobile's prime directive, the 4-4-2 was much more than just an overpowered engine in a cheap package. The 4-4-2 offered style and comfort from the outset. With high-grade materials and judicious application of bright trim work (and later even woodgrain trim), the 4-4-2 was a civilized, dignified musclecar equally at home at a country club or a drag strip.

Such refinement would continue to be Oldsmobile's hallmark throughout the musclecar era. While other manufacturers gave relatively little concern to anything but power and performance, Oldsmobile paid attention to the details. As a result Olds produced some of the most attractive, most drivable muscle of the period.

Oldsmobile's attention to details caught the eye of high-performance shifter manufacturer George Hurst, leading to one of the most well-known and interesting alliances in automotive history.

Aside from supplying the standard high-performance shifter on more musclecars than any other company, Hurst also dabbled in creating ultra-performance super cars, much like the Yenko Chevrolets, the Royal Bobcat Pontiacs, or the Tasca Fords. Hurst built one-off ultra-customs, such as the twin-engine, four-wheel-drive Hurst Hairy Olds, which he used as promotional exhibition vehicles at drag strips across the country. But he desperately wanted to build his own line of performance vehicles. His concept was simple: an executive hot rod. Hurst wanted a car that upper management would be comfortable driving to the office Monday through Friday—in 12 seconds flat.

He approached Olds with the idea just when the division had determined that it needed an "image" car to draw buyers into the showrooms. Thus, the legendary Hurst/Olds allegiance was formed. Based on the Olds Cutlass platform—the same model as the 4-4-2—Hurst was able to provide Olds with a convenient way to skirt around some internal GM edicts, namely the 400-ci displacement limit for the intermediate-size Cutlass. Hurst contracted Olds to supply both partially assembled 4-4-2s and custom-built Toronado 455s that were set up with loose tolerances to allow the engines to make more power through decreased internal friction. Hurst then mated the engines to the cars, made a number of lesser changes, added special paint striping, and sold the cars through Olds dealers. The plan was successful, despite the fact that only about 500 cars were built.

In the years that followed, Hurst repeated the process several times, even into the 1980s.

Meanwhile, with buyers flocking to Olds showrooms to see the outrageous Hurst/Olds hot rods, the job of selling less-expensive 4-4-2s became easier and easier. By 1970, GM had rescinded its cubic-inch limit, which allowed Olds to install its 455-cube W-30 engine into 4-4-2s right on the assembly lines, thereby negating much of the need for Hurst's creations. In the process, Olds proved it could build its own executive hot rod—one that's remembered and revered to this day.

1970 Oldsmobile 4-4-2 W-30

Dr. Oldsmobile, the GM division's fictional musclecar-mad scientist, had been working hard in his laboratory throughout the 1960s producing a number of the hottest musclecars of the era. For 1970, Oldsmobile outdid himself when he concocted the new W-30 4-4-2.

While other manufacturers were busy creating stripped-down race cars for the street, the good Doctor made the 4-4-2 a best-of-both-worlds combina-

tion. Like any good musclecar, the W-30 4-4-2 had power to spare; but it also had ample amenities to keep the car comfortable for long cruises—or quarter-mile blasts.

The muscle was provided by a new 455-ci Oldsmobile V-8. In the past, GM's top brass had a 400-ci displacement limit on all of its intermediate-sized passenger cars, including the 4-4-2, the GTO, the Chevelle SS, and Buick's GS. But with the competition powered by 426 Hemis, 440 Magnums, 428 Cobra Jets, and 429 Super Cobra Jets, GM had no choice but to match motors, inch-for-inch—or better.

Olds' Rocket 455 was a strong motor to start with, and had proven itself in Olds' full-size cars for years. But in W-30 trim, the 455 benefited from a hotter camshaft, increased compression, a free-flowing intake with large Rochester QuadraJet carburetor and cold-air induction system, dual exhausts, and more. The package was rated at 370 horsepower and an earth-moving 500 foot-pounds of torque.

1970 Oldsmobile 4-4-2 W-30

Specifications

Body	Base Price	Units Built
Hol. Coupe	$3,376	
Sport Coupe	$3,312	
Conv.	$3,567	
Total		3,100*

Engine

Std.	365-hp 455-ci 4-bbl. V-8
Opt.	370-hp 455-ci 4-bbl. V-8 (W30)

1/4-mile (typical)

ET.	14.3 secs.
Speed	100 mph

*no by-model breakdown information is available

Oldsmobile's 4-4-2 blended high performance and luxury into one solid package. In 1970, the 4-4-2's massive 455-ci engine was offered as the W-30 high-performance option that featured an aluminum intake manifold, 328-degree camshaft, and disc brakes.

With either a four-speed or heavy-duty version of the TH400 automatic, plus a Positraction-equipped heavy-duty rear axle assembly, the 4-4-2 W-30 could dash down the quarter-mile in less than 15 seconds on street tires. With better traction and a less restrictive exhaust system, the 4-4-2 W-30 was capable of dipping into the 13-second bracket—complete with its bucket seats, rich woodgrain interior trim, and other accoutrements. Further modifications put 12-second runs within reach.

Thanks to its impressive list of performance equipment and creature comforts, the 4-4-2 W-30 was hard to beat. In fact, there was only one way Dr. Oldsmobile could top it—by *un*topping it. Whether in convertible form or the more traditional hardtop form, many enthusiasts consider the Olds 4-4-2

The W-30 was derived from a 370-horsepower version of Olds' 455-ci "Rocket" V-8, which was fed cool, outside air by the fiberglass twin scoop Ram Air that had a flapper-door air cleaner. The 1970 W-30 had dynamite looks, especially in convertible form. Note the optional red inner fender liners.

Equipped with bucket seats, woodgrain dash, and a large tachometer and speedometer, the W-30's interior was a comfortable, attractive place to pass time—or pass just about anything else on the road, especially your competition.

W-30 to be the ultimate musclecar, combining stunning good looks with a lavish interior, and an almost unbeatable powertrain.

Sadly, just 3,100 W-30 4-4-2s were produced for 1970, and by 1971, the option had become a mere shadow of its 1970 self, suffering from lower compression, milder cam timing, and other changes that robbed the W-30 package of its soul. But for one brief year, the W-30 4-4-2 was as hot an Olds as one could find, and one of the hottest, best-mannered musclecars around.

BUICK: A SYNERGY OF STYLE AND SUBSTANCE

In GM's divisional heirarchy, Buick is one step beneath Cadillac: luxury car comforts without the luxury car price tag. But beneath the company's spit-polished, squeaky-clean image lurks a rebellious spirit that craves fun and excitement.

To the uninformed, "Buick musclecar" sounds like an oxymoron, or at least a mis-statement. Yet while performance cars weren't Buick's specialty, the straightlaced division still managed to put out some of the hottest vehicles in musclecar history.

In the early 1960s, Buick made a nod toward performance with its Wildcat and Riviera. When Chevy, Olds, and Pontiac introduced their new intermediate-sized muscle machines as 1964 models, Buick held off. Its entrant into this market was another year in coming—but well worth the wait. The 1965 Skylark Gran Sport, or simply GS, was a musclecar as only Buick could make it: loaded with comfort and conveniences, and *over*loaded with power.

To stand up to its powerful peers, the Buick GS came equipped with a 401-ci Buick V-8—which somehow squeaked past GM's 400-ci displacement limit for its midsize cars. A three-speed gearbox with floor shifter, dual exhaust, heavy-duty suspension, and other goodies rounded out the package. With 325 horsepower and 445 foot-pounds of torque, the GS took off as if shot from a catapult.

Buick's conservatives insisted the car still be a Buick, which meant retaining the features that had made Buick an outstanding buy as a family car: rich upholstery, extensive conveniences, and classic styling.

The GS walked that precarious line between style and substance well—perhaps too well, as the public barely took notice. Until 1970, that is.

In 1970, Buick took out all the stops to develop the ultimate GS: the GSX.

To ensure that the GSX looked like no other Buick, the car was available in only two colors: Apollo White or Saturn Yellow. Regardless of which a buyer selected, the car received bold black striping that ran along its sides and up and across the pedestal-mounted deck lid spoiler. The GSX hood had massive black stripes separated by the hood's center crease, a tachometer mounted in a rearward-facing scooplike bubble, and twin holes that provided cold air for the induction system of the car's 455 V-8. Most GSX Buicks were fitted with the top-option Stage 1 455, though a few were built with only the 360-horse standard 455.

Like the Hurst/Olds models of 1968 and 1969, the 1970 Buick GSX was an outstanding traffic builder for Buick dealers. And the car did a lot to change the company's image, making the public realize that Buick wasn't just a stodgy old man's car. It was a car for younger drivers and performance enthusiasts, too.

Sadly, the GSX was a one-hit wonder. Though Buick offered a GSX option on cars throughout the early 1970s, only the original commands much respect or admiration among enthusiasts or collectors today. For the most part, the 1970s saw Buick retreat to its comfort zone, providing Cadillac content at Chevrolet prices.

In the 1980s, however, the company mustered a performance resurgence as America caught NASCAR fever. Buick dechromed its midsized Regal, drenched it in ominous onyx black paint, and topped it off with an unusual powerplant—a turbocharged (and later intercooled) 231-ci V-6 that produced 245 horsepower.

The Buick Regal Grand National, or GN for short, made the world take notice of Buick at a time when GM's cars were often criticized for their "cookie cutter" looks. And conservative, luxurious Buick had the distinction of producing the quickest car in America when it assembled a limited run of

300-horsepower Grand Nationals, dubbed the GNX.

So, while Buick's modern lineup doesn't offer any true performance cars, the company "for the supercharged family" may just be waiting until the time is right to unleash its next X model. And if history is any indication, a new Buick X model would be nothing short of exceptional.

1970 Buick GSX

At first glance, Buick's 1970 GSX looked like a Pontiac GTO Judge or maybe Olds' new-for-1970 Rallye 350. As with both of those models, the GSX sported bold hood and side stripes, a deck lid spoiler, and vibrant colors—Saturn Yellow or Apollo White, take your pick. And in many ways all three models were similar.

But the GSX was hardly a copycat musclecar. Buick had plenty of experience building performance cars, including its Gran Sport (the "GS" in GSX), the Wildcat, and even the Riviera, so it didn't have to "cheat" to develop a powerful performance machine.

While the performance Buicks were handily capable of running with 4-4-2s, Road Runners, and Fairlanes, Buick went to great lengths to ensure that the

1970 Buick GSX

Specifications

Body	Base Price	Units Built
Hdtp.	$4,881	678
Total		*678*

Engine

Std.	350-hp 455-ci 4-bbl. V-8
Opt.	360-hp 455-ci 4-bbl. V-8 (Stage I)

1/4-mile (typical)

E.T.	14.2 secs.
Speed	101 mph

Buick's Gran Sport ("GS" for short) had often been overlooked as a musclecar—until the GSX came along. The top-shelf GS featured audacious styling with Ram-Air hood and rear deck spoiler. Only 678 of these big-block monsters were built in 1970.

One of the GSX's classic features was the hood-mounted tachometer with a 5,000-rpm redline.

Buick's awesome Stage 1 455 produced 360 horsepower, which was more than enough to allow some unmusclelike options, such as air conditioning and power steering. But the big-block had stump-pulling torque as well; the 510 foot-pounds rating was one of the highest of the musclecar era.

Skylark GS lineup was always something more than just another musclecar. The boys from Flint built in a high level of comfort and convenience. Things that were either extra cost or simply unavailable on other musclecars came as standard equipment on the GS.

The GSX took that philosophy to an eXtreme, if you'll pardon the pun. It offered both more muscle and more luxury. For power, the GSX started with a 350-horse 455-ci Buick V-8—the largest V-8 ever offered in the intermediate-sized Skylark body. Buyers with an insatiable craving for power could have their 455 served up in Stage I trim, which added 10 more horsepower on paper—a figure most enthusiasts argue was grossly underrated, citing countless victories against Hemi Mopars and SS 454 Chevelles as proof that the horsepower difference was much greater than Buick let on.

The GSX's performance package also consisted of the usual musclecar goodies: a manual four-speed transmission, a 3.42:1 heavy-duty rear axle assembly with a Positraction limited-slip differential, raised-white-letter (Buick referred to them as "billboard") tires, and dual exhaust. More unique were the GSX's standard power front disc brakes, its front *and* rear anti-roll bars, the rear deck lid spoiler, and, especially, the front spoiler.

Luxury touches on the GSX included standard bucket seats, a deluxe steering wheel, special instrumentation featuring a way-cool hood tach, styled steel wheels, power steering, power brakes, and rich-looking upholstery. Plus, unlike many other musclecars, the GSX was available with a vast assortment of convenience options, including air conditioning, power windows, a variety of sound systems, and virtually any other Skylark option. Most musclecar manufacturers, by comparison, eliminated such luxuries as air conditioning on top performance options more to discourage average buyers from purchasing barely civilized cars.

Unfortunately, the local Buick dealership wasn't exactly the musclecar set's first stop when they went shopping. As a result, just 678 GSXs were produced for 1970—491 were Saturn Yellow and the remaining 187 were bathed in Apollo White. Records indicate that 400 of the cars were equipped with the top-option Stage 1 engine, meaning that the average challenger who drew up beside a 1970 GSX at a stoplight had a *very* hard time beating it to the next light.

Based on its parts and performance, the 1970 Buick GSX was considered the baddest Buick ever. Not until the limited run of 547 GNX Grand Nationals in 1987 did the division build anything hotter.

CHAPTER 2

Ford Motor Company

The Pony Car Creator

It's been said that racing improves the breed. At Ford Motor Company that saying was practically a way of life. Henry Ford realized early on that nothing demanded more from a car than a good race. And while it was inevitable that parts would break, Ford used that opportunity to improve the parts so they wouldn't break again. In doing so, Ford developed a reputation not only for building performance cars, but also for commitment to quality.

Competing publicly in races had a second benefit: exposure. The better a manufacturer did at the races, the more recognition it got from the press, and thus from car buyers and, especially, enthusiasts. In short, drawing attention at the race track could draw the public to your dealerships.

As sales soon indicated, buyers like to drive winners, not losers. So, those three factors—quality, awareness, and vanity—all had a part in the "What wins on Sunday, sells on Monday" philosophy.

In the 1950s, two forms of motorsports dominated the hearts and imaginations of automotive enthusiasts—and garnered the lion's share of "support" from auto manufacturers: stock car racing and drag racing.

Ford was a stalwart competitor in both arenas; and despite a ban that prevented any "official" involvement in motorsports by the Auto Manufacturers Association, Fords were still a regular sight on victory lane.

Moving into the 1960s, manufacturer after manufacturer gradually discontinued its support of the AMA ban, Ford included. Practically within days of publicly announcing it would no longer support the AMA antiracing actions, Ford launched its "Total Performance" campaign, one of its most successful marketing efforts ever.

More important, Ford's engineering teams were now given budgets to improve both cars and parts for competition use—in contrast to the era of the AMA ban, when such projects were carried out on shoestring budgets. If

Ford hit the jackpot with its 1964 1/2 Mustang and sold over 500,000 copies in the first year. Based on the Ford Falcon, the Mustang was just what young Americans wanted—good looks and sporty performance—at a price they could afford. The Mustang was available with a variety of engines—the 170 inline six, a 200-ci V-6, a 260 V-8, and the hi-po 289 V-8.

The Mustang's interior came standard with lots of items buyers typically had to pay extra for on other models, including bucket seats and a floor-mounted shifter.

cars of the day are judged—milestones along the road of musclecar history.

1965 Mustang

While Pontiac's 1964 GTO marks the beginning of the musclecar era, the Ford Mustang's impact on the automotive landscape can hardly be overstated. With this model, derived from the humble Falcon, Ford created a new breed of performance automobile: the pony car.

Ford actually produced the Mustang to compete with Chevy's sporty Corvair in the sales race. Little did Ford know that the Corvair would soon be dealt a lethal blow from consumer advocate Ralph Nader, whose book, *Unsafe At Any Speed,* characterized the rear-engined sedan as a death machine. Fortunately for Ford, Mustang's platform—devised by Lee

money was available at all. The injection of money into the engineering departments resulted in an unprecedented increase in the number and quality of performance parts. New intake manifolds, new cylinder heads, entirely new engines, and even entirely new vehicle bodies were all designed to put Fords first on race day. And those same parts filtered onto the production lines, down to dealers' lots, and into the driveways and garages of John and Jane Q. Public.

Cars such as the slippery Torino Talladega that cheated the wind on NASCAR's high-banked superspeedways, or the 1968 1/2 428 Cobra Jet Mustangs that took the drag racing world by storm, were just two examples of how official involvement in racing led to new products—and a greatly improved performance image.

A side benefit of Ford's racing activities was a series of collaborative projects with established race shops. From its involvement with Carroll Shelby came the legendary Shelby Mustangs; work with stock car specialists Holman & Moody contributed to the development of the Boss 429 engine and other NASCAR innovations.

Many of the Fords from the Total Performance era set performance standards against which all other

1965 Ford Mustang

Specifications

Body	Base Price	Units Built
Coupe	$2,320.96	501,965*
Fastback	$2,533.19	77,079
Conv.	$2,557.64	101,945*
Total		680,989

Engine

101-hp 170-ci 1-bbl. I-6 (early)
120-hp 200-ci 1-bbl. I-6
164-hp 260-ci 2-bbl. V-8 (early)
200-hp 289-ci 2-bbl. V-8
210-hp 289-ci 4-bbl. V-8 (early)
225-hp 289-ci 4-bbl. V-8
271-hp 289-ci 4-bbl. V-8 (hi-po)

1/4-mile (typical)

ET   15.9 secs.
Speed   85 mph

*Includes early- and late-1965 production runs

The hi-po 289-ci engine cranked out 271 horsepower at 6,000 rpms and made the "Stang" a competent performer. The 289 featured a nodular iron crankshaft, heavy-duty connecting rods, and an oversized crankshaft balancer.

Iacocca, who would later lead Chrysler to salvation—was both sportier and safer than Corvair's.

The Mustang was safe for Ford in two ways: part vehicle design and part corporate risk-management. On the design side, Mustang did not follow the Corvair's rear-engine layout, which made it so unsafe in Nader's and the public's eyes. From a corporate standpoint, Mustang was a "safe bet," given that it was built on the same platform as the company's already successful and economical Falcon. The Mustang's budget-minded specifications also made it quite affordable.

The car's sporty character derived largely from its powerful engine lineup, which featured an exciting "hi-po" 271-horsepower 289 V-8. This motor was added to the option list in June 1964, just a few months after the model's April 17 introduction. With the hi-po 289 and a four-speed, the new pony car was a fast runner even among big-block competition.

Ford hit the mark with more than just the car's layout and performance. Mustang's stylish body, intentionally designed with a European flair, proved to be enticing to young American men and women. To ensure there was a Mustang for nearly any buyer's needs, Ford designers fashioned the key styling elements into three Mustang bodies: a coupe version, a fastback model, and a convertible.

Calling the Mustang anything short of a grand-slam sales success would be a gross injustice. More than 680,000 Mustangs were assembled for model year 1965, combining both 1964-1/2 and 1965 production figures. Only a small percentage of these cars were built with the hi-po 289. Most rolled off the assembly lines with either a 170-ci straight-six or 260-ci V-8—hardly brutal performers, but clearly satisfactory to a huge number of buyers.

Having stormed the market with the initial Mustang, Ford evolved the model along the trend toward bigger engines and greater horsepower. In the years to come, some of the most astounding musclecars would bear Ford's famous galloping-horse emblem, including the Cobra Jet Mach 1, the Boss 302, and the mighty Boss 429. These formidable descendents reinforce the 1965 Mustang's place in musclecar history.

1966 Shelby Mustang GT-350

From the moment the Mustang debuted, enthusiasts recognized its performance potential. The 260-ci

1966 Shelby GT 350H Mustang

Specifications

Body	Base Price	Units Built
Fastback	$4,428	1,000
		1,000

Engine

306-hp 289-ci 4-bbl. V-8

¼-mile (typical)

14.7 secs.

92 mph

Shelby interiors offered few creature comforts, but improved on base Mustang innards with a wooden three-spoke steering wheel plus a tachometer centered on the top of the instrument panel.

Shelby GT-350 Mustangs—including the GT-350H Hertz model—featured shock-tower and LeMans ("export") braces to strengthen the chassis. The engine was a modified version of the hi-po 289 that pumped out 306 horsepower.

V-8, available when the car was introduced, was not a fire-breather itself, but a sign of what was possible, and hopefully forthcoming.

Naturally, Ford could have built a souped-up Mustang on its own, but the company had all it could do to keep up with demand for the models already available. Besides, the company knew that the quickest way to develop a reputation of winning performance was to actually make winning performances. And what better way to accomplish that than by having a real race team build a race car out of a Mustang?

Ford already had a relationship with Carroll Shelby, who stuffed Ford drive trains into British two-seaters. Shelby called the cars Cobras, but the

Ford contracted Carroll Shelby to build special racing versions of the Mustang fastback called the GT-350. In turn, Shelby built 1,000 GT-350s for the Hertz rental car company that received the "H" designation. The cars featured black paint, gold striping, and Magnum 500 wheels.

competition called them bad news. With their small size, light weight, and abundance of power, the Cobras were ferocious on race courses and almost unbeatable.

Because of the reputation Shelby had developed building and racing Cobras, Ford logically concluded that a car with Shelby's name would get lots of attention at dealerships and on the streets. Ford approached Shelby about the idea and the rest, as they say, is history.

The first Shelby Mustangs, the 1965 models, were built at Shelby-American's airplane-hanger-turned-assembly-plant in California. Ford shipped semifinished fastback Mustangs to Shelby to be completed. The cars, as supplied by Ford, lacked hoods, back seats, exhaust systems, and emblems. And while the cars were equipped with Ford's top-of-the-performance-line powertrains—including the 271-horse 289 V-8, a Borg-Warner four-speed, and a 9-inch Detroit Locker rear axle assembly outfitted with oversized station wagon brakes—Shelby and company made numerous modifications to raise the cars to within a whisker of true racing specs.

The engines were outfitted with a high-rise aluminum intake manifold, Holley four-barrel carburetor, equal-length tubular exhaust headers, and some dress-up goodies such as the finned-aluminum Cobra valve covers. The upgrades added some 35 horsepower. To make sure that power could be put to use consistently, Shelby's team redesigned the suspension to improve the car's stability in corners. The front suspension geometry was radically altered, and new springs were installed that dropped the front end by roughly an inch. An oversized anti-roll bar helped keep the car level in the curves, while Koni shocks at all four corners kept the wheel movements under control.

By the time Shelby finished with the cars, the Shelby GT-350 Mustangs—and especially the competition version, the GT-350R—were about as close to real race cars as you could get on the streets, and about as far removed from stock Mustangs as imaginable. Too far, in fact, for Ford's taste.

Shelby was instructed to "civilize" the GT-350 for 1966, which he did—but just barely. He added air conditioning to the option sheet, along with a heavy-duty version of the C-4 three-speed automatic. In addition, the 1966 Shelby was available in six colors, which starkly contrasted with the Wimbledon White–only 1965s. Buyers responded favorably to the 1966 Shelby Mustangs, including Hertz Rent-a-Car, which put in an order for 1,000 Shelby Mustangs in special black paint with gold stripes and accents. At year's end, more than 2,200 Shelby Mustangs had been assembled.

Unfortunately, later Shelby Mustangs were gradually watered down into more Mustang and less Shelby, as Ford's control over production increased and Shelby's interest in the Mustang market waned. But it was the Shelby GT-350 that established the

Mustang as a true performance machine, with plenty of wins to prove it.

1969 Ford Mustang Mach 1

When America entered the jet aircraft age in the 1950s, the buzz was all about going faster, going

1969 Ford Mustang Mach 1
Specifications

Body	Base Price	Units Built
Fastback	$3,122	72,458
Total		*72,458*

Engine		
Std.	250-hp 351-ci 2-bbl. V-8	
Opt.	290-hp 351-ci 4-bbl. V-8	
	320-hp 390-ci 4-bbl. V-8	
	335-hp 428-ci 4-bbl. V-8	

1/4-mile (typical)	
E.T.	14.6 secs.
Speed	99 mph

The Mach 1's base engine was a 250-horspower 351 Windsor V-8 in 1969. The optional 335-horsepower 428 Cobra Jet V-8 (pictured) was accompanied by a Shaker hood and dual exhaust.

By 1969 the stakes and cubic inches had significantly increased in the musclecar wars. Ford responded with the Mach 1, which was available with 351, 390, and 428 V-8 powerplants. The high-performance package fastback featured a flat-black hood with racing-style pins, styled steel wheels, and tasteful graphics.

Mach 1 deck lids featured a subtle integrated spoiler lip, while the taillamp panel had a decal that outlined the panel. "Mach 1" bisected the stripe. Although not pictured, sport slats (louvers) and a deck lid spoiler were popular options.

higher, and who had "the right stuff" to pilot the aircraft to those new barriers.

A decade later, America was in the musclecar age and the buzz was about who could go quicker, faster, and who had the right stuff to pilot those street machines to record-setting runs.

In 1969, Ford had a Mustang for all reasons: economical six-cylinder models, models that excelled at road racing, models that were prime drag race equipment. And with the advent of the new Mach 1, Ford had what it believed was the right stuff—the ideal street Mustang.

The Mach 1 combined many of the best virtues of all the other Mustangs, which made it a truly exceptional car.

First, like the GT models, the Mach 1 had an elegant but racy appearance, inside and outside. The look was aggressive but understated, classy but subtle.

Borrowing from what it learned in road racing competition and in the development of the Trans-Am–inspired Boss 302, the Mach 1's "Competition" suspension system was tuned for precise handling on twisting, turning roads without a harsh, jarring ride.

Under the hood, Ford offered an assortment of engines, starting with the Mach 1's base 351 Windsor with two-barrel carburetion and 250 horsepower. Also available were a 351-4V rated at 290 horsepower and the 335-horse 428 Cobra Jet that was dominating drag races from coast to coast.

The 428 CJ was available in R-code form with a shaker-style hood scoop and Ram-Air induction, or the less obvious Q-code form, which had the same power rating but lacked the cold-air induction system. A third variant was possible: the Super Cobra Jet, or "SCJ" for short. Ironically, you couldn't just order the SCJ—you got it by default if you wanted either the 3.91:1 or 4.30:1 rear axle ratios. For the princely sum of $6.53 you got racing-style, heavy-duty connecting rods with cap-screw-style bolts; a unique crankshaft specifically machined for the LeMans-type rods; a flywheel and torsional vibration damper designed to work with the special crank and rods; and an engine oil cooler mounted ahead of the radiator. While the parts didn't add any power (at least according to Ford), they were worth their weight in gold in terms of increased durability under the severe stresses of competition-type use.

Naturally, a Mach 1 could be ordered with a manual or automatic transmission, whichever the buyer preferred.

Finally—and perhaps most important—the Mach 1 was an exceptional value. For as little as $3,122, a buyer could drive away from the local Ford dealer in one of the most attractive Mustangs ever. And 72,458 buyers did just that in 1969, making the Mach 1 Mustang one of the most popular musclecars ever.

The Mach 1 name would soldier on through 1978, appearing on three different generations of Mustang by the time the plug was pulled. Although that longevity doesn't count for much, the original Mach 1's combination of prestige, handling, power, and pricing made it a milestone in the history of musclecars.

1969 Ford Torino Talladega

As the 1968 NASCAR season drew to a close, word of Dodge's secret weapon, the aerodynamic Charger 500, had already gotten out—and the competition was scared. Charger was already a fierce competitor, thanks largely to the Hemi engine.

1969 Ford Torino Talladega

Specifications

Body	Base Price	Units Built
Hdtp.	$3,680	754
Total		754

Engine

335-hp 428-ci 4-bbl. V-8 (Cobra Jet)

1/4-mile (typical)

E.T.	14.9 secs.
Speed	95 mph

The Torino Talladega was Ford's secret weapon in stock car racing competition during 1969. Aerodynamic principles were being effectively applied in NASCAR, and Ford had to compete against the winged Dodge Daytona Charger. The Talladega featured an aerodynamically sculpted nose extension and front bumper.

While the street versions of the Talladega were powered by the 335-horsepower 428 Cobra Jet, the race versions typically carried Boss 429s.

Production Talladega interiors were only slightly more comfortable than their race car counterparts'. A bench seat and column shifter were standard.

A sleek body would only make the Charger that much tougher to beat.

Upset that Chrysler wouldn't let him drive a Charger 500, long-time Plymouth driver and NASCAR superstar Richard Petty went shopping for a new ride. He wasn't about to finish as an "also-ran."

Ford was only too anxious to bring Petty on board. And they had just the car to offer him: the new Torino Talladega, which had been created in response to the Charger 500. With the Torino Talladega's fastbacklike rear end and its extended front end—which tapered slightly and used a modified Fairlane rear bumper on its front end to slice through the wind more easily—Petty knew he had found a car with the right stuff to compete against the wind-cheating Chargers.

And compete it did. Petty won his first outing in a Ford, at Richmond, and took 8 more firsts that season behind the wheel of a Talladega, along with a number of close second- and third-place finishes. Still, Petty finished second in points, after fellow Talladega driver David Pearson, who racked up 11 wins and 31 other top-five finishes.

Interestingly, the street Talladegas weren't available with the thundering Boss 429 powerplant that powered Petty's and Pearson's NASCAR racers. Instead, civilian buyers had to settle for a 335-horsepower 428 Cobra Jet. But that substitution vastly improved the street-driving characteristics of the Talladega, since the Boss '9 was notorious for its cantankerous nature and need for frequent tuning. The 428-CJ, on the other hand, was docile and torquey, day after day.

There was little else about the Torino Talladega that was well suited to daily driving. Its extended nose added some 6 inches to the car's length and made it more difficult to drive, especially when attempting to park. And visibility out the gently sloped rear window was poor, due to large blind spots created by the massive C-pillars. And if that wasn't enough to deter most buyers, the bare-bones interior made few friends. The Torino Talladega was built for speed, not comfort. If a part didn't help the Talladega go faster, it wasn't available on the car.

The "no-frills" mentality even carried over to the exterior identification of the car. Unlike its Mercury sibling, the Cyclone Spoiler II, which featured bold red and white or blue and white paint highlighted by either "Dan Gurney Special" or "Cale Yarborough Special" decals, the Talladega was available in traditional Torino colors with only three small "T" emblems to identify it—one on the top of each door, and another on the gas cap.

The Boss 302 wasn't your average Windsor-based 302. It was as close to a race engine as you could buy off the showroom floor. The 5-liter developed 290 high-strung ponies and featured a cross-drilled forged steel crank, forged steel connecting rods, forged aluminum pistons, four-bolt main bearing caps, and massive valve ports for maximum breathing.

Despite the Talladega's regular visits to Victory Lane, it wasn't tremendously popular with the buying public. NASCAR rules dictated that Ford had to sell at least 500 copies of the Talladega for the car to be legal for competition; at year's end, only 754 Talladegas had been assembled (plus an estimated 519 copies of the similar Spoiler II Mercury).

Still, the very fact that Ford went to such great lengths to create a car capable of dominating NASCAR racing makes the 1969 Torino Talladega a memorable piece of musclecar history.

1970 Ford Mustang Boss 302 & Boss 429

Ford was humiliated. Though the Mustang won the SCCA Trans-Am manufacturers' championship

Ford's desire to conquer the SCCA Trans-Am series spawned the Boss 302 Mustang. With the goal of winning the highly coveted road racing series, Ford pulled out all the stops to produce the best-handling car possible. The production car featured wide 60 series tires, large spindles, gusseted shock towers, 0.72-inch front sway bar, high-performance shocks, stiff springs, 16:1 steering ratio, and 11.3-inch disc brakes.

1970 Ford Mustang Boss 302

Specifications

Body	Base Price	Units Built
Fastback	$3,720	7,013
Total		

Engine

290-hp 302-ci 4-bbl. V-8 (Boss 302)

1/4-mile (typical)

E.T.	14.8 secs.
Speed	96 mph

in 1967, it did so by a slim margin over the new kid on the block, Chevy's Camaro Z28. And the Z28 dominated the series in 1968, and again in 1969, winning the title both years. Things weren't much better in the world of NASCAR stock car racing, where Fords struggled for wins against the mighty Hemi Mopars.

Having wooed Bunkie Knudsen and Larry Shinoda from General Motors, Ford had inside information about the 1969 and 1970 Camaros long before they debuted. The Mustang engineering team put that knowledge to good use, refining the plans for its upcoming Mustangs to make them Camaro killers.

To reclaim the SCCA title, Ford built its own answer to the Z28—the Boss 302. In the past, Ford had relied upon Carroll Shelby's skunkworks facility to craft capable race cars. Shelby's GT-350 sported a number of modifications aimed at improving the

The Boss 429 Mustang had a dual role: homologate the Boss 429 semi-Hemi engine for use in NASCAR competition (even though Mustangs didn't race) and dominate drag racing.

Mustang's odds of winning on the track. While Shelby's Mustangs were fierce competitors on the track, their success failed to translate into the sales for which Ford had hoped because the cars were viewed as *Shelby*'s Mustangs, not Ford's.

Ford moved to correct this in 1968, by taking over production of the Shelby models. Yet even though Ford made no effort to conceal the fact that it was now building the Shelbys, the public still believed that Shelby was involved. Ford decided it needed an ultra-performance Mustang that was all its own.

For 1969, Shinoda gave them just what they were looking for in the Boss 302. With a completely reengineered 302 engine that featured a high-strength cylinder block, large-port heads, a race-ready cam, and other special touches, the Boss 302 had the pow-

er to compete. Suspension, steering, and brake system upgrades gave it the agility to compete. And thanks to subtle, yet characteristic styling cues, the cars were highly recognizable whether at speed or in the winner's circle.

The Boss 302 wasn't an immediate on-track success, but it did garner its share of sales in the showrooms, which was ultimately more important to Ford. In 1970, when the modestly updated Boss 302 did dominate the sport, Ford was hardly upset about the publicity and image the wins brought.

NASCAR racing was a different matter altogether. Ford had a good reputation thanks to its numerous wins, but the company wasn't comfortable with competition being so equal. Simply put, the NASCAR Fords needed more power to outrun the

The Boss 429 featured massive aluminum cylinder heads with semi-hemispherical combustion chambers. The 375-horse engine's heads were so wide that the Mustang shock towers had to be reworked to make room for the engine, which was installed by Kar Kraft for Ford.

Mopars. That power came from a new 429-ci engine with massive cylinder heads cast with semi-hemispherical combustion chambers, similar to the Chrysler Hemi's. The Boss 429, as the engine was named, was built for the sole purpose of out-muscling the Hemi in NASCAR competition.

Designing and building the engine was a relatively easy task for Ford. The hard part was making sure it sold enough to homologate the engine for use in NASCAR racers. The company needed to sell at least 500, but the statisticians calculated it was unlikely that enough Torino buyers would shell out the extra $1,200 to put a radical engine—the Boss 429—under the hood. However, NASCAR didn't require an engine used for racing to be available in a vehicle used for racing. And since the odds said Mustang buyers would fork over the extra money for the burly Boss 429 engine, the decision was made to create a special, limited-production model called the Boss 429, after the engine.

Construction of the Boss 429 Mustangs, however, was a complex and expensive proposition—and one far too complicated to carry out on the regular production lines. So Ford contracted a Michigan specialty car company, Kar Kraft, to modify partially assembled 428 SCJ–equipped Mustangs to receive the massive Boss 429. Each Mustang's shock towers had to be cut and relocated 1 inch outward to make enough room for the Boss 429's huge cylinder heads, which made the engine nearly 2 inches wider than a 428 CJ. Unique control arms and spindles also dropped the front end roughly an inch to improve handling and appearance.

Externally, the Boss 429 contrasted sharply with its brazen Boss 302 little brother. The Boss 429 sported an attractive hood scoop with a manually operated cold-air induction system, a shallow air dam under the front lower valance, and unassuming "BOSS 429" outline decals—one per fender. Oh yes, and every Boss 429 received a small metal ID tag on the driver's door with the letters "KK" (for Kar Kraft) and the car's sequence number. Like Chevy's "COPO" Camaros, the Boss 429 was a true sleeper: It didn't look like much, but when asked to, it could trounce its competition without breaking a sweat.

1970 Ford Mustang Boss 429

Specifications

Body	Base Price	Units Built
Hardtop	$3,979*	499
Total		*499*

Engine
375-hp 429-ci 4-bbl. V-8 (Boss 429)

1/4-mile (typical)
E.T.	14.1 secs.
Speed	102 mph

* price includes base SportsRoof model plus Boss 429 engine option; other mandatory, extra-cost equipment not included

As predicted, Ford had no trouble selling the required 500 units to legalize it for NASCAR use—859 units went down Kar Kraft's makeshift production line in 1969 and another 499 were built for 1970. Though it isn't entirely clear, it's generally believed Ford lost as much as $1,000 on every Boss 429 Mustang produced.

But the Boss 429 program was a success. The new engine—coupled with the Torino Talladega's sleek new nose—gave Ford's NASCAR race teams the muscle they needed to charge to the front, and stay there. Ultimately, Ford and Dodge battled quite evenly all season, nearly alternating wins from week to week.

Today, the Boss 302 and Boss 429 Mustangs are shining examples of how auto manufacturers could mass-produce race cars for the general public. Regardless of the ethical ramifications of such a move, history shows that the public eagerly received the Boss Mustangs, and their competition was most definitely intimidated.

Under the fiberglass hood breathed a standard Mustang 335-horspower 428 Cobra Jet that gave the GT-500 potent power, but it was hardly as exotic as the modified Shelby engines of just a few years earlier.

1970 Shelby Mustang GT-500

Just five years after Ford had approached Carroll Shelby about producing special Mustangs in order to build a performance reputation for the Mustang, Shelby found himself disenchanted with his relationship with Ford. As Ford exercised more and more control over the development and production of the Mustangs that bore his name, Shelby became less and less satisfied with the results. It wasn't long before Shelby asked Ford to dissolve their partnership.

Confident that the Shelby project had accomplished its mission of establishing the Mustang as a respected performance car, Ford agreed to Shelby's request. In fact, Ford no longer needed Shelby to produce special Mustang models, as the company had an abundance of high-performance Mustangs in the lineup, including the GT, the Mach 1, the Boss 302, and the Boss 429—in addition to the Shelbys.

Though a Shelby in name only, the 428 Cobra Jet–powered 1970 Shelby GT-500 was still a formidable, as well as a very exclusive, musclecar. Special styling, interior, and powertrain changes set it apart in its final year of production. Only 789 GT-500s were released in 1970.

67

1970 Shelby GT-500 Mustang

Specifications

Body	Base Price	Units Built
Hdtp.	$4,709	
Conv.	$5,027	
Total		789*

Engine

335-hp 428-ci 4-bbl. V-8 (Cobra Jet)

1/4-mile (typical)

E.T.	14.6 secs.
Speed	99 mph

* a by-bodystyle breakdown is not available, and the 789 total units figure is disputable, though generally considered accurate

With so many exciting Mustangs to pick from, it's no wonder that buyers decided to choose from Ford's own, often less-expensive offerings. And while Ford had conservatively estimated there would be demand for roughly 4,000 1969 Shelbys, the company found itself with an estimated 789 of those cars still on-hand at the end of the 1969 model year.

Rather than sell the cars to dealers as leftovers (and thus at fire-sale prices), Ford chose to update the remaining cars and sell them as 1970 models at full price. As part of the update process, Ford replaced the identification tags on the leftover 1969s with 1970 tags, applied some black stripes on the hood and a Boss 302-like chin spoiler.

Again available in both GT-350 and GT-500 trim, the 1970 Shelbys were, essentially, Shelbys in name only. Under all that Shelby-specific bodywork—the fiberglass fenders with brake cooling ducts, the fiberglass hood with its three forward-facing and two rearward-facing NACA ducts, and the fiberglass deck

lid and quarter-panel extensions—was mostly just typical Mustang mechanicals.

The GT-350's standard engine was the four-barrel–equipped 351 Windsor V-8, producing just 290 horsepower. Unlike previous Shelby engines, which featured extensive modifications, the 351W in the 1969–1970 Shelbys received only a high-rise aluminum four-barrel intake and aluminum Cobra valve covers.

GT-500s, such as the one pictured, continued to rely upon the 428 Cobra Jet big-block V-8 with its 335 horsepower and R-code cold-air induction, fed by the center, forward-facing hood scoop. Again, the cars were available with either a four-speed manual or three-speed automatic transmission. And the "Competition" suspension package featured the very same capable equipment found under Mach 1 models.

Likewise, the interior of the Shelbys was Deluxe Mustang fare, with the addition of a roll bar that not only improved the racy good looks of both the fastback and convertible models, but also added a degree of safety in the event the vehicle wound up with its wheels pointing skyward.

Although the 1969–1970 Shelby Mustangs were still plenty able to mix it up with Camaros, Firebirds, Challengers, and 'Cudas, they were hardly cut from the same cloth as the early, true Shelbys. But given the rarity and admirable performance of the 1970 Shelby Mustangs, those that survive today are highly prized treasures.

MERCURY DIVISION: FAST FORDS WITH HIGH FASHION

While Mercury's mission was to provide luxurious models at affordable prices, the company realized the importance of tapping into the burgeoning performance market. Apart from the additional sales and exposure, such a move would also help the company build brand loyalty among the young buyers in the hope of converting them into buyers of high-end (and highly profitable) luxury cars later in life.

Like its sister division, Ford, Mercury created a performance reputation the old fashioned way: by racing—and winning. Battles took place on drag strips and stock car ovals around the country.

Known more for its luxury, cars such as the 1969 Cougar Eliminator showcased Mercury's muscle-building talents. Larry Shinoda, who styled the Boss 302, developed the Eliminator package for Mercury. The semi-fastback, side stripes, and deck lid spoiler gave it a unique look.

Mercury built a limited run of Comets aimed at dominating drag strip competitions. A 289-powered model was cleared for competition in NHRA's B/FX class, and Mercury covered the A/FX class with Comets stuffed full of high-riser and SOHC 427s. Drag racing legends Dyno Don Nicholson, Eddie Schartman, and Hayden Proffitt all lit up the win lights in Mercurys; Dyno Don even did it in a Mercury Comet *station wagon*, which he believed had better weight transfer characteristics than the standard sedan—

something he credited for his 11-second class record and a season that saw only a single defeat.

And when it came to the NASCAR circuit, Comets—and later Cyclones—carried the Mercury name into Victory Lane. As the aero wars took center stage, Mercury was there with its Cyclone Spoiler and subsequent Cyclone Spoiler II.

Naturally, as word spread of Mercury's on-track accomplishments, its off-track business picked up, though never quite to levels that were completely commensurate with its finishes at the races. That meant that a significant portion of the buying public ended up missing out on the street versions of each of Mercury's racing models.

The buyers who didn't miss out were rewarded with cars that were every bit the equal of the more popular Ford performance models, but with more comfortable interiors and more stylized bodies. Mercury musclecars had the added advantage (for those buyers who valued it for some less-than-strictly-legal reasons) of not looking like musclecars nor did many people know much about their performance potential, so Mercury drivers had little trouble convincing unsuspecting victims to race them.

But when "performance" became a dirty word in the early 1970s, Mercury wisely refocused itself on the luxury car market. And though Mercury occasionally released performance cars throughout the remainder of the twentieth century—cars such as the imported Capri in the early 1970s, the 5.0-liter Mustang-based Capri of the 1980s, and the sporty Cougar at the turn of the century—its days of building musclecars were over. The surviving 1960s and 1970s Mercury musclecars have been left to preserve the memory of Mercury's hottest machines.

1969 Mercury Cougar Eliminator

An upscale Ford that's just right for taking down—or shaking down—the competition.

Despite all its market research, the various concept cars that were meant to test the waters, and the fact that the Mustang was going to be based on the Falcon underpinnings, the Mustang was still a huge financial risk for Ford Motor Company. Understandably, the company wasn't eager to let its Mercury division rush down a similar development path until the Mustang had proven itself.

Of course, following the sales stampede created by the 1965 Mustang debut in April 1964, there was little reason to hold back on plans for a Mercury pony car. In the fall of 1966 the Cougar hit showrooms featuring a number of refinements that differentiated it from the Mustang and uniquely qualified it as a Mercury, including softer suspension calibrations, a 3-inch wheelbase stretch, and of course the

Cougar Eliminators were available with a variety of engines, including the Boss 302 and base 351, but this particular 1969 model carried the legendary 428 Cobra Jet. With dual exhaust and a shaker hood, the 335-horsepower 428-powered Eliminator was a monster on the street.

unique front- and rearend treatments and other bodywork changes.

Though hardly the instant success that the Mustang was, the Cougars sold well—over 100,000 units a year during the first few years. For 1969 the Cougar was restyled and an exciting new performance model joined the line-up: the Eliminator.

The Eliminator, like Pontiac's GTO Judge, combined outstanding performance and a high measure of luxury with an unmistakable and aggressive appearance. Performance-wise, the Eliminator picked up where the previous year's GT model left off. Ride and handling were dictated by the Competition Suspension package, which offered taut handling without a jarring ride. More important to race fans were the engines, transmissions, and rear axle assemblies that were available—and there were several.

The base Eliminator engine was the 290-horse 351-4V, which was optionally available on Cougars. Up a step from that was the marginally more powerful Marauder 390 at 320 horsepower, or the Boss 302 with its 290 horsepower. The Cobra Jet 428 that appeared in late 1968 remained available, and for a very brief time the Boss 429 could be ordered, but

The Cougar's Mustang roots showed through inside, where the semi-cockpit-style instrument are obviously derived from the Mustang. A large analog tachometer and speedometer fed vital information to the pilot. Like other Ford products of the day, it featured the rim-blow steering wheel.

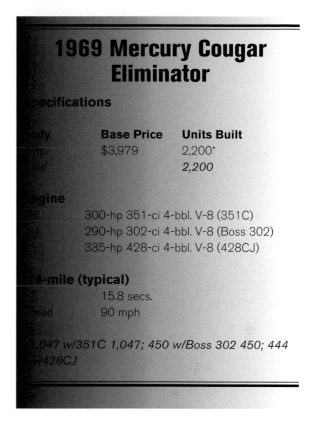

1969 Mercury Cougar Eliminator

Specifications

Body	Base Price	Units Built
Htp.	$3,979	2,200*
Total		2,200

Engine

300-hp 351-ci 4-bbl. V-8 (351C)
290-hp 302-ci 4-bbl. V-8 (Boss 302)
335-hp 428-ci 4-bbl. V-8 (428CJ)

1/4-mile (typical)

ET   15.8 secs.
Speed   90 mph

*1,047 w/351C 1,047; 450 w/Boss 302 450; 444 w/428CJ

only if you had connections—just two found their way under Cougar hoods.

Buyers interested in a great *driving* car were wise to select the Boss 302, which was the very same high-winding engine that highlighted the Boss 302 Mustang. It was widely known that the Boss 302's 290 horsepower and equal torque ratings were greatly under-rated. Though a bit twitchy for around-town driving, the Boss 302—and, indeed, the Eliminator—was in its element blasting down twisting, curving roads.

On the other hand, buyers who were more into short jaunts of, say, a quarter-mile or so, were better served by the Cobra Jet 428. As with the Boss 302, the CJ's 335 horsepower rating was somewhat less than believable, especially given the durability built into the engine when delivered in Super Cobra Jet form, with its LeMans-style rods, heavy-duty crank, and other fortified components. The big-block 428 also made for an excellent street warrior, though it lacked the handling prowess that the smaller, lighter Boss 302 afforded.

As improved as the Eliminator was over a typical Mustang, and as competent as it was on the street and race tracks, it just never caught on with the public. Still, in spite of its May 8, 1969, intro date and little promotional fanfare, Mercury dealers had little trouble moving 2,411 copies of the Eliminator by the end of the 1969 model production in July. But a full year of production in 1970 actually saw a dip in sales to 2,200 units, with just under half getting the base 351 Cleveland engine and the other half split evenly between Boss 302 and 428CJ engines. Such low production numbers hardly justified the engineering, marketing, and sales efforts that Mercury poured into the car. But as unsuccessful as the Cougar Eliminator was sales-wise, it nonetheless stands as one of the ultimate—and rarest—Mercury musclecars.

CHAPTER 3

Chrysler Corporation

Big-Block Thunder and Small-Block Lightning

When you've got the King of Stock Car Racing, Richard Petty, in your camp, it's hard to fathom how you could be viewed as anything but serious about performance. And for Chrysler's Plymouth division, Petty was merely the icing on a multilayer performance cake.

Beginning in the 1950s, Plymouth was making a reputation for itself as a performance car company, thanks to such models as the Fury and engines such as the original Hemi.

Along came the 1960s and drag racing literally took off. When it did, Plymouth was right there with its Super Stock 413 and 426 cars that cleaned the clocks of nearly anyone who bothered to run against them.

King Richard held court over NASCAR racing with his Petty Blue Plymouths (except for 1969 when he temporarily jumped ship to race a Torino Talladega for Ford). For 1970 Plymouth was right in the thick of things with Petty at the wheel of its winged warrior, the Superbird.

Plymouths were regularly winning in one form of motorsports or another, and on the street. With such cars as the GTX, the Road Runner, and the legendary 'Cuda, Plymouth was able to earn its reputation every day of the week, often one stoplight at a time.

It's interesting to look back at each manufacturer's contributions to the musclecar era, to see what kind of mark each left. For Pontiac, it's clear that the GTO created the musclecar market. For Ford, it was the creation of the pony car market. Plymouth made the musclecar market fun. The Road Runner took its name from the popular cartoon character, and Plymouth played the connection for all it was worth by applying decals of the character to the car's exterior, interior, and even underhood. The company even gave the car a "beep-beep" horn. In 1970, when the end of the musclecar was on the horizon, Plymouth drenched its performance models in outlandish paint colors such as Panther Pink and Plum Crazy.

Plymouth's 1964 Sport Fury was purpose-built to wage war on drag strips, and it soon proved a formidable opponent on the street thanks largely to its Super Stock 426. The Wedge-head 426 with a single four-barrel carb and 10.3:1 compression ratio developed 365 horsepower at 4,800 rpms.

The Super Stock 426 big-block was not an engine for the timid: the "weak" S/S 426 put out 415 horsepower; the hot 426 put out 10 more horsepower. Note the dual-quad cross-ram intake and exotic exhaust manifolds.

1964 Plymouth Super Stock 426

Specifications

Body	Base Price	Units Built
Ship.	$3,379*	
Total		n/a

Engine

Std.	415-hp 426-ci 4-bbl. V-8
Opt.	425-hp 426-ci 4-bbl. V-8

1/4-mile (typical)

E.T.	13.1 secs.
Speed	112 mph

Today, it's a sad fact that the Plymouth nameplate is no more. But during the 1960s and 1970s no manufacturer was more into musclecars than Plymouth. The milestone musclecars on the following pages are proof of that.

1964 Plymouth Sport Fury

Chrysler was no stranger to the drag strip. Nor did it find building a high-powered drag car any kind of mystery. So when drag racing competition started heating up in the early 1960s, it was no surprise to find Chrysler continually leading the pack with its "Max Wedge" engines.

By 1964, with the competition breathing down its neck with 409 Impalas, "swiss-cheesed" Super Duty Pontiacs, and quick-as-lightning Thunderbolts, Chrysler instructed its engineers to find more speed for the company's Super Stock offerings.

Starting with the simple logic that bigger is better, the engineers hogged out the aging 413 engine and came up with an additional 13 cubic inches of displacement. A new, short-runner, cross-ram-style intake manifold improved the engine's ability to

breathe, while dual Carter four-barrels mixed fuel and air in ample volume. Two compression ratios were available with different power outputs—the "low" compression version used an 11.0:1 ratio that developed 415 horsepower, while the high-compression 13.5:1 engine made 10 additional horses. Regardless of compression, Chrysler gave the Super Stock engines an exotic exhaust system that consisted of unique, free-flowing, individual runner cast-iron exhaust manifolds, 3-inch head pipes with a crossover and dump tubes, and low-restriction twin mufflers for keeping things reasonably quiet on the street.

Behind the Super Stock 426 engine, buyers could select either a heavy-duty four-speed manual gearbox or Chrysler's fortified 727 TorqueFlite, which was generally considered to be the preferable equipment due to the highly consistent times it allowed, plus its cushioning effect, which extended the life of such driveline parts as universal joints, axle gears, and axles.

With huge power and a seriously upgraded suspension system, the Super Stock Sport Fury was capable of catapult-like launches with a high-G pull that just didn't quit until the driver lost his nerves or the road ended—either of which happened in a hurry. On the strip, stock S/S Sport Furys could run low-14s out of the box with inexperienced drivers at the wheel. Experienced drivers could rip off 13s until the cows came home. And with some tweaking and a few carefully selected aftermarket parts, including headers and slicks, mostly stock S/S Sport Furys were honest-to-goodness 12-second cars.

Apart from their bulletproof powertrains, the Sport Fury and its sibling, the Polara-based Super Stock Dodge, had a weight advantage compared to their usual competition. At 3,400 pounds, the Chrysler twins were the lightest cars in their class. When GM and Ford tried to even the scales by swapping in lightweight hoods, fenders, and bumpers, Chrysler responded in kind, dropping the Fury's weight to just over the 3,200-pound NHRA class minimum.

But the Plymouths (and Dodges) would likely have continued their winning ways without any exotic weight-loss programs. The cars were simply that good on the strip.

In the showroom, the Fury proved to be one of Plymouth's most attractive models ever—a characteristic many Mopar enthusiasts still respect about the model. But even the non-Mopar-minded admit the Super Stock Sport Fury was an awesome performer—and a milestone of the times.

1967 Plymouth Belvedere GTX

When the automotive industry saw the public clamoring to get its hands on Pontiac's 1964 GTO, each manufacturer clamored on its own to catch up with Pontiac, and hopefully beat the GTO at its own game.

Plymouth's response to the GTO was the Belvedere, which evolved into the Belvedere GTX for 1967. The midsize Belvedere was a natural GTO combatant, with a similar size, weight, and general market.

But Plymouth had something that Pontiac couldn't compete with: an unlimited cubic-inch displacement policy. While GM hamstrung its intermediate models with a 400-ci cap, the Belvedere's designers had ready access to the Plymouth Super Commando 440, or the 426 Street Hemi.

For the performance-minded but cash-strapped, the 440 GTX was a bargain at $3,178 MSRP. Buyers got 375 horsepower, 480 foot-pounds of torque, a heavy-duty "Hemi" four-speed (or beefy TorqueFlite automatic), and a tough-as-nails 8 3/4-inch rear axle assembly. Armed with those items, the GTX more

The 1964 Sport Fury's interior was quite comfortable with bucket seats. Deluxe appointments included a console, a large-diameter steering wheel, and even a four-instrument gauge panel.

The GTX was fitted with the 375-horsepower Super Commando 440 V-8.

Standard GTX performance was provided by the 375-horsepower Super Commando 440, but the 425-horsepower 426 street Hemi was also available. At 3,545 pounds and 200.5 inches long, the GTX fit into the full-size musclecar category; but equipped with the killer 426 Hemi, it humbled most of its opponents.

This fully-appointed musclecar has bucket seats, console, rich carpeting, and a lot of chrome accents.

1967 Plymouth GTX

Specifications

Body	Base Price	Units Built
Hdtp.	$3,178	
Conv.	$3,418	
Total		12,690

Engine		
Std.	375-hp 440-ci 4-bbl. V-8	
Opt.	425-hp 426-ci 2x4-bbl. V-8 (Hemi)	

1/4-mile (typical)	
E.T.	14.6 secs.
Speed	96 mph

than matched any GTO's performance—and durability. But buyers who wanted to give a GTO no chance of keeping up could plunk down a couple hundred more dollars to equip their GTX with the mother of all performance engines: the awesome Street Hemi, which put 425 (under-rated) horsepower and 490 foot-pounds of torque at a driver's disposal—potential that Plymouth urged drivers to exercise with caution on the street.

With either engine, the GTX had what it took to win races—which it did in Top Stock Eliminator competition at the 1966 Springnationals, Winternationals, Summernationals, and World Championship Finals. With the Hemi, some fine-tuning, and a pair of slicks, a GTX could dash down the quarter-mile in the 11-second bracket.

The GTX also had what it took to win friends. Outside, GTX's styling was clean and classic, instantly attractive. Inside, it was simple but well appointed. No matter which way you sliced the GTX, it came up a winner.

Unfortunately, few Plymouth buyers recognized the GTX for the incredible buy that it was. By year's end, just 12,690 GTXes had rolled off Chrysler production lines, including 125 ultra-rare Hemi-powered units.

A year later, in 1968, the GTX found itself facing some serious competition from—of all places—Plymouth. When the new-for-'68 Road Runner hit the streets, it did so with bodywork identical to the GTX's—and a price that was $500 less. For most buyers, that savings more than offset the power difference between the Road Runner's 383 and the GTX's 440—and either could be had with the Hemi. A total of 44,599 Road Runners were sold—more than double the 18,940 GTXes that year.

GTX sales continued to dwindle in the coming years: 15,602 in 1969; 7,748 in 1970; and, finally, 2,942 in 1971. Even though the GTX never garnered huge sales, its performance record and its status as the big brother of the Road Runner preserve its seat at the musclecar table.

1970 Plymouth Superbird

If anyone doubted Chrysler's interest in winning NASCAR Grand National (now Winston Cup) races, they needed only a glimpse of the 1970 Plymouth Superbird.

From the Superbird's streamlined, wedge-shaped snout to its outrageous elevated rear wing,

Few cars make more of a statement than Plymouth's Road Runner–based Superbird. The front nose and rear wing created enormous downforce and gave the car a competitive advantage on NASCAR's high-speed ovals. Only 1,920 Superbirds were built for the street, making it one of the rarest Mopar musclecars ever made.

The Superbird's base engine was the 375-horsepower 440 Super Commando V-8, and the 425-horsepower street version of the 426 Hemi race engine was optional.

1970 Plymouth Superbird
Specifications

Body	Base Price	Units Built
Hdtp.	$4,298	1,920
Total		*1,920*

Engine

Std.	375-hp 440-ci 4-bbl. V-8
Opt.	425-hp 426-ci 2x4-bbl. V-8 (Hemi)

1/4-mile (typical)

E.T.	14.4 secs.
Speed	100 mph

there was no mistaking the Superbird for grandma's grocery-getter. No sir, the Superbird was built for speed—and lots of it.

NASCAR's first round of "aero wars" kicked off in 1969, when Dodge debuted the Charger 500 and Ford countered with its Torino Talladega. Mercury got into the action with its Cyclone Spoiler II. And late in the year, Dodge pulled out all the stops and debuted its futuristic-looking Charger Daytona, on which the Superbird was based.

The Charger 500 had been Dodge's first attempt at improving the aerodynamics of its NASCAR star. The 500's flush-mounted grille and semi-fastback rear window boosted lap speeds by several miles per hour on NASCAR's superspeedways, and more important, proved there was much to be gained from improving the shape of a car.

Unfortunately for Dodge, Ford was a fast learner, and the Talladega (along with its Spoiler II cousin) was immediately competitive with the slick Dodge. Chrysler's engineers went back to the wind tunnel with scale models looking for more speed, and increased stability. They rightly reasoned that a wedge-shaped nose cone fitted to the Charger would have two distinct effects. First, it would slice through the air rather than bash against it. Second, properly

shaped, the aero nose would act much like an air foil, increasing downforce on the front end and helping to keep the front tires firmly planted during cornering.

But the Daytona's nose had an unexpected side effect: there was so much downforce on the front end that the rear of the car actually began to lift at speed, creating an incredibly loose handling condition. To restore stability, engineers experimented with a number of deck lid spoilers, but none generated enough rear downforce to counter the pressure on the front of the car. None, that is, until the engineers crafted an airplanelike wing and positioned it nearly 2 feet above the deck, between two massive supports. The height got the wing up into "clean" air, and the designers made the blade angle adjustable, allowing pit crews to tune the downforce for specific track conditions—more angle made more downforce, which was handy for shorter tracks, while big tracks required less blade angle.

Plymouth, which had been limping along at the races with its aerodynamic-as-a-brick Road Runner and GTX twins, had its engineers looking over the Dodge boys' shoulders during the aero and track tests of the Daytona. The Rapid Transit Authority then came up with some subtle enhancements for its

The Superbird measured 221 inches long and its wing was 24 inches high, 58 inches laterally across the back end, and 7.5 inches wide. It produced a maximum downforce of 600 pounds on the race track. The race version of the winged wonder was the first stock car to go over 200 miles per hour. The Superbird was so dominant in races that NASCAR banned the use of tall wings in 1971.

version of the winged wondercar, including a relocated and enlarged grille positioned on the underside of the nose, and slightly shorter rear wing supports to suit the needs of the Road Runner's roofline.

The Superbird was an immediate success, winning eight races during the 1970 season, while its less streamlined sibling, the Road Runner, racked up roughly another dozen victories on shorter tracks. Not a bad scorecard, considering Plymouth had only two wins during the previous year, both of which came before the Charger 500, Talladega, and Spoiler II debuted.

Bound by NASCAR rules, Plymouth had to offer the Superbird—complete with pointed proboscis and stratospheric spoiler—to the general public. As attention-getting as the aero devices were, they weren't exactly great street machines. The long nose made it hard to judge how close you were to cars ahead while parking or coming to a stop. The smallish grille limited cooling ability at street speeds. And the wing hampered rearward visibility, and even limited how far the trunk lid could open.

1971 Plymouth 'Cuda
Specifications

Body	Base Price	Units Built
Coupe	$3,156	6,228
Conv.	$3,412	374
Total		*6,602*

Engine

Std.	250-hp 383-ci 4-bbl. V-8
Opt.	290-hp 340-ci 3x2-bbl. V-8 (AAR)
	375-hp 440-ci 4-bbl. V-8
	390-hp 440-ci 3x2-bbl. V-8
	425-hp 426-ci 4-bbl. V-8 (Hemi)

1/4-mile (typical)

E.T.	13.9 secs.
Speed	104 mph

The Hemi was the ultimate Barracuda engine, but a variety of performance engines were available including the 335-horsepower 383 and the 390-horsepower 440 Wedge motors for the cost-conscious. A high-revving, triple two-barrel, 290-horsepower 340 was available in the AAR 'Cuda, which was Dodge's homologation special for Trans-Am road racing.

Despite their Road Runner roots, which gave the cars the necessary equipment to run well on the street—including standard 440 Super Commando or optional 426 Street Hemi power—Superbirds didn't exactly fly off dealers' lots. In total, some 1,800 were constructed and sold, many ultimately at deep discounts, just to get rid of them.

But the Superbird represented a definite high-water mark in musclecar aerodynamics—and it proved on race tracks that it had the muscle to put those sleek lines to good use. On those terms, no other musclecar even came close.

1971 Plymouth 'Cuda

When the Barracuda debuted in mid-1964, it was anything but a musclecar. But in true Ugly Duckling style, the Barracuda grew to become the envy of the musclecar market. Each year, Plymouth refined the Barracuda, transforming it from a Corvair- and Falcon-fighter to a fearsome Mustang- and Camaro-killer.

At no time was the 'Cuda—introduced in 1969 as a separate performance-oriented version of the Barracuda—more refined than 1971. When Plymouth first unleashed the 'Cuda option, it did so to address power shortcomings in the aging fastback Barracuda. In 1970, the Barracuda lineup was redesigned with a Camaro-esque long hood/short deck body that rippled with muscle.

For 1971, the one-year-old body was updated to smooth the design's few rough edges. Under the hood, the 'Cuda engine lineup was warmed-over from 1970 and most engines were re-rated to reflect the auto industry's move to the Society of Automotive Engineers (SAE) net horsepower ratings—which more realistically indicated how much power an engine would produce as installed in a production vehicle, rather than on an engine dynamometer. (Of course, any deliberate horsepower understatements by manufacturers in previous years still make comparisons tricky.) Otherwise, the 340, 383, both the four-barrel and six-barrel 440s, and the legendary Hemi were unchanged. GM and Ford made quick and drastic changes in their 1971 performance engine line-ups, making the 'Cudas appear all the more awesome.

Thanks to the chassis and suspension systems introduced in 1970, the 'Cuda continued to be one of the best-handling cars on the market, especially when equipped with the lightweight but plenty powerful 340 small-block engine, which produced a re-rated and still underrated 235 horsepower in 1971. Naturally, the straightline crowd was more attracted to the 440s and Hemis, but at $884 (plus the cost of the mandatory four-speed and other heavy-duty options) the elephant motor was a stretch for all but a lucky 115 'Cuda buyers—just 7 of whom went for their Hemi in a convertible body.

As exciting and powerful as the 1971 'Cuda was, there was still one area in which it couldn't compete with Camaros and Mustangs: sales. Those models sold more than 100,000 units each, whereas the entire Barracuda line didn't even account for 19,000 registrations that year—and just 6,602 were 'Cudas.

The following year, Chrysler detuned its musclecar program. The 'Cuda engine lineup was gutted. The only "performance" engine kept on the option list was the 340, which picked up 5 horsepower on

The Barracuda was first released in 1964, but the 1970 E-Body Barracuda joined the upper echelon of musclecars and was a genuine challenger to the Camaro and Mustang. With the exception of the Dart, the Barracuda was the lightest and smallest Mopar musclecar in 1970. When equipped with a Hemi, it became the fastest Mopar.

The short deck and long hood emulated the Mustang and Camaro, but the clean lines and distinctive styling were all Mopar. The 'Cuda featured a blacked-out taillamp panel and was available with a deck lid wing and rear window slats.

paper but was obviously far less powerful than the lower-rated 340 of 1971.

For the brief span of one model year, the 1971 'Cuda was the pinnacle of Chrysler musclecar creation, and for many today, the ultimate musclecar ever.

1971 Plymouth GTX

Chrysler was the last of The Big Three auto makers to respond to the government's and the insurance industry's pressure to scale back performance and exhaust emissions. While GM and Ford dramatically cut power for 1971—both in real terms through detuned engines, and on paper through a revised (net) horsepower rating system—Chrysler continued into 1971 as if the musclecar wars were still being waged.

One of Chrysler's last true musclecars was a descendent of one of its first—the Plymouth GTX. For 1971, the Satellite lineup—which included both the Road Runner and the GTX—was completely

restyled with a new "fuselage"-style body that featured a long, low, wide look with a semi-fastback rear end treatment and a wraparound front bumper and recessed grille. Unlike the "slab" sides of the previous Belvedere body design, the new model had nicely sculpted sides with a strong feature line that separated the midsection from the lower body. The new shape proved as functional as it was fashionable when the King of Stock Car Racing, Richard Petty, was able to continue his winning ways behind the wheel of a 1971 Plymouth, conspicuously lacking GTX or Road Runner logos.

Inside, the cars were equally updated with all-new everything. Thoroughly modern—and even a bit futuristic—the new models were an immediate sensation in Plymouth dealerships, especially in two-door form. (Four-door models were actually remarkably different, sharing not a single body panel, and featuring a far more traditional, though similar, appearance.)

The same Super Commando 440 lurked beneath the curvaceous new sheet metal. A big revision to the power rating system dropped output to 330 *net* horsepower.

Under the GTX's new hood—which featured two simulated vents in standard form or a new, forward-facing, pop-up "Air-Grabber" cold-air induction system optionally—things were somewhat less than all new, which was a good thing in light of detuning by GM and Ford.

The GTX came with a re-rated version of the tried and true Super Commando 440, while the Road Runner continued to feature a 383 in exchange for a $600 savings. The 440, despite its new 305 SAE net horsepower rating, had yet to be castrated; it still had its high compression, its lopey cam, its large-port heads, and rich jetting in its Carter AFB four-barrel carb. As such, the GTX was one of the hottest performers of 1971, still able to rip off low-14-second passes with ease, while would-be challengers struggled to just break into the 14s.

In addition to the sleek new shape, new interior, and hot-as-ever engines, the 1971 GTX was the best-handling GTX to date, thanks to its extra-heavy-duty

The redesigned GTX received a contemporary long-hood, short-deck style, and a semi-fastback profile in 1971. The new body rippled with muscle and injected new life into the Mopar musclecar lineup.

The GTX's new, space-age interior was as attractive as the exterior and far more inviting than the previous generation's.

1971 Plymouth GTX

Specifications

Body	Base Price	Units Built
	$3,733	2,942
		2,942

Engine

305-hp 440-ci 4-bbl. V-8
330-hp 440-ci 3x2-bbl. V-8
350-hp 426-ci 4-bbl. V-8 (Hemi)

¼-mile (typical)

14.8 secs.
94 mph

suspension system that was designed for more than just straightline acceleration. The brakes were also improved, which made the car a better—and safer—driving machine.

At year's end, however, fewer than 3,000 buyers saw fit to order a GTX, perhaps in part because of its $3,733 base price. The powers that be at Plymouth weren't impressed by the GTX production figures, and with the big 440 slated for extinction thanks to emissions regs, the GTX quietly disappeared from the product line.

DODGE: HAIL THE RAPID TRANSIT SYSTEM

It's almost a universal law that when you talk about musclecars, you have to at least mention a Dodge. The reasoning is simple: Dodge was so much a part of the musclecar movement that the two are practically inseparable.

Ironically, Dodge didn't have that many musclecars to hoot and holler about.

Sure, initially there were the Max Wedge Super Stock Dodges. Then in 1966 the Charger joined the lineup, and four years later the Dodge Boys finally joined the pony car race with its Challenger. There was also the Coronet, and the Super Bee. But by and large, there were few Dodge models aimed at the youthful musclecar market.

Perhaps the reason enthusiasts link Dodge so readily to the musclecar era isn't so much its cars, but the muscle behind them: Dodge's engines.

Though Chrysler Corporation shared the Dodge engines with the Chrysler and Plymouth lines, many enthusiasts think of the Hemi as a Dodge powerplant. And when they think of the beautiful (and powerful!) triple two-barrel setup on the RB big-block, they call it a "Six Pak"—Dodge's name for the system. (Heck, even Chevy fans call the Corvette Tri-Power setup a Six Pak!) And the 440 that the Six Pak comes on is generally called a "440 Magnum," even though that's just Dodge's name for it; Plymouth's 440 was the Super Commando.

Some have argued that Dodge's performance reputation was artificially inflated due to prominent roles in car movies such as *Bullitt, Vanishing Point,*

Dirty Larry, Crazy Mary, and even the TV series *The Dukes of Hazzard.*

But while the publicity no doubt helped solidify Dodge's reputation as a powerhouse, the company's accomplishments on race tracks left little doubt in anyone's mind about whether Dodge deserved its recognition as a musclecar maker. Dodge's Charger 500 was a terror on NASCAR's high-banked ovals in 1969. And less than a year later Dodge dropped the hammer on its NASCAR cruise missile, the winged and pointy-beaked Charger Daytona. Both were cars that sent the competition back to the trailers.

Like the Super Stock Dodges in the early part of the decade, the late-1960s and early-1970s Dodges did an outstanding job on drag strips, too, thanks largely to the mighty Hemi.

Dodge realized the importance of aerodynamics in stock car racing and attempted to harness the power of the wind with its sleek 1969 Charger 500's flush grille and semi-fastback rear window. With a 426 Hemi and 3.23 rear-end ratio, the automatic-equipped car sprinted through the quarter-mile at 14.01 seconds at about 100 miles per hour.

Whatever the reason, 1960s and early-1970s Dodges are known for their muscle. They were then, and they are today. A compilation of musclecar milestones wouldn't be complete without at least a few of the many deserving Dodges.

1969 Dodge Charger 500

While many musclecars were born to square off against a competitor in a battle of rapid acceleration, Dodge's 1969 Charger 500 was built for victory on the high-banked, high-speed ovals of NASCAR Grand National (now Winston Cup) racing. In fact, the "500" designation in the name represented the number of production units the company had to build to legalize the car for NASCAR competition—something the company did with only a handful to spare.

Starting with the B-body–based Charger from 1968, Dodge made the industry's first real science-based aerodynamic improvements to help the car achieve higher speeds. Two significant areas were addressed: Charger's standard, recessed grille; and the sail-panel roofline at the rear.

Replacing the recessed grille with a flush-mounted, Coronet-like grille minimized a major point of drag from the front end, and aided down-force that helped keep the front wheels firmly planted while cornering.

Charger's normal rear styling utilized two "flying buttress"-like sail panels, flanking a recessed rear window. The look was dramatic and exciting on the street, but the recessed window created a low-pressure zone that promoted aerodynamic lift of the rear end, destabilizing the car at high speeds. Complicating matters further, the massive sail panels acted like rudders in crosswinds, leading to some hair-raising rides for high-speed drivers.

The fix for the rear of the car was similar to that of the front: flush-mount the window with the peaks of the sail panels, creating a semi-fastback styling that smoothed the air stream over the car, allowing air to flow down the rear window, across the deck lid, and off the subtle lip at its rear edge. As it had with the front, removing the recessed area greatly enhanced downforce, and thus increased high-speed stability.

With the Charger 500's body capable of supporting sustained triple-digit speeds, racers finally had the ability to tap into the full power of Dodge's

While the Charger 500's body was designed to slice through the wind, the already-legendary 426 Hemi was designed to suck in gobs of it and convert it to race-winning horsepower—425 horsepower in street trim.

Charger interiors were among the finest available. Bucket seats were both comfortable and supportive, while six gauges in the instrument panel kept a driver well informed of the machine's status.

engines—namely, the 440-ci, Wedge-"B-motor" and the legendary 426 Hemi. The latter was available to the public in 425-horsepower "Street Hemi" form.

The Mighty Mopars proved to be formidable opponents, especially with driver Bobby Isaac at the wheel of the K&K Insurance–sponsored 1969 Charger, which won nearly half of the races that season. And the effectiveness of the aerodynamic alterations wasn't lost on the competition; Ford and Mercury each took their high-bank warriors to the wind tunnels and developed unique front-end treatments for them, creating the Torino Talladega and the Cyclone Spoiler II. General Motors, which had only unofficial participation in NASCAR racing at the time, passed on the investment necessary to streamline its eligible models.

The Charger 500 showed Chrysler—and the automotive world—that aerodynamics was every bit as important as engine power. The company would hammer the point home the following year with its radical pair of "winged warriors," the Charger Daytona and Plymouth Superbird. Their pointed nose cones and 3-foot-tall, adjustable deck lid spoilers produced incredible downforce, allowing the cars to run at more than 220 miles per hour during testing at the 2.6-mile Talladega Superspeedway—well beyond the safe limits of the day's tire technology.

But the Charger 500 had impact far beyond the musclecar wars and the high-banked battles. Years later auto manufacturers would incorporate some of the lessons learned from the Charger 500 and the later wing cars into everyday production vehicles, not for high-speed performance but rather highway-speed fuel economy. Rarely can a musclecar lay claim to improving fuel mileage, but the Charger 500 can.

In the end, the Charger 500 was a one-year-only model that drew barely enough buyers to qualify it for competition use; the general public knew little, if anything, about it. Yet because of its aerodynamics, the Charger 500 has had a lasting effect on nearly every car buyer since, making it a noteworthy combatant in the musclecar wars.

The recessed grille on standard Chargers acted like a parachute, slowing the cars, but the 500's flush Coronet-like grille prevented that and was responsible for a noticeable increase in speed of several miles per hour, depending on the track. The "500" indicated the number of Charger 500s Dodge built—the very same number NASCAR required in order for the car to be legal for competition use.

1969 Dodge Charger 500

Specifications

Body	Base Price	Units Built
Hdtp.	$3,860	500
Total		500

Engine

Std.	375-hp 440-ci 4-bbl. V-8
Opt.	425-hp 426-ci 2x4-bbl. V-8 (Hemi)

1/4-mile (typical)

E.T.	13.9 secs.
Speed	104 mph

CHAPTER 4

American Motors Corporation

Bold, Brash, and Eclectic

Mention "American Motors" to most Americans old enough to remember the company and the first image that usually pops into their minds is the Pacer — or the Gremlin. But musclecar enthusiasts don't think like most people. Maybe that's why they tend to remember AMC's successes, rather than those two arguable failures.

AMC intially denounced other auto manufacturer's involvement in the marketing of performance cars, and lost a lot of ground in doing so. When the company realized that performance was what the buying public wanted, it threw all its engineering, marketing, and executive weight behind its own performance programs. A light had gone on at the top of the company, with AMC suddenly convinced that it needed its own contenders on the street and the race track. Of course, many believe that AMC's very survival *did* depend on it succeeding in the musclecar market. And amazingly enough, AMC made remarkable progress in a very short time.

The company's first effort was a slightly souped-up Rambler. The following year, the Rambler was upgraded with a 343-ci V-8 that really caught people's attention. In 1969—with George Hurst's help—AMC unveiled the SC/Rambler, complete with a 315-horse 390 under the hood, making the car more than a match for any Chevy II/Nova, even if its styling was a little dated by then.

Despite running a distant fourth (of four) in sales and size, AMC led the way in several performance markets. The AMX, which stood for American Motors eXperimental, was a two-seat personal sports car along the lines of the 1950s Ford Thunderbirds. Wielding 390 power, impressive handling, dynamite styling, and comfort to boot, the AMX was a delightful performance car.

AMC's answer to the Chevy II/Nova SS was the SC/Rambler, which it codeveloped with shifter mogul George Hurst. Just 1,512 units were produced, including 1,012 with this "A" paint scheme. Along with the potent 390, the SC/Rambler featured a torque-linked rear axle, front disc brakes, AMC/Warner Gear T-10 four-speed with heavy-duty clutch, and a Model 20 rear axle.

The enormous and fully functional Ram-Air hood scoop helped boost horsepower and pushed the car to 14.3 seconds at 100.8 miles per hour.

The AMX's big brother, the Javelin, was another sure thing, thanks to its outstanding styling, thrilling performance, and exceptional value.

AMC didn't just build these cars for the street and claim they performed—they took the cars racing. Out on the track, the little AMCs were equally impressive. The Javelin faired well in SCCA Trans-Am competition right from its first race, and won the manufacturers' championship in both 1970 and 1971. In drag racing, AMX and Rambler models—and later, Gremlins—were fairly common sights and were rarely defeated easily.

But the one venue in which AMC had the most difficulty succeeding was the most important one: dealers' showrooms. No matter what AMC did to improve its image, no matter how many races it won, no matter how great its new cars were, and no matter how "catchy" its advertising campaigns, the public just wasn't buying enough AMC models to keep the company afloat.

Today, surviving AMC models such as the AMX, the Javelin, the Rebel Machine, the SC/Rambler, and others are bold reminders that tiny AMC once took on the big boys on the streets and strips of America—and won.

1969 1/2 AMC/Hurst SC/Rambler

Little AMC was doing its best in 1969 to catch up to the Joneses—The Big Three Joneses. The company had publicly stated in 1964 that it would have nothing to do with the performance wars being staged between GM, Ford, and Chrysler. But with sales projections growing bleaker by the day, the company was forced to take drastic action or suffer the consequences.

The company realized that passing on the performance car market just didn't make sound financial sense, so in 1965 it began working on a number of projects aimed at creating a performance image.

By 1969, AMC blasted onto the racing scene with a vengeance. It was running Javelins in SCCA Trans-Am competition, and with the help of George Hurst (the Hurst in "Hurst Shifters") the AMX was doing damage in professional drag racing. While the company was working on street versions of the Javelin Trans-Am and the AMX drag car, both of those were largely competitors for pony cars such as the Camaro and Mustang. That left AMC absent from a number of performance car markets.

Although the company hadn't yet formulated a strategy for competing with other makers' midsize and full-size musclecars, the company did have something for the compact-car market.

The Rambler American was AMC's answer to Chevy's Chevy II (later renamed Nova) and Ford's Falcon. But those models were soon uprated. Ford's performance Falcon was something called the Mustang (the two shared a common platform), and Chevy created the Nova Super Sport and stuffed its engine bay with a hot 327-ci V-8. AMC initially responded with the 1966 1/2 Rogue, but the Rogue's 225-horse 290 V-8 proved to be no match for the Chevy 327 or the Mustang's hi-po 289.

A year later, AMC rolled out the 1967 1/2 Super-Americans, which evened the score somewhat, thanks to the 280-horsepower 343 V-8. The Super-Americans were good, but they had their problems.

When AMC got the idea to redo the Super-American for 1969, they asked George Hurst to apply to the Rambler some of what he learned prepping 53 AMXes for Super Stock duty. The cars he created were the Hurst SC/Ramblers—the "SC" stood for "SuperCar."

The first course of action was to improve the SC/Rambler's engine. The trusty 343 was ousted in favor of the AMX 390 with its 315 horsepower. Curing one of the factory limitations of the Super-Americans, AMC installed a factory dual-exhaust system fitted with Thrush glasspack mufflers.

Chassis flex had been a common complaint about the Super-Americans, to such a degree that tales of broken windshields weren't uncommon. Things would only get worse with the 390's boosted torque. To remedy the problem, the SC/Rambler chassis was reinforced at key structural points.

The 390 was linked to a T-10 four-speed via a heavy-duty clutch, and a T-handle Hurst shifter (of course) poked through the floorboards. Out back, the AMC Model 20 rear axle assembly was fitted with 3.54:1 gears and a Twin-Grip limited-slip differential, while AMX Torque Links were reengineered to fit the American chassis to control wheel hop and aid handling. Front disc brakes were made standard to haul the car down from speed safely and swiftly.

To make sure an SC/Rambler wasn't mistaken for a garden-variety, little ol' lady's Rambler, the car was given flamboyant red and blue accents. Initially, the SC/Rambler paint scheme consisted of massive red side stripes, blue graphics on the hood, and blue Magnum 500–styled steel wheels with redline tires. A fiberglass hood sported a boxlike scoop that angled upward to ingest cold air as it rushed over the car, and a huge blue arrow pointed into the scoop with red "390 CU.IN." bisecting the arrow's head from its stem. AMC built 500 SC/Ramblers with this paint scheme, then revised it with a more subdued "B" paint appearance. It was still a white car, but the B version did away with the huge red sides in favor of a much narrower, 2-inch red lower body stripe above blue rocker areas. The hood also lost the bold graphics, though it did retain the hood pins and cables. Five hundred "B" cars were built. When those were sold, a third batch consisting of 512 SC/Ramblers was built with the original "A" paint scheme, for a total of 1,512 SC/Ramblers.

Regardless of the paint treatment, all the SC/Ramblers were the same inside (and in every other respect, since there were no options). Each car featured gray vinyl front seats that weren't buckets but were more like individual minibenches. The seats, which had red, white, and blue-striped headrests, were too close together for a console or even an armrest. A wood, three-spoke steering wheel gave orders to the front wheels, while a standard Rambler dash was jazzed up only slightly with a Sun tach that was secured to the steering column with a stainless-steel hose clamp.

The SC/Ramblers were fearsome on the streets or the track, thanks to their envious power-to-weight ratio. And at the SC/Rambler's $2,998 sticker price, it was one of the best bargains of the musclecar era— especially given its ability to blast down the quarter-mile in just 14.1 seconds as it did for *Road Test* magazine's testers.

The one-year-only SC/Rambler was, indeed, a match for its competition—and just about any other car it could come across on the streets. But, once again, despite building a better mousetrap, AMC just couldn't sell enough cars to make the SC/Rambler a

1969 AMC Hurst SC/Rambler

Specifications

Body	Base Price	Units Built
Hdtp.	$2,998	1,512
Total		*1,512*

Engine

315-hp 390-ci 4-bbl. V-8

1/4-mile (typical)

E.T.	14.2 secs.
Speed	100 mph

worthwhile venture. Besides, the Rambler was in its last year of production, with the new Hornet waiting in the wings to replace it.

1969 AMC AMX California 500 Special

American Motors wasn't exactly known for building performance cars in the 1960s. After all, AMC—the company formerly known as Nash—brought us the Rambler and the Metropolitan, which were successful if a bit plain, as well as the Gremlin and the Pacer, which have the dubious honor of having been voted two of the ugliest cars ever by *Car & Driver* readers.

Credentials such as those are, perhaps, what make AMC success stories—the AMX—so interesting.

The AMX grew out of the 1965 skunkworks Project IV program, which created four concept cars: the AMX, the AMX II, the Cavalier, and the Vixen. While the Cavalier and Vixen were more mundane in nature, the AMX and AMX II were designed with sportiness in mind. The AMX show car was styled as a 2+2 with a unique "Ramble" (in homage to the company's Rambler models) seat in place of a trunk. When show crowds voiced strong interest in the AMX's attractive styling, the company quickly enlisted the talents of Italian metalworkers at Vignale to construct a functioning AMX prototype.

When the Vignale AMX joined the Project IV tour, reaction became even stronger, and the AMX was fast-tracked for production—with a few select changes. Wiser heads prevailed and nixed the Ramble seat to avoid potential legal troubles, and, in fact, the 2+2 seating configuration was killed entirely. Fortunately, deletion of the Ramble seat had little effect on the AMX's attractive profile. To cut production costs, the AMX was engineered to ride on a shortened Javelin chassis.

The 1968 AMX styling was perfect for competing with the recently redesigned Mustang and the GM pony car twins, the Chevy Camaro and Pontiac Firebird. The AMX's long hood with simulated, side-facing vents, attractively sculpted sides, and a fastback rear end and massive, muscular C-pillars was sporty, yet tough.

Had it not been for another AMC skunkworks project, those looks would have been only skin deep. Fortunately, the company's all-new 290 was an economical base engine, whose 343- and 390-ci versions proved to be capable performance engines, serving up 280 and 315 horsepower, respectively. The beauty of the AMC 290/343/390 engine was that it produced big-block power without traditional big-block bulk and heft. Weighing in under 600 pounds, the engines compared quite favorably to the big-blocks offered by the Big Three, which tipped the scales anywhere from 750 to 850 pounds. Though the AMC engine may have been down a bit on power, compared to the Chevy 396, Ford's 428, or Chrysler's 426 Hemi, its power-to-weight ratio made it a good competitor and gave the AMX better handling capabilities since it had less weight over the front wheels.

Of course, in the 1960s, the measure of a musclecar was its quarter-mile elapsed time. Even here, the AMX could run with the big boys, with box-stock runs of 14.3 seconds. Still, AMX trap speeds of

With the AMX's 315-horse 390, the SC/Rambler was serious competition for the Chevy Nova and Dodge Dart. With a number of Group 19 (AMC high-performance) parts, the SC/Rambler could run in the mid- to low 12s.

AMC cars had a personality all their own. Other than the Corvette, the AMX was the only two-seat musclecar of the era. This 1969 AMX California 500 Special wears Trendsetter Sidewinder sidepipes, and special brass plaques on the hood blisters identify it as a 500 Special.

The AMX's base engine was a 290-ci V-8, but a 343, 360, and the stellar 390 V-8 were also available. The 390 had a 4.17 by 3.57-inch bore and stroke and pumped out 315 horsepower.

AMX interiors had a look similar to that of the 1969 Mustang, thanks to the twin-cockpit design. The short-wheelbase muscle/sports car featured large, easy-to-read analog gauges, bucket seats, and a floor shifter for both automatic and manual transmissions.

94 miles per hour indicated a horsepower shortage compared to its competition, which often ended the quarter-mile dash at better than 97 miles per hour.

A tasteful appearance and good performance were often enough to win buyers, but AMC could not afford to take chances. An inviting interior was fitted between the doors, though one accommodated just two occupants. Richly upholstered bucket seats plus stylish door panels and a simple, yet pleasing instrument panel and dash kept a driver and passenger comfortable, informed, and in control of an AMX at any speed.

By all respects, the AMX was a fine piece of work, and AMC had every reason to be proud. But the competition had the upper hand on the sales floor. In its first year, 1968, dealers sold just 6,725 AMX models. In the following 12 months, they put through orders for 8,293. But for the model's third and final year, a mere 4,116 were constructed.

Fortunately for AMC, the AMX was never purely about generating impressive sales figures. To be sure, that would have been a delightful coincidence. In truth the AMX was as much about drawing buyers to AMC dealerships as it was about its own sales figures. In that respect, the AMX was a quantifiable

1969 AMC AMX California 500

Specifications

Body	Base Price	Units Built
Hdtp.	$3,297	8,293
Total		*8,293**

Engine

315-hp 390-ci 4-bbl. V-8

1/4-mile (typical)

E.T.	14.6 secs.
Speed	96 mph

* *includes: 284 "Big Bad Orange"; 195 "Big Bad Blue"; and 283 "Big Bad Green"*

success, and many enthusiasts credit the car—for a while, at least—with changing the outlook for a foundering AMC. Keeping a sinking corporation afloat is something few musclecars can lay claim to.

1970 AMC Javelin Trans-Am

Since its introduction in 1968, AMC's Javelin had been steadily improved, both in appearance and performance. The press had given the car rave reviews, especially in comparison articles in which the Javelin was pitted against Camaros, Mustangs, and other pony cars.

The Javelin had sold well—more than 50,000 units in 1968, and 40,000 in 1969—but still wasn't a smashing success in the performance car market.

Having returned to profitability in 1969, AMC was convinced it had rounded a corner and was on its way to a profitable recovery. So the notion of spending a bunch of money on a bona fide racing program wasn't nearly as far-fetched as it had been when money was considerably tighter.

AMC didn't kid itself. It knew it couldn't feasibly compete in organized drag racing or stock car racing, where engineering and cost demands knew no bounds. The SCCA's Trans-Am series offered high visibility and better odds of winning events. With these prospects on the horizon, AMC launched an all-out assault on the Trans-Am series with the goal of capturing the manufacturers' championship.

There was only one problem: AMC didn't have the know-how to field competitive cars. The solution to this dilemma was to contract Roger Penske's organization to field Javelins. Penske's shops built the cars and SCCA pro Mark Donahue drove them. Together, the pair was almost unstoppable. After early development pains, the Javelins eventually succeeded in taking home 5 first-place trophies, of the 11

awarded that season. (Donahue would do even better in 1971, scoring the first win of the season, plus six more in a row to take seven of the first nine events—and the manufacturers' championship.)

AMC wasted no time in capitalizing on its performances in Trans-Am racing. Ads—some of the boldest of the entire musclecar era—screamed "From zero to Donahue in 3.1 years" and "Donahue puts his mark on the Javelin." Another interesting ad showed a race-ready Javelin and a 1970 Javelin side by side and told of the virtues of "A Javelin for the track. A Javelin for the road."

The Javelin for the road was one of the 100 Javelin Trans-Ams assembled to homologate the car for Trans-Am competition. Each of the 100 were mandatorily painted in a bold and patriotic red-white-blue hash paint scheme. Also standard was the 315-horse 390 engine, dual exhaust, a limited-slip differential, a Hurst-shifter four-speed, front disc brakes, heavy-duty springs and shocks, front and rear

AMC's performance workhorse, the 390 V-8, was the Javelin's top engine option. Due to the added weight and size, the Javelin posted slower quarter-mile times than the AMX. Still, the 315-horse 390 pushed the Javelin to 15-second E.T.s in the low-90-mile-per-hour range, which weren't too shabby.

AMC and Penske Racing selected the Javelin for use in SCCA Trans-Am competition and handily won the championship. This 1970 Javelin's wild red, white, and blue paint scheme celebrated its racing accomplishments.

The Javelin instrument panel featured a clock on the far left, a huge speedometer in the middle, and an equally large tachometer on the right. A Hurst T-handle shifter was mated to a four-speed Warner Gear T-10 transmission.

spoilers, fat F70x14 tires, and a 140-mile-per-hour speedo plus a tach to keep tabs on the engine.

The outrageously painted Javelin Trans-Ams drew throngs of fans and speed freaks to AMC dealers. Yet, while an interesting curiousity, few inspired buyers to plunk down money for the unique appearance. But eventually, the 100 models were sold, legalizing the car for competition—or so AMC thought.

Before the start of the 1970 racing season, the SCCA changed the Trans-Am homologation rules. Instead of just 100 models, AMC now had to sell a total of 2,500! Realizing buyers wouldn't possibly buy 2,400 more copies of the tricolor Javelins, AMC quickly decided to make better use of its association with Roger Penske and, especially, Mark Donahue. The Javelin Trans-Am package was changed; it now came in any standard Javelin color, and it was renamed the Mark Donahue Special 1970 Javelin. Donahue's signature was written on the rear of the deck lid spoiler that he helped design, based on the one he used on his race car. The car proved much more popular—even in flamboyant colors such as

Big Bad Orange, Big Bad Green, or Big Bad Blue—and AMC handily sold 2,501 Donahue specials.

The very fact that AMC funneled so much effort and expense into a performance program at a time when the company was literally on the verge of collapse is remarkable and showed AMC committment to establishing itself as a respected player in the performance car market. But despite all the money, despite all the race wins, and despite the Javelin's rave reviews and the fact that it proved to be a formidable competitor on the streets and race tracks of America, the Javelin just wasn't what enough buyers were looking for.

AMC continued its support of Trans-Am racing in 1971, extending its backing to a second team, Roy Woods Racing. But with Ford, GM, and Chrysler officially out of Trans-Am, the competition was minimal and AMC won the manufacturers' crown with almost no effort. Per its contract with Penske, AMC continued its support for 1972, but promptly pulled the plug on its Trans-Am adventures at the end of the season, despite winning its second straight manufacturers' championship. Two years later, the Javelin drifted off into obscurity, and a few years later, so did AMC.

1970 AMC Javelin Trans-Am

Specifications

Body	Base Price	Units Built
Hdtp.	$3,995	100
Total		*100*

Engine

325-hp 390-ci 4-bbl. V-8

1/4-mile (typical)

E.T.	15.1 secs.
Speed	91 mph

CHEVY
MUSCLE CARS

Mike Mueller

Acknowledgments

The author would like to thank every car owner whose pride and joy appears within these pages. It was the cooperation, patience, and, above all, hospitality of each of them that made this book possible. In order of appearance, these lucky men and women are:

Randall and Patti Fort of New Smyrna Beach, FL, (1970 Chevelle SS 454); Roger and David Judski of Roger's Corvette Center, Maitland, FL, (1969 ZL1 and 1967 L88 Corvettes); Ervin Ray of Tavares, FL, (1966 Corvair Turbo Corsa); James Hill of West Palm Beach, FL, (1963 Nova SS convertible); Tom and Nancy Stump of North Liberty, IN, (1967 Nova SS); Dan Bennett and Jim Beckerle of Festus, MO, (1969 Nova SS 396); Steven Conti of St. Petersburg, FL, (1967 SS Camaro convertible); Paul McGuire of Melbourne, FL, (1967 Z/28 Camaro); Jim and Gina Collins of Hollywood, FL, (1967 SS 396 Camaro); Bill and Barbara Jacobsen of Silver Dollar Classic Cars, Odessa, FL, (1968 SS 396 Camaro); Mick Price of Atwood, IL, (1969 Yenko Camaro); Jim Price of La Place, IL, (1969 ZL1 Camaro); Scott Gaulter of Waukee, IA, (1964 Chevelle SS); Floyd Garrett of Fernandina Beach, FL, (1965 Z16 Chevelle SS 396); Bob and Christa Gatchel of Clermont, FL, (1966 SS 396 Chevelle); Roger Adkins of Dresden, TN, (1969 L89 SS 396 300 Deluxe sedan); Fred Knoop of Atherton, CA, (1969 COPO 427 Chevelle)—photo shoot courtesy of Roger Gibson, Roger Gibson Auto Restoration, Kelso, MO; Mick Price of Atwood, IL, (1969 Yenko Chevelle); Lukason and Sons Collection of FL, (1970 LS6 Chevelle convertible); Carl Beck of Clearwater, FL, (1970 SS 396 El Camino); Walter Cutlip of Longwood, FL, (1958 Impala convertible); Marty Locke of Lucasville, OH, (1961 Impala SS 409); Jerry Peeler of Clermont, FL, (1962 Bel Air 409); Frank Ristagno of Philadelphia, PA, (1964 Impala SS 409 convertible); Don Springer of Tampa, FL, (1967 Impala SS 427 convertible); Jim and Carol Collins of Hollywood, FL, (1969 Impala SS 427 convertible); courtesy Sullivan Chevrolet of Champaign, IL, (1970 454 Caprice); John Young of Mulberry, FL, (1954 Corvette); Ed and Diann Kuziel of Tampa, FL, (1962 Corvette); Lukason and Sons Collection of Florida (1965 396 Corvette).

Introduction
The Bow Tie Legacy

Chevrolet's fortunes took a major upswing when the "Hot One" came along in 1955. Featuring the division's first overhead-valve V-8, the famed 1955 Chevy left Chevrolet's tired "Stovebolt" image in the dust as an unbeatable performance reputation was born almost overnight.

Chevrolet's fiberglass two-seater also received Ed Cole's OHV 265 cubic inch V-8 that same year, saving Zora Arkus-Duntov's Corvette from possible extinction. Meanwhile, thanks to Daytona Beach race car builder Smokey Yunick, 1955 Chevys had become formidable forces in NASCAR's short track division. At Yunick's urging, Chevrolet hired long-time performance product manager Vince Piggins in 1956, laying a base for a racing parts program that would help keep Chevy street performance offerings at or near the top of the heap for nearly two decades.

Chevy's small-block V-8 quickly became the hot rodder's choice, as well as a base for countless high-performance factory models. Then along came the 348 cubic inch big-block in 1958, the forerunner of the legendary 409. Introduced in 1961, the 409 roared to many victories on NHRA drag strips under Bel Air and Impala hoods.

By 1965, the full-sized 409s were displaced by lighter, high-powered intermediates. Chevrolet had introduced its A-body model, the Chevelle, for 1964, followed by the 396 cubic inch Mk IV big-block V-8 in 1965. The Mk IV transformed the Corvette into a real screamer, made the Super Sport Chevelle a crowd-pleasing success, and later did the same for the 1967 Camaro and 1968 Nova.

In 1966, the 427 cubic inch Mk IV big-block was born as an option for full-sized models and Corvettes. With Piggins' help, 427s also found their way through the Central Office Production Order (COPO) pipeline into Camaros and Chevelles three years later, despite GM's 400 cubic inch limit for intermediates and

Borrowing the lightweight, stamped steel, ball-stud rocker arm design created by Pontiac engineers, Chevrolet's 265 cubic inch overhead-valve V-8 was a high-winding powerplant with loads of potential. Introduced in 1955, the first in a long line of Chevy small-block V-8s, it was rated at 180 horsepower with a four-barrel carb and dual exhausts.

pony cars. (GM had passed an anti-racing edict in 1963 and was trying to downplay performance.) The ZL1 aluminum 427 Camaro and L72 cast-iron 427 Chevelle, both limited edition COPO creations built for 1969, stand among Chevrolet's hottest products, surpassed only by the 1967–1969 L88 aluminum head 427 Corvettes and their more exotic 1969 ZL1 427 siblings—all impressive, but well beyond the average customer's reach.

On a more realistic scale, 1970 was the pinnacle year for Chevrolet performance. This was due in no small part to the lifting of the 400 cubic inch limit for its smaller model lines and the resulting creation of the SS 454 Chevelle. In 450 horsepower LS6 trim, the 1970 SS 454 may well have represented Detroit's strongest regular-production muscle car, with low 13-second quarter-mile runs possible right off the truck.

But by 1971, tightening federal emissions standards had brought on drastically lowered

Two of Chevrolet's most powerful offerings, the 1967 L88 (in back) and 1969 ZL1 Corvettes. Both cars were drastically underrated at 430 horsepower, with more than 500 horses at the ready from both the aluminum head L88 and all-aluminum ZL1 427 big-block V-8s. While a mere twenty L88 Corvettes were built for 1967, only two ZL1s were produced two years later.

compression ratios and stifling pollution control equipment. Detroit's muscle car era came to an end in a morass of rising insurance rates and escalating safety and environmental concerns. Chevrolet's street performance legacy basically went dormant after 1972, re-emerging less than a decade later when technology began to meet the demands of the modern performance market.

Perhaps Detroit's most popular muscle car, Chevrolet's Super Sport Chevelle reached the pinnacle in SS 454 form for 1970. In base trim, the SS 454 featured the 360 horsepower LS5 454 cubic inch big-block. The king of the hill, however, was the LS6, which pumped out 450 horsepower worth of mid-sized muscle.

Chapter 1

Big Guns
Full-Sized Flyers from 409 to 454

In the beginning—before Camaros, before Chevelles, before Sting Rays—there was the 409, Chevrolet's legendary, lyrical, performance powerplant. When the 409 was introduced in 1961, big cubes in big cars represented the only way to fly as Detroit's muscle car wars were just beginning to heat up. For Chevy, escalation had begun in 1958, the year engineers transformed the 348 "W-head" truck engine into the first beefed-up Bow Tie big-block V-8. With triple two-barrel carbs, the 348 initially maxed out at 315 horsepower, but by 1961 it was producing 350 horses.

That same year, Chevy engineers upped the ante again, recasting the W-head V-8's block to make room for 409 cubic inches. And to showcase the new 360 horsepower 409, Chevrolet introduced the Impala Super Sport, a classy hardtop that would reign supreme as one of the 1960s top full-sized performers.

In typical fashion, the 409 progressed up the performance ladder each year, receiving two four-barrel carbs in 1962 to raise output to 409 horsepower, then reaching a maximum of 425 horsepower in 1963. But by 1965, the coming of the 396 cubic inch Mk IV big-block V-8 spelled the end for the antiquated 409, which had dropped to 400 horses in top tune. Production of 400- and 340-horsepower 409s for 1965 reached 2,828, bringing the five-year total to 43,755.

Introduced midyear in 1965, the 396 cubic inch big-block helped diehards forget all about the 409. Offered in two forms, 325- and 425-horsepower, the 396 Mk IV was an instant suc-

Once Chevrolets began putting on considerable weight in the late 1950s, engineers responded with more horsepower and torque. Beginning in 1958, the additional power came courtesy of the 348 cubic inch "W-head" V-8. Also introduced in 1958, Chevy's decked-out Impala weighed as much as 300lb more than the previous year's topliner, the 1957 Bel Air.

cess, reaching sales of nearly 60,000 for the year. In 1966, another Mk IV big-block was introduced as the 396 was bored and stroked to 427 cubic inches, identical to the Mk IV's forefather, the Mk II "Mystery Motor" that had first appeared for NASCAR action at Daytona in February 1963. Although maximum 427 output, at 425 horses, was the same as the 396, that power was achieved at 800 less rpm.

Chevrolet's top Mk IV big-block was an option for all full-sized 1966 models and became the star of the Impala Super Sport line in 1967 with the arrival of the SS 427. Offered along with the standard Impala SS, the SS 427 reappeared in 1968, and again in 1969, as the last of the full-sized Super Sports. Although the SS imagery was gone, buyers of full-sized Chevys in 1970 could still order the 390 horsepower 454, and in 1971 the detuned 365 horsepower 454 remained available. By then, however, luxury was the main selling point as big car performance had long since faded away.

The 348 was originally designed for truck duty and is easily recognized by its valve covers, which resemble a *W* or an *M* depending on your perspective. With one four-barrel carburetor and 9.5:1 compression, Chevy's first Turbo-Thrust 348 was rated at 250 horsepower. Exchanging the four-barrel for three Rochester two-barrels upped output to 280 horsepower. At the top was the maximum performance Super Turbo-Thrust 348 featuring a solid-lifter Duntov cam, 11:1 compression, and the same three Rochesters; output was 315 horses.

Introduced shortly after the famed 409 made the performance scene early in 1961, the Impala Super Sport represented icing on the cake. Chevrolet's Super Sport kit, an optional package for the Impala line (originally, brochures even advertised a stillborn four-door model), was rolled out to showcase the new 409, though the venerable 348 was an available 1961 SS power source. Exterior SS treatment included spinner wheel covers and "SS" badges on the rear quarters and deck lid. Only 453 1961 Impala Super Sports were built; 409 production for 1961 was a mere 142 units.

Although nearly identical in outward appearance to its 348 forerunner, the 1961 409 was quite different internally with a beefier block, forged aluminum pistons, and a more aggressive solid-lifter cam. Compression was 11.25:1; output was 360 horsepower at 5800rpm. Fuel/air was supplied by a Carter four-barrel on an aluminum intake that was painted in early cars despite the fact that the paint quickly peeled. Dressed up with chrome by many owners, the 1961 409 was originally delivered with painted valve covers and air cleaners. This 409 is incorrectly equipped with a 348 single-snorkel air cleaner; 1961 409s had dual-snorkel units.

Left
Super Sport interior modifications included a sport steering wheel with a column-mounted 7000rpm tachometer, a Corvette-style grab bar on the passenger side of the dash, and a bright floor plate housing the shifter in four-speed cars.

Although the preferred 409 application for the sake of image was the Super Sport Impala, drag racers were better off choosing the lighter, less expensive Bel Air "bubbletop" coupe. Nineteen sixty-two Bel Airs—like this 409 horsepower dual-quad 409 version—were a common sight in NHRA winners' circles.

In 1962, revised heads and a hotter cam upped 409 output to 380 horsepower with a single four-barrel carburetor. Priced at $428, the 380 horsepower 409 was only the beginning. Sixty dollars more added twin Carter AFBs, increasing the 409's advertised maximum rating to 409 horsepower at 6000rpm. Painted valve covers were the norm in 1962; in 1963 chrome dress-up became standard 409 fare. Total production of 1962 409s was 15,019.

*S*he's real fine, my 409.

—The Beach Boys, *409*

The most outrageous 409 was the Z11 factory drag package, which first appeared in very limited numbers in late 1962 for NHRA A/FX competition. Z11 components included replacement heads, pistons, and cam for the 409 horsepower 409, along with a special two-piece intake manifold. Also included were aluminum fenders, inner fenders, and hood. In 1963, aluminum front and rear bumpers were added to the Z11 option group, as was a special 409 stroked to 427 cubic inches. The 1963 Z11 was easily identified by its NASCAR-style cowl plenum air cleaner setup. Laughably underrated at 430 horsepower, the Z11's actual output was more than 500 horses.

Right
The distinctive anodized aluminum bodyside trim pieces with their swirl pattern had become a Super Sport trademark in 1962, but truly stood out running down the bodyside of a 1964 Impala SS. Easily the most popular among Detroit's sporty full-sized crowd, the 1964 Super Sport attracted 185,325 buyers. This 409-equipped 1964 SS convertible features the optional wire wheel covers in place of the familiar flat Super Sport spinners.

In 1963 and 1964, Chevrolet offered three different 409s. At the top was the dual-quad 425 horsepower version, RPO L80. Next down the ladder was the single-carb 400 horsepower L31. Tamest of the bunch, and the only 409 available with an automatic transmission, was the 340 horsepower L33. This 1964 L33 V-8 was one of 8,864 409s built for 1964, down from a high of 16,902 the previous year.

Right
New for 1967 was a Super Sport package built specifically around an engine option: the Impala SS 427. Powered by the 385 horsepower 427, the 1967 SS 427 was offered in hardtop or convertible form and featured heavy-duty suspension, a special domed hood, a blacked-out rear cove panel with "SS 427" identification, and unique "SS 427" crossflags on the front fenders. Only 2,124 of these high-priced, high-powered showboats were built.

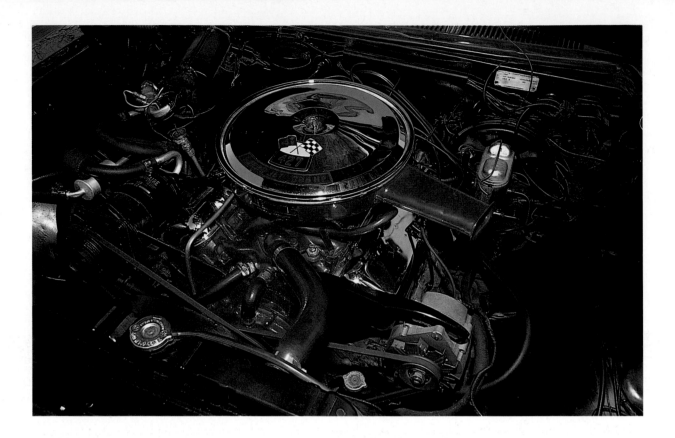

Included with the SS 427 package, and optional on other 1967 Chevys, the L36 427 produced a maximum 385 horses at 5200rpm; maximum torque was 460lb-ft at 3400rpm. Compression was 10.25:1. Even with all that torque, throwing a two-ton 1967 Impala around was no easy task. According to *Car Life*, a 1967 SS 427 went 0–60mph in 8.4 seconds; quarter-mile time was 15.75 seconds at 86.5mph.

Right
The last Impala Super Sport came in 1969, and it went out with a bang as the SS 427 was the only model offered. Absent was a special domed hood (used in 1967) and fender "gills" (a 1968 SS 427 feature); in their place were large "SS" fender badges and a custom grille. Nearly unnoticeable "427" badges were incorporated with the front fender marker lights. Production for the last of the three SS 427 models was 2,455.

Listed under RPO Z24, the SS 427 package for 1969 included this 390 horsepower 427 Turbo-Jet. Mildly modified cylinder heads and pistons made for a five horsepower increase compared to the 1967 and 1968 L36s. Maximum torque remained the same at 460lb-ft, but came 2000rpm higher at 3600 revs.

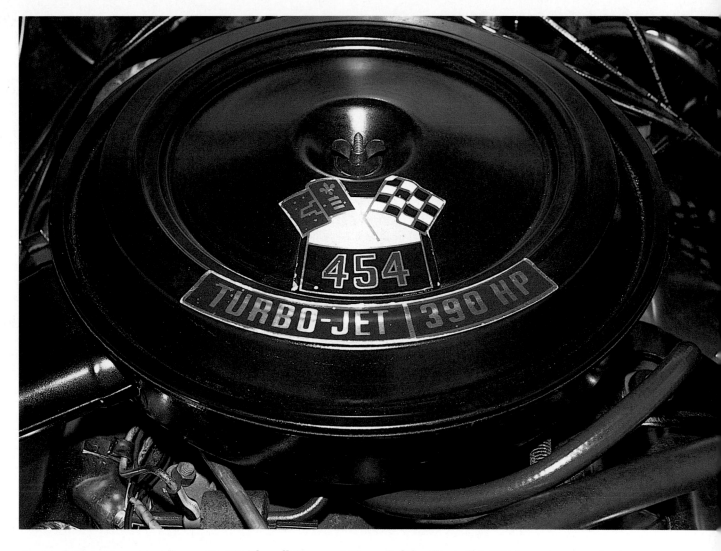

As standard equipment under an SS 454 Chevelle's bulging hood, the LS5 454 was rated at 365 horsepower. In full-sized applications, Chevy's LS5 carried the Corvette's 390 horsepower output rating. At 500lb-ft, torque output was the same for all LS5 applications, as were 10.25:1 pistons.

SS 427: just the ticket for the sporting man who likes some room to move around in.

—1967 Chevrolet advertisement

By 1970, the Super Sports were gone but an Impala or Caprice customer in search of full-sized performance could still check off Chevy's biggest big-blocks as an option. This Caprice sport coupe is powered by the LS5 454. Along with all that big-block brute force, this Caprice also features many of the comforts of home, from power door locks, seats, and windows, to a tilt wheel and AM/FM stereo. Performance options include the 15in Rally wheels, F40 sport suspension, and G80 positraction rear end.

Chapter 2

Mighty Mites
Corvairs and Novas

Chevrolet performance models came in all shapes and sizes, not the least of which were the compact Corvairs and Chevy IIs. Introduced in 1960 and 1962, respectively, both models were initially offered as budget-minded competition aimed at the foreign compacts that had gained a foothold in the American market in the late 1950s.

Many customers, however, looked at the Corvair as a Euro-style sportster. In 1961, 42.5 percent chose the optional bucket seats, followed by 64.6 percent in 1962 and 80.5 percent in 1963. By 1965, the only body style available was a sporty hardtop roofline offered in both four- and two-door form. Enhancing the sporty image were various optional performance packages, beginning in 1962 with heavy-duty, sintered-iron brakes, a positraction transaxle, and special handling equipment.

Big news for 1962 was the Monza Spyder, a true performance Corvair powered by a turbocharged version of Chevrolet's air-cooled, 145 cubic inch six-cylinder opposed engine. With 10lb of boost, the turbo upped the pancake six's output to an impressive 150 horsepower. Both convertible and coupe Spyders were produced for three years, though the turbo option carried on after the Spyder's demise. For 1965 and 1966, the turbocharged Corvair Corsa six-cylinder displaced 164 cubic inches and was rated at a healthy 180 horsepower.

The performance angle was initially a bit tougher to come by for Chevy II buyers. No ifs, ands, or buts about it, the first Chevy II was a 100 percent budget buggy with power coming

Along with being the last year for the Chevy II designation, 1968 was also the first year for the SS 396 Nova, which was offered through 1970. Almost identical to its 1968 forerunner, this 1969 SS 396 Nova features optional Rally wheels. SS 396 exterior trim included the blacked-out grille with "SS" badge and "396" identification in the front marker lights.

Although the Monza Spyder had been discontinued after 1964, a turbocharged Corvair was still available in 1965 and 1966. Available only on Corsa hardtops like this 1966, the **turbocharger option featured no external imagery—like the earlier Spyders—save for a small, round emblem on the deck lid. The chin spoiler was a standard Corsa feature in 1966.**

from either a frugal 90 horsepower 153 cubic inch four-cylinder or a 120 horsepower 194 cubic inch six. Although a V-8 swap was made available midyear as a dealer option, its price tag ran as high as 75 percent of a 1962 Nova sports coupe's sticker.

Performance imagery came along in 1963 with the Super Sport option. First offered on Impalas in 1961, the SS package for Novas included special trim and wheel covers, bucket

seats, instrumentation, and a deluxe steering wheel. True performance debuted in 1964 with the first optional Chevy II V-8, the 195 horsepower 283. Two years later, Chevrolet's little Nova joined super car ranks with the addition of the L79 option, a 350 horsepower 327 that transformed a Chevy II into a polite 15.10 second quarter-mile contender.

Small-blocks were the limit for Chevy II customers until 1968, when the 396 big-block

became available early in the model run. Standard power for the 1968 Nova SS 396 came from a somewhat mild 350 horsepower big-block, with a serious 375-horse version also listed. According to *Popular Hot Rodding*, a 375 horsepower SS 396 Nova could run the quarter in 13.85 seconds, topping out at 104mph. SS 396 Novas were dropped after 1970, leaving the 270 horsepower 350 cubic inch small-block as the top power choice in 1971.

A revised turbocharger and an increase in displacement from 145 cubic inches to 164 cubic inches helped pump up output from the Spyder's 150 horsepower to 180 horsepower in 1965. Here, a Saginaw four-speed sends this 1966 turbo six's torque through a 3.55:1 positraction transaxle.

With bucket seats, a four-speed stick, and an attractive dash layout featuring full instrumentation, a turbocharged 1966 Corsa Corvair offered as much sporty imagery inside as it did performance beneath its rear deck lid.

Right
A Nova SS convertible was offered only in 1963, the same year the Super Sport equipment was first made available to Chevy II buyers. Six-cylinder power was as hot as it got for the 1963 Nova SS, though an ultra-expensive (roughly $1500 or more) dealer-option V-8 swap was listed. Super Sport Nova production for 1963 reached 42,432, with no breakdown given for sports coupe or convertible. The 1963 Nova Super Sport's exterior features included SS wheel covers (from the 1963 Impala Super Sport), special beltline trim, "Nova SS" emblems on the tail and rear quarters, and a silver rear coverpanel.

Priced at $161, the Super Sport option for the 1963 Chevy II Nova added bucket seats, a deluxe sport steering wheel, and a four-gauge (oil, ammeter, temperature, fuel) instrument cluster. A bright molding spanned the center of the dash, and a "Nova SS" emblem was added to the glovebox. Powerglide-equipped Nova Super Sports got a floor shifter with an attractive chrome plate (all three-speed cars included column shifts).

Right
The Chevy II's body was restyled in 1966, while the Nova SS was recharged with the addition of the optional L79 327 V-8. Featuring a Holley carburetor, 11:1 compression, and big-valve heads, the L79 produced 350 horsepower. Sadly, the L79 option was discontinued for 1967, the year in which front disc brakes were first offered. This yellow 1967 Nova SS shows off its attractive, slotted Rally wheels, which were included when front discs were ordered.

N ova SS: a quick looking
coupe you can order with
the toughest block on the block.
—1968 Chevrolet
advertisement

Like Chevelle SS 396s, a big-block Nova Super Sport featured a blacked-out rear cove panel with an "SS" badge in the center. An "SS" steering wheel was also included inside. This gold 1969 SS 396 Nova is one of 5,262 equipped with the 375 horsepower big-block; another 1,947 were built with the 350 horsepower 396. Total 1969 Nova Super Sport production, including small-blocks, was 17,654.

This innocuous badge incorporated into the side-marker light on both front fenders was the only clue to the presence of a 1969 SS 396 Nova. Priced at $280 above the cost of a Nova coupe, the standard Super Sport featured a 350 cubic inch small-block V-8. Price for the 350 horsepower SS 396 package was $464; the 375 horsepower version cost $596.

Left
Fitted with 11:1 compression, a big Holley four-barrel on an aluminum intake, free-breathing heads, and solid lifters, the 375 horsepower 396 was a no-nonsense muscular powerplant, "a very serious engine to stuff into an unsuspecting Chevy II," according to *Car and Driver*. Performance was equally serious at 14.5 seconds through the quarter-mile. Top speed was an estimated 121mph.

Chapter 3

Mid-Sized Muscle
From Chevelle to Monte Carlo

Chevrolet general manager Semon E. "Bunkie" Knudsen introduced the Chevelle in August 1964 to rave reviews, both from the press and from the car-buying public. Chevy's popular new A-body was smart looking, easy to handle, and offered ample comfort. Performance potential was also present, though it would be more than a year before that was fully tapped.

Initially, the best a performance-minded Chevelle customer could do was to add the $162 Super Sport equipment group, which featured more sporty flair than anything else. Even mundane six-cylinder power was a Super Sport option in 1964 and 1965; but midway through the 1964 model year, the 327 cubic inch small-block V-8 was made available. Then in 1965 the truly hot 350 horsepower L79 327 appeared as an option.

Really big news came in February 1965 when Knudsen again did the introductory honors, this time for Chevy's first SS 396 Chevelle, the fabled 1965 Z16. The limited edition Z16 was powered by a 375 horsepower 396 mated to a Muncie four-speed and loaded with a host of options that ran its bottom line up to about $4,200. Publicity was the driving force behind the Z16's existence. Only 201 examples were built—200 hardtops and one mysterious convertible. The lone drop-top was built as an executive car. It was eventually sold off, and its final fate remains unknown to date.

Credit for inspiring COPO 9562 Chevelle production basically goes to Don Yenko, who ordered ninety-nine 427-equipped A-bodies for his Chevy dealership in Canonsburg, Pennsylvania. When the Chevelles arrived, they were converted into Yenko Super Cars. Graphics and badges identical to the Yenko Camaro's were added, as were optional Atlas five-spoke mags on request. Of the ninety-nine 1969 Yenko Chevelle SCs built, twenty-two were four-speed cars, and seventy-seven were equipped with Turbo-Hydramatics, like this Fathom Green example.

After 1965, Chev elle Super Sports came only with the 396 cubic inch Mk IV V-8—no more small-blocks or six-cylinders. Offered in more affordable, less plush form, the base 1966 SS 396 Chevelle relied on a 325 horsepower 396, with 360- and 375-horse big-blocks available at extra cost. Carrying a price tag right around $3,000, Chevrolet's SS 396 quickly raced to the forefront of Detroit's super car scene.

In 1969, the SS 396 package was improved greatly with the addition of front disc brakes and the F41 sport suspension group as standard equipment. As for power options, new for 1969 was the aluminum head L89 option for the L78 375 horsepower 396, features that didn't change output on the street, but saved considerable weight at the track. Also new was the COPO 9562 Chevelle, a rare 427-powered variant created in order to supply Don Yenko

With its 115in wheelbase (identical to the 1955 Chevy), super clean slab sides, and scalloped rear wheel openings, Chevrolet's 1964 Chevelle clearly picked up where the famed "Hot One" had left off. The crossflag fender emblem on this 1964 Chevelle Super Sport indicates the presence of the optional 327 cubic inch V-8, introduced in three power levels midway through the model year. The L30 327 was rated at 250 horsepower, while the L74 put out 300 horses. At the top was the mysterious 365 horsepower L76 Corvette 327, a true performance powerplant that was officially offered then quickly cancelled before true production got underway. No more than a handful were built; this 1964 SS was assembled to L76 specs by its owner to demonstrate an ultra-rare breed.

The Super Sport option group for the 1964 Chevelle was identified by special trim on the upper body line, rockers, and wheel openings; SS wheel covers; and "SS" badges on the rear quarters and back cove panel. Super Sport Chevelle hardtop production for 1964 was 57,445 for V-8 cars and 8,224 for six-cylinders. Standard power for a V-8 Chevelle SS in 1964 was a 195 horsepower 283 cubic inch small-block.

with base models for his Yenko Super Car transformations.

Once GM's 400 cubic inch limit for intermediates was lifted after 1969, the sky became the limit. Chevy's SS 396 remained available—with actual displacement at 402 cubic inches. But the top dog was the SS 454, available in two forms—the 360 horsepower LS5 and the

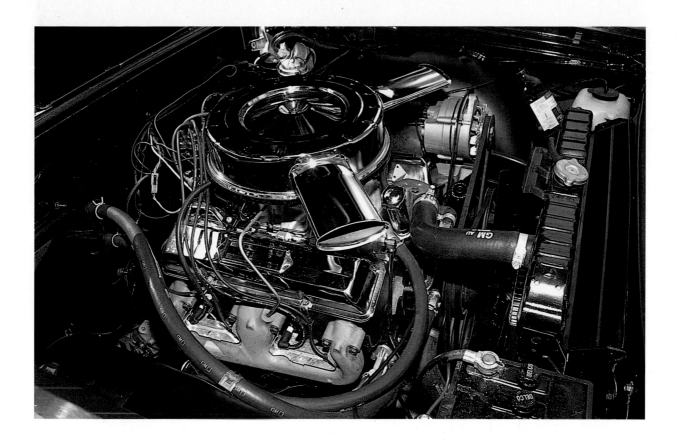

450 horsepower LS6. The latter engine's greater horsepower was attributable in part to closed chamber heads with bigger valves, 11.25:1 compression, a 0.520in lift cam, and a 780cfm Holley four-barrel. Able to leap tall buildings in a single bound, the 13-second LS6 ranks as one of the greatest super cars of all time. But the LS6 legend was short-lived. Although initially offered again, this time in 425 horsepower tune, the LS6 454 Chevelle failed to reappear in 1971, a victim of skyrocketing insurance rates, growing safety concerns, and impinging emissions standards.

By 1971, the Chevelle SS was again made available, though now with small-block power

Reportedly the A-body chassis made it difficult to equip the 365 horsepower L76 327 with large enough exhaust manifolds, which helped kill the project before it ever got off the ground. A certified street killer, the L76 small-block featured a solid-lifter "special performance cam," 11:1 compression, a big four-barrel carb on an aluminum intake, and a dual-snorkel air cleaner. According to rumors, a prototype L76 Chevelle ran 0–60mph in six seconds.

for the first time since 1965. The SS 454 managed to stick around through 1972, still a force to be reckoned with, but only a mere shadow of its former self. After 1973, all that remained were memories.

Z16 Chevelles differed from 1965 small-block Super Sports in back, where the "Malibu SS" rear quarter script was removed (reinstalled up front) and the tail dechromed. Less ornate 300 series taillights were installed, as was a blacked-out rear cove panel and a "Malibu SS 396" deck lid badge. A base 1965 V-8 Chevelle SS was priced at $2,600. Throw in the $1,501.05 for RPO Z16, along with the cost of a few other options, and the overall sticker got heavy in a hurry.

Left
A limited edition, fully loaded teaser for the big-block Chevelle bloodline to come, 1965's Z16 was both high-priced and high-powered. All 201 Z16s were equipped with the 375 horsepower 396 cubic inch Mk IV V-8 backed by a Muncie M20 four-speed with 2.56:1 low—an automatic transmission wasn't available. Gold-line rubber with simulated mag-style wheel covers, a blacked-out grille, "396 Turbo-Jet" fender emblems, and the transplanted "Malibu SS" badge (from the rear quarters to the front fenders) were all included in the Z16 deal.

Appearing first in 427 cubic inch "Mystery Motor" form at the Daytona 500 in February 1963, Chevrolet's Mk IV big-block V-8, RPO L37, was introduced for street duty in 1965. The 396 cubic inch mill became an option for Corvettes and full-sized models and was made the heart of RPO Z16. Under Z16 Chevelle hoods, the L37 396 was rated at 375 horsepower. Unlike the 425 horsepower Corvette 396, which used a solid-lifter cam, the Chevelle big-block relied on hydraulic lifters. Other L37 features included a Holley four-barrel, aluminum intake, and 11:1 extruded aluminum pistons.

Standard 1965 Z16 interior included bucket seats, front and rear seatbelts, AM/FM four-speaker stereo, a 160mph speedometer, 6000rpm tach, oil gauge, and dash-mounted clock. Optional equipment seen here includes power windows and a sport steering wheel with simulated woodgrain rim. As with exterior paint, Z16 interior color choices numbered only three: black, white and red, with red not offered with the Crocus Yellow paint. Regal Red and Tuxedo Black finishes were the other two exterior choices.

Chevelle SS396. And the SS doesn't stand for "Standing Still."

—1967 Chevrolet advertisement

This cowl plenum intake system was offered over dealers' parts counters for 1966 Chevelle SS 396s (the setup had first appeared on the rare 1963 Z11 A/FX Impala), though it would become better known as a Z/28 Camaro option the following year. A rare Chevelle feature, this NASCAR-style induction setup sits atop a 375 horsepower L78 396, of which 3,099 found their way under SS 396 hoods in 1966. Also featured on this car is the M22 Muncie "Rock Crusher" four-speed, one of only eighteen ordered by 1966 SS 396 buyers.

Right
For one year only, the SS 396 package, RPO Z25, was offered on both the top-line Malibu hardtops and convertibles, and on the lower priced 300 series models, making an SS 396 sedan possible in 1969. No breakdowns are available, but this Hugger Orange SS 396 300 Deluxe sedan is certainly a rare bird, especially when you consider it's powered by an aluminum-head L89 396. All 1969 SS 396s, regardless of body style or model line, came with 14x7in five-spoke sport wheels.

148

Aimed at racers who preferred cutting weight wherever possible, RPO L89 added a pair of lightweight aluminum cylinder heads to the 375 horsepower L78 396. Output for the L89/L78 big-block V-8 remained the same. Only 400 L89 Super Sport Chevelles were built for 1969, with estimates claiming as many as six of the aluminum-head 396s installed in SS 396 300 Deluxe sedans.

The 425 horsepower L72 427 carried no identification under a COPO Chevelle's hood, leaving some believing it was just another 396. Much hotter than even the 375 horsepower L78, the L72 featured 11:1 compression, a 0.520in lift, solid-lifter cam, and an 800cfm Holley four-barrel carb. COPO Chevelles turned low 13 second quarter-miles. Although exact production figures aren't available, it is known that Chevrolet built ninety-six L72 V-8s for COPO Chevelles with Turbo-Hydramatics (code MP) and another 277 425 horsepower 427s for four-speed COPO 9562 applications. The 373 total represents engines built, not cars assembled.

Right
Somewhat of a mystery still today, the 1969 COPO 9562 Chevelle was a little-known variation on the big-block A-body theme. Like the COPO Camaros, this Chevelle was equipped with the L72 427 Corvette V-8. COPO Chevelles featured the SS 396's hood, exhaust extensions, grille, and blacked-out tail treatment (with "SS 396" badges removed front and rear), but the car wasn't a Super Sport. Both the SS 396 bodyside stripes and Rally wheels were optional, with the Rallys being 15x7in units; optional Malibu Rally rims in 1969 were fourteen-inchers, while all SS 396s rolled on their own exclusive 14x7in five-spoke wheels.

The L72 427 under Yenko Chevelle hoods was rated at 450 horsepower. A set of Doug Thorley headers was offered as a Yenko option, but few were ordered. According to *Super Stock & Drag Illustrated's* Ro McGonegal, a 1969 Yenko Chevelle could trip the lights at the far end of the quarter-mile in 13.31 seconds at 108mph—on street tires.

Right
Considered by many as the king of the muscle car hill, the 1970 LS6 SS 454 Chevelle ranked easily among Detroit's quickest performance machines, achieving low 13-second quarter-miles with relative ease. Breaking into the 12-second bracket was also possible with a few modifications. This LS6 convertible, looking somewhat plain without the typical cowl induction hood and optional striping, is one of about twenty built (some production estimates also go as high as seventy-five). Total 1970 LS6 production—convertible, hardtop, and El Camino—was 4,475.

Left
Car Life claimed the 450 horsepower LS6 454 was "the best super car engine ever released by General Motors." Free-breathing, closed-chamber heads; 11.25:1 compression; a 0.520in lift, solid-lifter cam; and a 780cfm Holley four-barrel atop a low-rise aluminum manifold were among the LS6's supporting cast. Torque output was an impressive 500lb-ft at 4000rpm. The twin-snorkel air cleaner shown here is one of three types used on LS6 454 Chevelles.

Previous pages
From 1966 on, El Camino models could be
equipped with nearly all features common to
Chevelle Super Sports—including the 396 big-
block V-8. It wasn't until 1968, however, that they
actually wore Super Sport badges . For 1968 only,
the SS 396 El Camino was a separate model in
itself. From 1969 to 1970, the SS 396 package,
RPO Z25, was listed as an option for El Caminos,
as it was in Chevelle ranks. In 1971, the SS 396's
RPO number changed to Z15. This 1970 SS 396 El
Camino is equipped with the popular optional
cowl induction hood and 350 horsepower big-
block.

Above
Joining Chevrolet's A-body ranks in 1970 was the
Monte Carlo, a personal luxury car that could also
be outfitted in Super Sport garb. Offered in both
1970 and 1971, the SS 454 Monte Carlo was a
classy torque monster fit with heavy-duty
suspension. Exterior identification consisted only
of two small "SS 454" rocker badges and twin
chrome exhaust extensions in back. This 1970
Monte Carlo SS 454 is one of 3,823 built; another
1,919 rolled out in 1971.

Standard power for the 1970 SS 454 Monte Carlo was the Chevelle's 360 horsepower LS5 454. Compression was 10.25:1 and maximum torque was 500lb-ft at 3200rpm.

Chapter 4

A Breed Above
Camaro: Chevrolet's Pony Car

In August 1964, General Motors officials gave the go-ahead for the F-car project, Chevrolet's response to Ford's pony car progenitor, the Mustang. Chevy's F-body Camaro, introduced on September 29, 1966, hit the ground running, making up more than two years of lost time in short order.

Initially, the hot Camaro package featured the ever-present Super Sport option group, which included the 295 horsepower 350 cubic inch small-block, a special hood with simulated air intakes, an accent stripe on the nose, SS badging, and wide-oval red-stripe rubber. The original Camaro SS was a certified eye-catcher, but no match for Ford's potent big-block GT Mustang. Chevrolet solved this problem in November 1966 when the big-block 396 Mk IV V-8 was made an optional Super Sport power source—first in 325 horsepower trim, followed later by the 375 horsepower L78 version.

Yet another impressive introduction came in November 1966, this one for the legendary Z/28, intended to homologate the Camaro platform for competition in Sports Car Club of America (SCCA) Trans-Am competition. The Z/28's 302 cubic inch V-8, one of Detroit's hottest small-blocks, was created by installing the 283's crankshaft in a 327 block. This ploy allowed Chevy to stay within SCCA racing's 305 cubic inch legal limit. Conservatively rated at 290 horsepower, Chevy's hybrid small-block was described by *Car and Driver* as "the most responsive American V-8 we've ever tested."

A revised accent stripe up front represented the most noticeable Camaro SS change for 1968. Rally Sport options for 1968 totalled 40,977; Super Sport production was 27,884. Note the restyled Rally wheel with its large center cap, again a feature included with the optional front disc brakes. In 1968, SS 396 Camaro buyers could choose from three big-block V-8s, as the 325 horsepower and 375 horsepower 396s were joined by a 350 horsepower version.

The 302 would remain the heart and soul of the Z/28 through 1969.

F-body news for 1968 included recognizable exterior emblems for the Z/28 and two additional 396 big-blocks. The 350 horsepower 396 joined the 325- and 375-horse versions on the SS equipment list, as did the rarely seen L89 aluminum head option for the L78 396. Retaining the L78's 375 horsepower rating, the L89 option simply lightened the load for race-minded customers.

Revised sheet metal helped make the

Priced at $210, the Super Sport package for the 1967 Camaro featured a distinctive accent stripe up front, fake air inlets on the hood, "SS" badging, and a 295 horsepower 350 cubic inch small-block V-8. Later in the year, the nose stripe would become an option for all Camaros. This 1967 SS convertible also features the Rally Sport equipment group, which added hideaway headlights. The mag-style wheel covers were optional. Camaro SS production for 1967, coupes and convertibles, totaled 34,411. RS convertibles numbered 10,675.

exceptionally stylish 1969 Camaro perhaps the most popular edition of Chevy's long-running F-body pony car performance package. Power options were basically unchanged with one major exception—the exotic ZL1 427. Featuring an aluminum block and heads, the race-ready ZL1 was created using the Central Office Production Order system, a quick way to cut corporate red tape, as well as avoid upper office roadblocks. COPO ZL1 Camaros were brutally fast, scorching the quarter-mile in nearly 13 seconds flat. Chevy performance guru Vince Piggins and Illinois Chevrolet dealer Fred Gibb put their heads together and used COPOs to build fifty ZL1 Camaros for Gibbs' lot in La Harpe, Illinois. Another nineteen COPO 9560 ZL1 Camaros were built for various other dealers across the country.

Another Chevy dealer, Don Yenko of Canonsburg, Pennsylvania, turned to Piggins and his COPO pipeline in 1969 to supply Yenko Chevrolet with factory-built 427 Camaros which he would then convert into Yenko Super Cars. Listed under COPO 9561, the L72 425 horsepower cast-iron 427 Camaro became the base for the 1969 Yenko Camaro, a high-powered hybrid capable of low 13-second quarters.

A stunning restyle shaped the Camaro image for 1970. For the first time, the Z/28 package was not powered by the 302, a variation of the Corvette's hot 360 horsepower LT1 350 cubic inch small-block taking its place. More of an off-the-line warrior, the 1970-1/2 Z/28 offered quarter-mile performance in the low 14-second range.

Listed under RPO L48, the Camaro Super Sport's 295 horsepower 350 featured 10.25:1 compression, hydraulic lifters, and forged steel rods and crank. With a few minor tuning tricks, courtesy of performance dealer Bill Thomas, *Hot Rod* managed a best quarter-mile run of 14.85 seconds at 95.65mph in a 1967 L48 SS Camaro. *Car and Driver's* results were considerably slower at 16.1 seconds 87mph.

A good ZL-1 . . . would produce somewhere in excess of 500hp without any attention to detail whatsoever.
—Tom Langdon in *Chevrolet Big-Block Muscle Cars*

Left
The SS package's price jumped to $263 when the L35 325 horsepower 396 big-block was announced as a Camaro Super Sport power choice early in the 1967 model run. The attractive Rally wheels on this Rally Sport SS 396 Camaro signify the presence of the optional front disc brakes. The vented 14in Rally rims were included with the RPO J52 front discs.

Rated at 325 horsepower, RPO L35 was the base 396 big-block for the 1967 SS Camaro. The hotter 375 horsepower L78 396 waited in the wings, but the cost of admission was nearly double that of the L35. The impressive 375 horsepower 396 featured a durable four-bolt main bearing block, while the 325 horsepower L35 had two-bolt mains.

Left
Fifteen-inch Corvette Rally rims and contrasting hood stripes represented the only exterior identification for Chevrolet's first Z/28 Camaro, introduced November 29, 1966, at Riverside International Raceway in California. The legendary Z/28 fender badges wouldn't come until March 1968. Z/28 equipment included front disc brakes, F41 sport suspension, quick-ratio steering, 3.73:1 gears, a Muncie four-speed, and the sensational 302 cubic inch small-block. Only 602 Z/28s were built for 1967.

The Z/28's hybrid 302 was conservatively rated at 290 horsepower and featured 11:1 compression, a hot solid-lifter cam, L79 327 heads with big valves, transistorized ignition, and an 800cfm Holley four-barrel on an aluminum intake. Modeled after NASCAR racing induction tricks designed by Smokey Yunick, the cowl induction air cleaner was a $79 option delivered in a Z/28's trunk to be installed by the dealer.

Previous pages
Chevy performance proponent Vince Piggins first suggested building the Z/28 in August 1966 to homologate the package for SCCA Trans-Am competition, where Mustangs and Plymouth Barracudas would be the Camaro's main rivals. Piggins' first choice for the car's name was "Cheetah," but in the end it was the optional group's RPO number that got the nod. Little known in its first year, the Z/28 jumped considerably in popularity for 1968, reaching sales of 7,199, followed by 19,014 in 1969.

Although the Z/28 Camaro was better suited for race action at the track, it could be equipped with all Camaro luxury and convenience options, including the Rally Sport package with its hideaway headlights. Here, this uncommonly plush 1967 Z/28 interior includes optional deluxe Parchment appointments, the sporty center console and gauge cluster.

With solid lifters and 11:1 compression, the L78 375 horsepower 396 was clearly meant for some serious action. When backed by a Muncie four-speed and 3.31:1 positraction gears, an L78 SS 396 Camaro could easily run the quarter-mile in the 14-second range. Special-duty differentials with stump-pulling ratios like 4.10:1, 4.56:1, and 4.88:1 promised even more.

Left
Race-minded Chevy dealer Don Yenko first
began transplanting 427s into Camaros at his
Canonsburg, Pennsylvania, facility in 1967. In
1969, he ordered a special run of COPO 9561 F-
bodies—Camaros equipped with 425 horsepower
Corvette 427s. Distinctive Yenko graphics and
badges, 427 emblems, and a choice between the
standard COPO equipment 15in Rally rims or
optional Atlas five-spoke mags were part of the
Yenko package.

Although some minor confusion exists concerning
exactly how many 1969 Yenko Camaro SCs were
built, the widely accepted—and presently
documented—figure is 201. COPO 9561 L72
Camaros were also sold by Chevrolet, with 1,015
425 horsepower 427 V-8s produced for F-body
applications in 1969. The ZL2 air induction hood
was a standard COPO 9561 feature, while the
"Yenko/SC" striping and 427 badges were
installed at Canonsburg. This SC's vinyl roof was a
factory option.

The big news isn't the gauges . . . it's what the gauges are connected to!

—1966 Chevrolet advertisement

The L72 427 lurking beneath a Yenko Camaro hood featured a cast-iron block and heads and an advertised 450 horsepower. An 800cfm Holley four-barrel fed the beast, a solid-lifter cam helped deliver the juice, and 11:1 pistons squeezed the mixture. Backed by an M21 Muncie four-speed and standard 4.10:1 positraction gears, the L72 transformed a Camaro into a quarter-mile terror— 12.80 at 108mph off the lot with street rubber and optional Doug Thorley headers, according to *Super Stock & Drag Illustrated's* Ro McGonegal. Slicks and tuning tricks lowered those figures even further to an astonishing 12.10 seconds at 114mph.

All 1969 Yenko models, Camaro or Chevelle, got custom headrest covers featuring the "sYc" logo for Yenko Super Car. Joining the 201 Yenko Camaros in 1969 were another ninety-nine similarly bedecked 427 Yenko Chevelle SCs.

Conservatively rated at 430 horsepower, the 12:1 compression ZL1 427 easily put out more than 500 horses, demonstrated by its ability to run the quarter in nearly 13 seconds flat. ZL1 427 features included an iron-sleeved aluminum block and open chamber aluminum heads, along with an aluminum bellhousing and transmission case. These helped keep engine weight down in the 500 pound range; a ZL1 big-block weighed no more than a small-block V-8.

Right
Other than the ZL2 air induction hood, no exterior clues give away the identity of an awesome 1969 ZL1 427 COPO 9560 Camaro. Along with that hood and the 430 horsepower all-aluminum 427, COPO 9560 equipment also included a heavy-duty Harrison radiator, transistorized ignition, special suspension, and a 14-bolt rear end. Mandatory options included front disc brakes and a choice between M21 or M22 "Rock Crusher" Muncie four-speeds and the Turbo-Hydramatic 400 automatic. Typical ZL1 stickered at nearly $7,300. Only sixty-nine were built.

Chapter 5

America's Sports Car
Classic Corvettes

Forty years and a million models after it first set rubber on American roads, Chevrolet's Corvette remains as this country's premier sports car. This achievement shouldn't be dimmed by the fact that it has basically reigned for four decades as this country's *only* sports car. Pretenders to the throne have been few, and save for Carroll Shelby's uncivilized Cobra, itself a match only as far as sheer brute force was concerned, the Corvette has remained unequalled .

Beginnings, however, were humble. The first-edition 1953–1955 Corvette was somewhat awkward and weakly-received; the public considered it more of a curiosity than anything. Insufficient market interest almost cancelled Harley Earl's 'glass-bodied baby in 1954, but V-8 power saved it the following year. Zora Arkus-Duntov's growing involvement with the car also helped to turn things around. By 1956 Chevrolet had itself a winner. A startling restyle, combined with some serious performance engineering courtesy of Duntov, put the 1956 Corvette on the right track. Armed with two four-barrel carburetors, the 1955 Corvette's polite 265 cubic inch V-8 was transformed into 1956's 255 horsepower bully.

Fuel injection debuted in 1957, landing the Corvette's enlarged 283 cubic inch small-block into the newly created "one-horsepower-per-cubic-inch" club (Chrysler had broken the barrier the year before with the 300B's 355 horsepower 354 cubic inch hemi). Although early

Optional side exhausts and standard four-wheel disc brakes debuted in 1965, but the really big news came up front in the form of the Corvette's first big-block, the 396 cubic inch Mk IV V-8. The 396 Mk IV, nicknamed "porcupine head" for its canted-valve design, was a direct descendant of the 427 cubic inch Mk II engine that shook the NASCAR troops at Daytona just as GM was closing the door on factory racing activities in February 1963. A special bulging hood was included when the 396 Turbo-Jet was ordered.

Chevrolet's fiberglass Corvette two-seater was offered only in Polo White when introduced in 1953. Three additional shades were added in 1954: Pennant Blue, Sportsman Red, and black. In all, 3,640 1954 Corvettes were built, less than one-third of Chevy's projected total. Opinions varied concerning styling and performance. But even though the car's creator, Zora Arkus-Duntov, wasn't happy with the 1953–1954 Corvette's performance, handling and acceleration were above average by American standards of the time; 0–60mph took 11 seconds, and the car topped out at 105mph.

versions of the injected V-8 were often disagreeable and difficult to maintain, it would remain as the top Corvette performance option through 1965. The 327 was the last fuel-injected Corvette engine of the 1960s, achieving a maximum output rating of 375 horsepower before it was displaced by the brutish 396 cubic inch Mk IV big-block V-8 in 1966.

Partial restyles in 1958 and 1960 freshened the Corvette's face, but paled in comparison to 1963's makeover. The body was Bill Mitchell's idea, with final lines penned by Larry Shinoda. Looking an awful lot like Mitchell's Stingray racer of 1959, the all-new Corvette Sting Ray was as innovative underneath as it was stunning on top, thanks to Duntov's devotion to

Powering the 1953, 1954, and early 1955 Corvettes was Chevrolet's 235 cubic inch Blue Flame six-cylinder, based on the same "Stovebolt" six that served more mundane duty under standard passenger car hoods. As a Corvette powerplant, the 235 six featured three Carter carbs, a relatively radical high-lift cam, 8:1 compression, and a split exhaust manifold feeding dual exhausts. Maximum output was 150 horsepower at 4200rpm. This 1954 Blue Flame six uses twin air cleaners in place of the three "bullet-type" breathers installed in 1953. Complete chrome dress-up was also available for these engines.

Looking much sleeker, the second-generation 1956–1957 Corvette was not only more popular than its predecessor but also more civilized, with the addition of roll-up windows and a removable hardtop. Performance improvements included various chassis updates to improve handling and optional twin four-barrel carburetors in 1956, followed by fuel injection in 1957. This black beauty is one of 6,339 Corvettes built for 1957; 1956 production was 3,467.

independent rear suspension. In reference to the 1963 Sting Ray, Duntov told *Car and Driver*, "I now have a Corvette I can be proud to drive in Europe." Offered both as Corvette's first coupe rendition, as well as in typical topless fashion, Shinoda's timeless Sting Ray shape lasted through five model runs, and

many feel the Corvette was never better.

Performance enhancements during the span included the aforementioned big-block introduction for 1965, a powerful package that was pumped up to 427 cubic inches in 1966. The awesome aluminum head L88 option for the 427 appeared in 1967, followed by the

In 1957, engineers bored out the Corvette's small-block V-8 to 283 cubic inches and upped the output ante to one horsepower per cubic inch with the optional Ramjet fuel injection setup. Actually, the Ramjet option was available in two forms, the 283 horsepower version with 10.5:1 compression and the 250 horsepower 283 fuelie with a 9.5:1 ratio. Also new for 1957 was a four-speed manual transmission. According to *Road & Track*, a four-speed 283 horsepower fuelie Corvette could go 0–60mph in 5.7 seconds. Quarter-mile time for the same car was a sizzling 14.3 seconds.

ultimate big-block Vette, 1969's all-aluminum 427 ZL1.

Meanwhile, Mitchell and Shinoda had turned out another new Corvette look for 1968. Featuring what would become General Motors' familiar "Coke-bottle" body, the fifth generation Corvette was, in *Car and Driver*'s opinion, "the best yet."

In 1970, the optional 370 horsepower LT1 350 cubic inch V-8 appeared, balancing the brutish big-block boulevard Vettes—which had reached their pinnacle that same year in LS5 454 cubic inch form—with a well-rounded agile road rocket. Not since the fuel-injected 327 had disappeared after 1965 had Corvette buyers been able to combine serious small-block power with a well-balanced, road-hugging stance. The LT1 small-block and 454 big-block carried the Corvette banner high into Detroit's post-performance years—the LT1 falling by the wayside after 1972, and the 454 doing the same two years later.

Left
The last of the solid-axle Corvettes, the 1962
model foretold the coming of the classic Sting Ray
in 1963 through its boat-tail rear, which had first
appeared in 1961. Although its grille was devoid of
the earlier models' teeth, the 1962 Corvette's quad
headlight front end was a direct descendant of the
design introduced for 1958. Top performance
option in 1962 was the 360 horsepower fuel-
injected 327 cubic inch V-8. Total 1962 Corvette
production was 14,531.

The Corvette's 283 cubic inch V-8 was bored and
stroked to 327 cubic inches for 1962. In basic
tune, the 1962 Corvette 327 was rated at 250
horsepower. Three other 327s were available, the
300- and 340-horse carbureted small-blocks and
the king-of-the-hill 360 horsepower fuel-injected
version.

Sports cars are by their nature controversial: they arouse the interest of the adolescent— and of those reaching second childhood.

—Roy Lunn, SAE paper 611F
in *American Muscle*

Befitting its name, the totally restyled 1963 Corvette Sting Ray featured its own "stinger," a spine that ran the length of the car; it began as a center bulge on the hood, and ended in this split window design on the coupe model's boat-tail rear. Duntov didn't like the idea, nor did drivers who preferred seeing what they were about to back over. But Bill Mitchell insisted the split window theme remain, which it did for one year only.

A serious performance powerplant with solid lifters and 11:1 compression, the 1965 Corvette's 396 Turbo-Jet produced maximum power of 425 horsepower at 6400rpm. Maximum torque was 415lb-ft at 4000rpm. All this brute force translated into a 0–60mph time of 5.7 seconds and quarter-mile performance of 14.1 seconds at 103mph. Reported top end for a 1965 396 Corvette was 136mph.

Left
In 1966, the 396 Turbo-Jet became the 427 Turbo-Jet, available in 390- and 425-horse forms. A triple-carb option in 1967 pumped up output to 435 horsepower, but the most potent Corvette power choice that year was actually advertised at five fewer horses. Given a 430 horsepower factory rating, the rare L88 427 probably put out somewhere between 500 and 600 real horses. Only 20 L88 Corvettes were produced for 1967.

Obviously built for racing, L88 427 features included aluminum heads, beefy internals, a 0.540/0.560 solid-lifter cam, 12.5:1 compression, a huge 830cfm Holley four-barrel, and an open-element air cleaner. Knowing a racer would quickly replace it anyway, the L88's exhaust system remained typical stock Corvette hardware. Backing up the L88 was a 10.5in heavy-duty clutch and a lightweight nodular iron flywheel.

This is the kind of car that goes a long way to encouraging irresponsible behavior on the public streets.
—Randy Leffingwell,
American Muscle

In 1969, the awesome L88 Corvette was superseded by the outrageous ZL1, an all-aluminum 427 also laughably rated at 430 horsepower. Again, actual output was more like 560 horsepower, but who was counting? Factory numbers games mattered little once behind the wheel of a ZL1 Corvette. Press tests put performance at a shocking 12.1 seconds through the quarter-mile, topping out at 116mph. Of course, that much speed didn't come cheap; the ZL1 option cost around $3,000. Only two were built.

Weighing some 100lb less than the aluminum-head L88, the ZL1 kept its weight down by using an iron-sleeved aluminum cylinder block. Everything the L88 was, the ZL1 did one better. Internals were even beefier, and a modified solid-lifter cam featuring revised ramp profiles was included, as were big-valve, open chamber aluminum cylinder heads. Compression remained the same, but pistons were reinforced.

In contrast to the brutal big-block Corvettes, the LT1-equipped models, introduced in 1970, were well-balanced performers; agile as well as muscular, they took many enthusiasts back to the fuelie's days when Corvettes were more sports car and less quarter-mile warrior. For 1970, the hot 350 cubic inch LT1 small-block was rated at 370 horsepower. In 1971 that rating dropped to 330 horsepower, and the final rendition was advertised at 255 net horses. This 1972 LT1 Corvette is one of 1,741 built. Production in 1970 and 1971 was 1,287 and 1,949, respectively. All LT1s got a distinctive hood modeled after the 1968–1969 L88/ZL1 design.

HEMI
MUSCLE CARS

Robert Genat

Introduction

Hemi! One word says it all. At a car show or drag race, a Hemi-powered car stops people in their tracks. It's the one musclecar that knows no manufacturer-biased boundaries. Although many of the most die-hard Ford and GM enthusiasts won't admit it, they hold the Hemi engine and Hemi-powered musclecars in high esteem.

By the late 1960s, the Hemi upped the performance ante so high that the others couldn't even compete. Soon, it was Hemi versus Hemi, with all the others racing each other at the back of the pack. In NASCAR racing, the Hemi's performance tipped the scale so far that it was banned. It was so powerful, so potent a machine, and so far above the competition that the playing field had to be leveled.

In pure stock form, the Hemi was more than the equal of the other engines. When modified, it was unbeatable. The Hemi engine had more potential for pure horsepower than any other musclecar engine. In addition, these monster engines were installed in some of the finest-looking cars Chrysler ever offered.

During the few years that the Hemi was available, approximately 11,000 were delivered. In sheer numbers, the Hemi production was a mere grain of sand in the desert of automotive-production history. But to automotive enthusiasts and historians, the era of the Hemi was monumental. Every gearhead remembers the first Hemi car he saw. It may have been at a drive-in, at the drag strip, or on a smooth strip of onyxlike asphalt. Those who have competed against a Hemi on the street or the track know what it's like because they are so hard to beat.

For the 1966 model year, Chrysler faced a costly dilemma. In order to race its Hemi engine in NASCAR, Chrysler had to build assembly-line versions. The company knew that its image on the track heavily contributed to showroom sales, so it created street going Hemis for 1966. Unfortunately, Chrysler didn't realize any profits from those models. Fitting the large Hemi into the engine bay of the Dodge Coronet and the Plymouth Belvedere and Satellite models was relatively easy. Designers beefed up the drive train and suspension to complement the Hemi's immense horsepower potential.

To make the Hemi streetable, Chrysler's engineers had to detune the powerful race engine. The aluminum heads were replaced with cast-iron versions. The compression was dropped by 2 1/4 to 10.25:1, so it could run on premium pump gas. The cross-ram intake was replaced with an aluminum manifold fitted with two Carter AFBs in tandem. For cold weather operation, a choke was provided along with manifold heat. Cast-iron exhaust manifolds replaced the tubular exhaust headers. The Hemi's horsepower rating was listed as 425 at 5,000 rpm, but Chrysler engineer Tom Hoover once stated that the street Hemi actually produced 500 horsepower at 6,000 rpm, a number Chrysler was hesitant to advertise.

The Hemi cars featured in this book cover only the years 1964 through 1971. These cars were either built at a Chrysler assembly plant or by a subsidiary under contract to Chrysler. In NASCAR racing, the race teams obtained engines and chassis through special racing channels (i.e., the factory race shops), not from the dealership's showroom floor. The Daytona Chargers and Super Birds, spawned by NASCAR competition and delivered to the general public, are prominently featured.

This book covers a wide range of Hemi-powered cars; some have been restored to perfection and others are original low-mileage survivors. A few are never driven and many others are cruised to car shows and occasionally used for daily errands. (Following one photo session, the owner was hungry and took his rare Hemi car through a local fast food drive-through.) Three of the Hemi cars in this book were raced extensively, have since been restored to their factory-fresh glory, and are now driven on the street. One of the race cars is still actively raced.

The street Hemi engine was first released in 1966 to satisfy NASCAR's rules requiring that the engine be production based. In this same basic form, the street Hemi was installed in 11,000 Dodges and Plymouths through the 1971 model year.
Chrysler Historical

The Fabulous Chrysler B-Bodies

Coronet, Belvedere, GTX, RT, Road Runner, and Super Bee

In 1966, Chrysler's mid-size cars were not as flashy as their contemporaries from General Motors and Ford. General Motors' and Ford's muscle-cars were given special trim and badges announcing their high-performance heritage to the world. On the street, it was easy to spot a Pontiac GTO, a Chevy 396SS, or a Ford Fairlane GT. Chrysler took a much more low-key approach to its musclecars, especially the Hemi. It would have been difficult at night on Woodward Avenue to read the small HEMI badging on the side of a 1966 Belvedere or Coronet. But as soon as the light turned green, the Hemi would be gone like a shot.

All 1966 B-bodies, from both Dodge and Plymouth, were built on the previous year's platforms. The Dodge Coronet was offered in four trim levels:

The 1969 Road Runner continued the momentum of the 1968 model. In the Road Runner, the public was offered a highly identifiable musclecar at a low price. In addition, engine options and creature comforts were available at an extra cost.

197

the base Coronet, the Coronet Deluxe, and the Coronet 440 and 500. The 440 and 500 were only used to distinguish the differences in the series of cars and had nothing to do with engine size. The 1966 Coronet featured a finely sculpted body in both sedan and hardtop versions. Car buyers were accustomed to seeing something new each year, and the new Coronet didn't disappoint its fans. The big news was the addition of the powerful 426-ci street Hemi engine to the option list. Dodge now had a full-fledged musclecar. Unfortunately, the new Coronet didn't have the visual appeal to match its horsepower, but that would soon change. Hemi sales were brisk, with over 740 Coronet customers checking the box on the order sheet for the elephant engine.

Like the Dodge Coronet, the 1966 Plymouth Belvedere and Satellite both had gracefully contoured sides. At 116 inches, the Plymouth rode on a wheelbase one inch shorter than the Coronet.

In 1966, the Hemi engine came in a wide variety of models, including this Coronet Deluxe two-door sedan. Looking more like grandma's grocery-getter, this sedan surprised more than a few people on the street.

The April 1966 issue of *Car and Driver* featured a road test of a new Hemi-powered Plymouth Satellite. In the article's opening paragraph, the writer makes reference to the previous month's edition, in which the magazine compared six of the hottest new "Super Cars." Unfortunately, the Hemi wasn't delivered in time for that issue's test. If it had been, it would have resoundingly trounced every car there. "Without cheating, without expensive NASCAR mechanics, without towing or trailing the Plymouth to the test-track," the writer said, "it went faster, rode better, stopped better, and caused fewer problems than all six of the cars tested last month." It was interesting to note that prior to the test, the Hemi Satellite had been driven by magazine staffers from Detroit to New York and then used as a daily driver for a week. The only complaints about the new Plymouth were the location of the tachometer (on the console) and the less-than-impressive styling. The demand was high for

For 1966 the entire Dodge line was restyled. The Coronet 500 was the top-of-the-line model, but compared to its 1966 muscle-car contemporaries, it lacked panache.

Plymouth's new Hemi power, and more than 1,500 were sold in Belvedere I, Belvedere II, and Satellite models in 1966.

The Plymouth Belvedere and Dodge Coronet returned in 1967 with only a few changes to the grille and taillights, but the new top-of-the-line models, the Plymouth GTX and the Dodge R/T, made their debuts. The GTX was Plymouth's first shot at musclecar styling, and it was dead center on target. Available only in a two-door hardtop or convertible, the 1967 GTX featured twin nonfunctional hood scoops. A quick-fill racing style gas cap

The 1966 Plymouth Belvedere/Satellite models, like the Dodges, were restyled. The availability of the Hemi engine in showroom models, like this Belvedere convertible, allowed NASCAR competitors like Richard Petty to race Hemi-powered cars on the track.

was prominent on the left quarter panel. Dual sport stripes and chrome road wheels were optional. When they were added, the GTX had the sporty styling musclecar buyers were looking for. The 440-ci V-8 producing 375 horsepower was standard. The 426 Hemi was optional, but it came with a heavy-duty suspension. The GTX's interior featured saddle-grain vinyl with an attractive tooled leather insert on the seats. Front bucket seats with a center console were standard, and the rear seats were styled to look like bucket seats. The GTX sold well and 125 Hemis made up a fraction of the total of 12,690 units that reached dealers. In the 1967 Plymouth line of Belvederes, Satellites, and GTXs, there were just slightly fewer than 200 equipped with the Hemi engine.

Dodge introduced its own version of the musclecar, the R/T (Road and Track). The R/T was a Dodge version of the Plymouth GTX. It featured a grille that was similar in styling to that of the Charger's, but the Dodge R/T's headlights were exposed. Three large nonfunctional louvers adorned the center of the hood. Available in only two-door hardtop and convertible body styles, the R/T rode on a heavy-duty suspension. Bucket seats were standard and chrome road wheels were optional. The R/T also featured the 375-horsepower 440 as standard equipment. In 1967, street Hemi

The 426 Hemi engine installed in the 1966 Coronets and Belvederes was a detuned version of the race Hemi that had a lowered compression ratio of 10.25:1 and a milder cam. The only transmissions available were a four-speed manual and a heavy-duty TorqueFlite.

Announcing the Hemi 426 Plymouth Belvedere

Now what this country needs is a dragstrip with a couple of good hairpin curves.

The Hemi-powered Plymouth Belvedere: a high-performance 426-cubic-inch hemispherical-head V-8. Dual four-barrel carbs. Dual-breaker distributor. High-lift, high-overlap cam. Special plugs, pistons and double valve springs. Low back pressure dual exhaust

system. Blue Streak Special tires. Wide-rim wheels. Oversize front torsion bars. Sway bar. Added-leaf, high-rate rear springs. Firm-Ride shocks.
And every Belvedere Satellite has: Front bucket seats. Center console with glove box. Deep-pile carpeting.

Padded instrument panel. Safety-Rim wheels. 3-speed automatic or 4-on-the-floor stick, optional.
Like an iron fist in a velvet glove, the Hemi 426 Plymouth Belvedere.

PLYMOUTH DIVISION ✦ **CHRYSLER** MOTORS CORPORATION

Plymouth ...a great car by Chrysler Corporation.

In 1966, the marketing staff at Plymouth didn't waste any time advertising the new Hemi engine's availability or its performance potential. Plymouth placed ads like this one touting the new Belvedere in enthusiast magazines.

engines were installed in 283 Dodge R/Ts, and 117 Hemi engines were installed in the balance of the 1967 Coronet line. While the 1967 Plymouth GTX and Dodge Coronet R/T were outstanding musclecars, complete performance and styling packages (à la GTO and SS396) for the B-body Dodge and Plymouth B-bodies would have to wait until 1968.

In 1968, with one giant leap, Chrysler made a major advancement in the musclecar wars with the release of the new Road Runner. It was the shot in the arm Plymouth needed. The 1967 GTX with all the musclecar options cost considerably more and never had the streetwise look of the GTO. Plymouth decided to strip its newly restyled mid-size entry of any frills, then add a performance engine package and a whimsical cartoon name. With the Road Runner, Plymouth had a low-priced factory hot rod that was capable of kicking any GTO's butt at any stoplight.

The 1968 Plymouth line included the base Belvedere, Road Runner, and GTX. They were all restyled in a smoother, more integrated look. The wheelbase remained at 116 inches, but the track width, front and rear, increased by one-half inch. The GTX also came with bucket seats, a center console, and lots of imitation wood-grain trim. The exterior featured extra chrome trim along the rocker panel and around the wheel openings. A few inches above the rocker panel were two horizontal

The 1967 Plymouth GTX was the first Hemi car whose appearance equaled its performance. Nonfunctional hood scoops were standard on the GTX, but the sport stripes were optional.

The 1967 GTX's stylish interior had front buckets and a chrome center console in which the tachometer was mounted. The "Inland" shifter, named for its manufacturer, selected the gears for the four-speed transmission. It wasn't until 1968 that Hurst shifters became standard equipment.

body stripes that terminated with a large GTX chrome emblem just in front of the rear wheel opening. The GTX's hood featured twin side-facing vents within which the engine size was inset in small chrome letters. Drive-in restaurant regulars and musclecar enthusiasts knew that the 1967 GTX came with a standard 440-ci engine, as did the 1968 model. Once again, the Hemi engine was an option and 446 was so equipped.

Opposite
Chrome road wheels were an option on the 1967 GTX, but red line tires were standard. In addition to the Hemi badges on the front fender, there was a small one on the rear edge of the deck lid.

The 1967 Plymouth GTX had clean sculpted sides that made an exciting styling package. The racing style gas cap on the left quarter panel was also part of the GTX package.

The 1967 GTX was available in either a hardtop or a convertible. Although the 1967 models used the same sheet metal as the 1966, the grille was modified to accept quad headlights. Dale Amy

As nice as the GTX was, the Road Runner got all the press in 1968. Its beauty was in its simplicity. Stripped of all extra chrome, it looked as docile as a librarian's sedan. The Road Runner was initially introduced as a two-door coupe. The hardtop would be introduced later in the model year, but

The 1967 GTX was touted as Plymouth's "Supercar." The standard engine was a 440 with a TorqueFlite, and the only optional engine was the Hemi. Even though Plymouth had finally put together a true musclecar package, the GTXs didn't sell well. A total of 2,500 GTXs were sold in 1967 and only 125 were equipped with the Hemi. This GTX convertible is one of 17 built. Dale Amy

The 1967 R/T featured the same grille as the Charger but without the hidden headlights. On top of the hood were three large simulated louvers. This Hemi-powered R/T convertible was one of only two built in 1967.

no convertible Road Runner models were offered in 1968. The grille was the same egg crate design as the Belvedere, but it was accented in black. The Road Runner used the same hood—with side-facing nonfunctional vents—as the GTX. A small chrome plate near the front edge of the doors discreetly announced that this was a Road Runner. To the rear of this Road Runner emblem was a small decal of the crafty little bird at warp speed. A standing version of the bird was placed on the Road Runner's deck lid. As the year progressed, a decor group was added to the Road Runner, which included a deck lid decal featuring the bird at full speed, trailed by a cloud of dust.

The Road Runner's bench seat interior was initially offered in blue, parchment, or black and silver. When Plymouth introduced the Decor Group, it added gold, red, green, black, and white to the interior color list. Bucket seats were not a Road Runner option in 1968.

The standard engine for the Road Runner was a special version of the 383, producing 335 horsepower and 425 foot-pounds of torque. A four-speed transmission was standard, and a column-shifted TorqueFlite was optional. There was only one optional engine for the 1968 Road Runner—the Hemi. Like the 383, the Hemi came standard with a four-speed, but the TorqueFlite was a no-cost

In 1967 Dodge introduced its new performance model, the R/T (Road and Track). Like the GTX, it came standard with a 440 engine and a host of heavy-duty performance-oriented features. And like the GTX, the only optional engine was the 425-horse-power 426 Hemi.

option. The Performance Axle Package, which included the Dana Sure-Grip rear axle, was a required option. Along with the Hemi engine option came a larger radiator, power front disc brakes, and 15-inch wheels with F-70 Polyglas tires. In 1968, a total of 1,011 customers paid the extra $714 for the Hemi option; of these, 840

Next page
Plymouth's introduction of the Road Runner in 1968 was big news. The finely trimmed GTX was still available, and it featured the same hood as the Road Runner with side-facing nonfunctional scoops. The GTX also had twin body side stripes that terminated at the GTX emblem on the quarter panel. Mopar Muscle

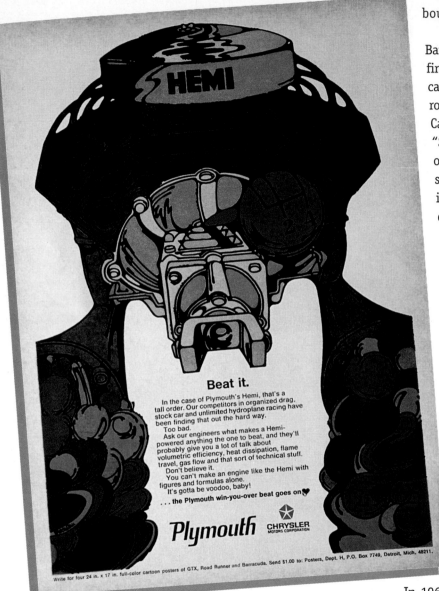

The artwork of Peter Max was fashionable in the late 1960s. Plymouth took advantage of it in this slick Hot Rod magazine advertisement to promote the Hemi engine.

bought coupes and 171 bought hardtops.

In the early and mid-1960s, Charlie Di Bari was the spark plug who provided the fire to the successful *Melrose Missile* race car program. The Di Bari family owned Melrose Motors and soon became the northern California Mopar high-performance Mecca. "Shortly after the Road Runners came out," recalls Di Bari, "we wanted to do something that would create a stir, calling more attention to the car and to the dealership. At that time, if you had a minimum of five cars, you could have any car painted a special color. We had five Road Runners painted Omaha Orange. They came in and went right out! We didn't want to have all orange cars, so then we had some painted school bus yellow and then a bright green color. Those were the first three, and the most dominant, of the special colors we came up with." The brightly colored Road Runners were an immediate hit, and soon customers were clamoring for them. Plymouth's marketing personnel in Detroit saw how fast the market was scooping them up. Vivid colors were formerly reserved for trucks but were now part of Chrysler's new musclecar palette.

In 1968 the mid-size muscle market was filled with a host of competitors. Fresh designs and a long list of performance options were what it took to stay in the game. Dodge reskinned its Coronet with slippery sheet metal that featured sculpted quarter panels. The successful R/T option returned in both hardtop and convertible models. With the R/T, the customer had the choice of side stripes or

HEMI ROAD RUNNER: 0-105 IN 13.5 SECS.! ONE OF THE REASONS MOTOR TREND NAMED IT...

CAR OF THE YEAR

See facts, figures, NHRA acceleration times—Page 127.

Bumblebee stripes. The standard engine for the R/T was the 440-ci engine. In 1968, 220 Dodge R/Ts were sold with the Hemi engine.

The big news for Dodge in 1968 was the release of the Super Bee option, which hit the Dodge showrooms in February 1968. It was designed to be a low-priced performance car in the same mold as the 1968 Road Runner. Based on the 440 coupe, the Super Bee featured swing-out quarter windows and had the same power-bulge hood as the R/T. Bumblebee stripes and a circular Super Bee logo on the quarter panel appeared on the rear of the car. The Super Bee's standard engine and transmission was a 335-horsepower 383, backed by a four-speed. The Hemi was optional and 125 were delivered in 1968.

In 1969, the Road Runner was named Motor Trend *magazine's Car of the Year. Never missing a chance to stomp the competition on the street, track, or in print ads, the marketing staff at Plymouth proudly heralded the announcement. The text of the ad went on to describe the quarter-mile times a stock Hemi Road Runner clocked, and the few simple modifications required to improve those times.*

In 1969, the Road Runner returned with a vengeance. Plymouth sold 80,000, almost double the previous year's total. Only minor changes were made to the 1969 model's grille and taillights. The Road Runner was still the low-priced performance king, but the price was increasing and the option

213

Carter AFB Carburetors

Most gearheads consider the Carter AFB to be the first true performance carburetor. Compact and simple in design, it was the carburetor of choice for the early Mopar and GM musclecars. Carter AFBs were also fitted to the Street Hemi engines.

The Carter Carburetor Company was founded in 1909 by Will Carter. Old Will was a born tinkerer and inventor who had only five years of formal education. In 1910, Carter patented his Model C carburetor. It was an updraft design with three distinct circuits for low, intermediate, and high speeds. In 1911, the company produced the first downdraft carburetor. Starting in 1925, Carter carburetors began showing up as standard equipment on a variety of production cars and trucks. In 1952, Carter released the world's first four-barrel carburetor designated the WCFB (Will Carter Four Barrel). It was constructed from three separate castings and weighed 18 pounds. Archaic by today's standards, the WCFB was a turning point in high-performance fuel delivery systems. It first saw Mopar musclecar action atop the 1957 Chrysler Hemi 392-ci engine.

The WCFB was a wonderful carburetor, but it only flowed at 385 cfm, too little for the emerging large displacement engines. In 1957, Carter introduced its AFB (Aluminum Four Barrel). Depending on the model, it flowed 450 or 625 cfm. The new AFBs soon started popping up in single or dual configurations on a number of Mopar and General Motors musclecar engines.

The new AFB featured a two-piece design cast from aluminum. It was much lighter than the WCFB and flowed better. Like the WCFB, the AFB had a mechanical link between the primary butterfly shaft and the secondary butterfly shaft. This allowed for positive opening of the secondary butterflies. The secondary side also featured an air valve. This air valve temporarily restricted air flow through the secondary butterflies until the engine could use the extra air/fuel mixture available. The air valve increased driveability by eliminating the bog that would take place by the sudden opening of the secondaries. All carburetors have a system for enriching the mixture when under full-throttle conditions. Most other carburetors have what is commonly called a power valve. The Carter AFB has a pair of metering rods that serve that function. Under normal conditions, these rods restrict the flow of fuel through the main metering jets. Under full throttle, when vacuum is at its lowest, the rods are pulled out of the jets, allowing for greater fuel flow. It's a simple system that has a great degree of flexibility for those who wish to fine-tune their carburetors. The rods can be changed for a richer or leaner mixture in a matter of minutes, without taking the carburetor apart.

Carter AFBs first appeared on the cross-ram manifolds of the (modern day) Hemi engines in 1964, but were quickly supplanted by Holleys. When the street Hemi was released in 1966, the Carter AFB was the carburetor of choice. The AFB's compact size allowed it to be comfortably mounted in tandem. The rear carburetor is the primary of the pair and has a choke. Its primary barrels are nearly centrally located on the intake manifold and feed the entire engine under normal low-speed operation. The front carburetor is the secondary of the pair and is connected by what Chrysler called "staged linkage" (hot-rodders know this type of linkage as progressive). This linkage allows the front carburetor to sit idle until it's needed. When the throttle is all the way to the floor, both carburetors are wide open.

Carter AFBs were the only carburetors used on the street Hemi. The rear carburetor had a choke and was used for low-speed operation. At full throttle, both carburetors opened up to provide maximum performance.

The 1969 Road Runner was available in three body styles: a two-door coupe, a hardtop (shown), and a convertible. The cartoon character adorned each door and the center of the deck lid. Also on the left side of the deck lid was a small Hemi emblem. The 15-inch wheels were standard with the Hemi option.

list was expanding. A convertible Road Runner joined the coupe and hardtop models. Power windows, center console, and bucket seats were new to the option list. Standard on any Hemi and optional for the 383, was a Fresh Air hood. This hood was also used on the GTX. It was similar to the hood on the 1968 Road Runner, except the vents were vertical. Extending under the hood was a system of ductwork that directed fresh air to the engine. Added to the 1969 Road Runner engine option list was the three two-barrel carburetor-equipped 440. Dubbed the 440 Six-Barrel, it came with a nasty-looking black scooped hood and many of the Hemi's heavy-duty suspension components. This powerful engine offered Hemi-style acceleration at half the cost.

Motor Trend magazine selected the 1969 Road Runner as the Car of the Year. In multi-page ads celebrating the fact, Plymouth copywriters went on to give the specific numbers the potential buyers wanted to hear—quarter-mile times and speeds. In stock form, a 1969 Hemi Road Runner, equipped with a TorqueFlite and 4.10 rear axle, consistently ran the quarter-mile in the mid-13-second range at speeds of 105 miles per hour. The next day, the same car was brought back to the track with a few bolt-on performance additions. A Racer Brown cam and kit were added along with a set of Hooker headers. Run with the headers open, the Hemi Road Runner's elapsed times dropped by seven-tenths of a second and speeds improved by five miles per hour.

While overall sales of the 1969 Road Runner increased, the number of buyers opting for the Hemi decreased slightly. The hardtops led the list with 422 Hemis, followed by the coupes at 356, and the convertibles at a lowly 10.

Like the Road Runner, the 1969 GTX saw only minor changes. The grille was redesigned and a GTX emblem was added to the center. In the rear, the taillights were recessed. The body side stripes and chrome molding were removed from the rocker panel and replaced with a flat black lower-body treatment. The GTX shared the Road Runner's Fresh Air hood on its standard 440 and optional Hemi. The success of the Road Runner took a bite out of GTX sales, with only 15,608 units delivered in 1969, which was down 3,300 units compared to 1968 sales. Hemi sales were down accordingly, with only 198 hardtops and 11 convertibles delivered.

In 1968, many options were added to the Road Runner, including bucket seats. An 8000-rpm tachometer was integrated into the right side of the instrument cluster. If someone forgot what model of car they were riding in, all they had to do was look at the right side of the instrument panel to see the smirking face of the little bird.

The 1969 Dodge performance lineup made very few changes to the R/T and Super Bee from their 1968 models. Bumblebee stripes on both models were revised to a single broad stripe. Both the R/T and Super Bee were available with an optional pair of dummy side scoops, which were attached to the leading edge of the quarter panel. The Super Bee, only available as a two-door coupe previously, was now available in a hardtop, and bucket seats were an option. The most significant change for both models was the addition of the Ram Charger hood. Standard with the Hemi and optional with other performance engines, the Ram Charger hood fed fresh air to the carburetors. On the surface of the hood were attached two forward-facing wedge-shaped scoops. Under the hood was a large fiberglass fixture that fed fresh air to the air cleaner. Models with the optional Hemi engine had HEMI

In 1970, both the Plymouth and Dodge were restyled. The Dodge's dual loop grille received mixed reviews, and Plymouth R/Ts featured nonfunctional quarter panel scoops and twin hood scoops that were functional. When the model was equipped with a 426 engine, a small HEMI emblem was placed on each hood scoop.

spelled out in small chrome letters on the outboard side of each scoop. In 1969, a total of 258 Super Bees and 107 Coronet R/Ts were equipped with the Hemi engine.

In 1970 the Dodge Coronet was restyled with a unique front-end treatment. The grille had a wide

split in the center, and each side was fitted with a halo-style bumper that tapered as it reached toward that split. It had the look of someone with large nostrils scowling. This would be the final year for the Coronet R/T and Super Bee. In 1971 both of these models would be listed as Charger options.

But in 1970, R/T and Super Bee meant performance. The R/T was available in both hardtop and convertible body styles, whereas the Super Bee was available only in a two-door coupe or hardtop. The R/T side scoop was redesigned with a single forward-facing opening. Bumblebee stripes were again part of the R/T and Super Bee option and could be deleted. With the 1970 Super Bee, the customer could opt for an alternate set of stripes, known as the "reverse C-stripes." They were two hockey stick-style stripes that traced the quarter panel character lines. A larger circular Super Bee decal was placed at the point where they met on the rear of the quarter panel. With the Hemi option, on both the R/T and Super Bee, the Ram Charger hood was standard. The musclecar insurance crackdown was in full swing in 1970, and performance cars including the R/T and Super Bee suffered. Sales in 1970 for the Super Bee were 15,506 units and 2,615 for the R/T. A mere 38 1970 Super Bees were sold with the Hemi option. Hemi-equipped 1970 R/Ts are even more rare, with just 14 sold, and only 1 of those was a convertible. These would be the last Coronet-based cars available with the Hemi engine, and the only mid-size Dodge Hemis sold in 1971 would be Charger Super Bee and Charger R/T models.

The 1970 Road Runner and GTX models were also restyled and were a little more mainstream compared to the 1970 Dodge Coronet. Plymouth's designers were able to use the roof and doors from the 1969 model and add new quarter panels, taillight treatment, and new front-end sheet metal for a fresh look. The quarter panels featured more-rounded corners and had a small nonfunctional scoop on the leading edge. The twin vertical vents were removed from the hood, and a power dome was added. The new Air Grabber scoop was standard on the Hemi-equipped GTXs and Road Run-

The 1970 Dodge R/T's interior was well appointed. A wood-grain and chrome console divided the two standard high-back bucket seats covered in Shallow Elk grain vinyl. The instrument panel also featured wood grain appliqués. The two large dials on the left side of the instrument cluster are the speedometer and tachometer/clock combination.

ners. The driver could flip a switch under the instrument panel that would open the trap door Air Grabber scoop. Wonderfully creative graphics on the side of the scoop would then be visible as outside air was directed to the engine. This scoop won big style points on the street.

The 15-inch wheels, which had been a standard part of the GTX and Road Runner Hemi package, were no longer required, and all Hemis came standard with 14x6-inch wheels, with the 15-inch wheels becoming an option. The Road Runner was available in a two-door coupe, hardtop, or convertible. The GTX, available only as a hardtop, had a twin body stripe that started at the leading edge of the front fender and swept rearward into the quarter panel scoop. Like their brothers over in the Dodge camp, the Plymouth executives were able to

The completely restyled 1971 Road Runner had the rounded look of the new body that made the car look larger than it actually was. When a Hemi was ordered, an Air Grabber hood scoop was included in the center of the domed hood. The Hemi engine was indicated by decals above the side marker light. Dale Amy

read the writing on the wall—musclecar mania was winding down. In 1970, only 152 buyers specified a Hemi engine in the Road Runner, and GTX customers were just as reluctant, buying only 72 Hemis.

In 1971, the only Hemi B-body was the Plymouth Road Runner and GTX. The Belvedere name was dropped and all two-door models were hardtops that were now called Satellite Sebrings. Ply-

mouth offered no convertible in 1971. Both the 1971 Road Runner and GTX were based on this fully redesigned Satellite Sebring. The new Plymouth offerings and the Dodge Chargers now shared the same 115-inch platform, although the Plymouth body was 2.2 inches shorter. The new body appeared larger and more rounded than the 1970 model. The front end had a long, low hood line that extended out to a flush fitting halo-style

Aggressive front and rear wheel-opening flares highlighted the clean styling of the 1971 Road Runner. Road Runner graphics were placed on the quarter panel just above the wheel opening and enclosed in a circle on the right side of the deck lid. Only 55 Road Runners were equipped with the Hemi engine in 1971, the last year of production. Dale Amy

bumper. The grille and headlights were sunk deeply into the bumper. The full wheel openings were flared out slightly. This feature, along with a wider track, gave the new Road Runner and GTX a very aggressive look. Both the GTX and Road Runner offered body-colored bumpers as an option, and a transverse strobe stripe was optional for the Road Runner. It ran from the rear wheel opening forward across the C-pillar and roof and then back down the C-pillar to the other rear wheel opening. With the Hemi engine, the Air Grabber hood was again standard.

In 1971, the curtain officially came down on the musclecar era. A total of 55 Hemi-powered Road Runners and 35 Hemi-powered GTXs were sold that year. Emission constraints and auto insurance surcharges had finally sucked the oxygen out of the musclecar atmosphere.

2

The Winged Wonders and Chargers

Charger, Charger Daytona, Plymouth Superbird

Chrysler's management was unhappy with the public's poor response to the 1962 Plymouths and Dodges. Sales for that year were dismal compared the rest of the industry. Chrysler's management wanted its cars to have a cleaner, more mainstream design. Elwood Engle, a Ford designer, was hired to replace Virgil Exner, Chrysler's premier designer during the 1950s. Engle was given the formidable task of reshaping Chrysler's look and doing it in minimal time. To make Engle's task more monumental, two new cars were added, the Plymouth Barracuda and the Dodge Charger.

The Dodge Charger was conceived as an upscale personal luxury car in the same mode as the Buick Riviera, Olds Toronado, and Ford Thunderbird, but less costly. The new Charger was to lead the Dodge

Continued on page 39

In 1970, the final year for the second-generation Dodge Charger, the Charger R/T had large rear-facing scoops added to the doors. The placement of the scoops required the relocation of the HEMI badges from the doors to the front fenders. Dale Amy

223

Heading the Dodge Rebellion advertising program in 1966 was the smartly styled Charger. It was built on the Coronet platform, and Chrysler designers incorporated a full-width grille that cleverly disguised its hidden headlights and parking lights in amongst the vertical bars.

A full-length console, mounting an optional clock, split both the 1966 Charger's front and rear bucket seats. The chrome instrument panel's two center pods contained the 150 mile per hour speedometer and the 6,000-rpm tachometer.

Four V-8 engines were available in the 1966 Charger, including the 426 Hemi. In 1966, all Hemi engines came with a large chrome-plated air cleaner and black crinkle-painted valve covers. Adjusting the valve lash was a lengthy project because items like heater hoses had to be removed in order to take off the large valve cover.

The 1966 Charger's full-width taillight matched the design theme of the front end, and the rear window's outer edges curled up to meet the sweeping roof line.

For the second-generation Dodge Charger, Chrysler designers were determined to create a car that looked completely different from the Coronet. Their vision was a car that looked as though it could be driven directly from the street to the high banks of Daytona. The new Charger featured a wedge-shape body, fastback roofline, and aggressive bulges around each full wheel opening. Dale Amy

226

Continued from page 35

Rebellion advertising theme in presenting a new image of performance and clean, inventive design.

The 1966 Charger shared its platform with the 117-inch wheelbase Coronet. Both cars shared the front- and side-sheet metal, but the Charger's fastback roof line dramatically set it apart. Because of the Charger's hardtop design, a considerable amount of body structure had to be added in the areas of the C-pillars and the upper rear deck. Dodge designers made small but significant changes to the Coronet's quarter panels. The rear wheel openings were enlarged and shaped the same as the front wheel openings, which gave the Charger an aggressive, sporty stance. The leading edge of the quarter panels received two horizontal depressions that simulated air intakes. The sides of the Charger were clean and devoid of any trim other than a thin belt line molding, a rocker panel molding, and thin wheel lip moldings. The large triangular sail panel was accented with a tasteful CHARGER name plate.

The Charger's front-end treatment was also bold. Within the large rectangular opening was a full-width grille with hidden headlights. The grille consisted of a series of thin vertical chrome bars, whose density concealed the split lines for the headlight doors and the parking lights. Even when the headlight doors were open, the lights were fully trimmed. It was a small detail that few manufacturers took time to master with hidden headlights. One plague that afflicts cars with hidden headlights are doors that fail to open or close completely. This "lazy eye" look neutralizes the overall effect of hidden headlights and makes noncustomers out of potential customers. Chrysler engineers were given the job of designing a fail-proof mechanism. To accomplish this, they gave each light its own heavily geared electric motor.

Mr. Norm's Hemi Charger

In 1968, Dodge high performance dealer extraordinaire, Norm "Mr. Norm" Kraus, drove a new Hemi-powered Charger R/T. "I had a '68 Charger street Hemi with a pearl paint job—it was gorgeous," recalls Kraus. The technicians at Grand Spaulding Dodge were always experimenting with cams and other engine components and Kraus' Charger was one of the test beds. "I wanted a top-end cam because I lived 25 miles from the dealership and spent a lot of time on the expressway. We also curved the distributor and put a set of headers on the car, but I never ran them open. I always felt the engine breathed a little better with the headers. A lot of guys tried to egg me on to race them. They knew who I was and the route I took to work. I'd be cruisin' in my Charger listening to the music, and I'd look to my left, and here's a guy pointing (giving the all-American signal for "Do you want to race?"). I really frowned upon street racing, but every once in a while I'd have to see how well our engine package worked. I'd inch 'em up saying no-no-no. So instead of going 55, now we were at 65. Then I'd nod and we'd both hit it. That Hemi would take off—it was something beautiful. That Charger was a great street car. Gas at that time was pennies compared to now, so you didn't care about the mileage. I always drove a Hemi and enjoyed it."

The modifications made to the 1969 Dodge Charger 500 were designed for NASCAR competition. The grille was pulled forward, flush to the edge of the opening. The hidden headlights were dropped in favor of exposed quad units, and the A-pillars received a special piece of bright trim.

When the driver pulled the light switch, a red light illuminated on the instrument panel until the headlight doors were fully open. An override switch was provided to open the doors in icy weather or to clean the headlight lenses.

The rear of the Charger carried the same wide rectangular one-piece look as the front. Within a thin chrome molding was a large single taillight lens. Widely spaced individual chrome letters spelled out

CHARGER across the width of the lens. The 1966 Charger looked long, low, and wide. In addition, the execution of the exterior sheet metal and details was crisp and contemporary.

The Charger's interior was as fashionable as its exterior. It featured individual seating for four. The front seats were Chryslers new clamshell-design buckets. The rear seats were also buckets, with backrests that could fold down, converting the

In the rear, the Daytona 500's rear window was blended flush with the C-pillars, creating a smooth flow of air over the roof. The rear window placement and subsequent roof modifications required a severe shortening of the deck lid. The taillight treatment and quick release-style gas cap were standard on all Chargers, but the transverse Bumblebee stripes were only on the Charger 500.

small luggage compartment into one of extended length. Splitting the seats was a full-length console, trimmed with a die-cast chrome plate with a brushed aluminum appliqué. At the forward end, a clock was mounted in a chrome housing. In keeping with the sporty theme, all 1966 Dodge Chargers with optional engines came with a floor-mounted shifter for either the TorqueFlite automatic or four-speed manual transmission. The instrument panel held four large chrome-rimmed pods. The two pods in the center housed the speedometer and a 6,000 rpm tachometer.

Dodge defined the Charger's performance image with the selection of standard and optional engines. The 318-ci 230-horsepower V8 was the base engine, and the 361- and 383-ci engines and the 426-ci street Hemi were optional. Along with the Hemi engine came a heavy-duty suspension, which featured 11-inch brake drums.

Even though it was introduced late in the model year, the 1966 Dodge Charger sold well. Of the 37,344 that were produced, 468 were equipped with the Hemi engine. Drag racers didn't latch onto the Charger like the NASCAR crowd did. The sleek aerodynamics and extra weight were counterproductive to the drag-racing credo. But down South, the good ol' boys of NASCAR saw the advantages of the slick roof line and powerful Hemi engine. David Pearson, driving a Dodge Charger, won the NASCAR Grand National championship.

Even Wile E. Coyote on an Acme rocket sled would have a hard time catching this Lemon Twist-colored Superbird. Based on a 1970 Road Runner, it featured much of the same wind-cheating design tricks that were used on the Daytona 500. All Superbirds came with Rallye wheels.

Only 135 Superbirds were powered by the Hemi engine. The rest of the 2,000 produced were equipped with a 440. Even though all other Hemi-equipped 1970 Road Runners were equipped with the Air Grabber hood, the Superbird was not. The distinctive Road Runner "Beep Beep" horn is at the left edge of the radiator tank. It's painted a shade of light purple and features the smirking face of the bird on a decal that states, "Voice of the Road Runner."

The Superbird's rear window was supported by two angled vertical stabilizers. The PLYMOUTH script on the quarter panel was done in the same font and size as on the side of Richard Petty's race car.

Chrysler didn't want to alter a successful car, and it made only minor changes to the 1967 Charger. The 440-ci engine was added to the option list. But in 1967, sales of the Charger were dismal—less than half those of the previous year. Sales of the Hemi engine dropped even more dramatically, down to 118.

For the 1968 model year, Chrysler designer Bill Brownlie was determined to create a Charger that looked completely different from the Coronet. His vision was a car that could be driven directly to the high banks of Daytona but could also be toured on the street. Design staff members got busy and submitted their renderings to Brownlie. The designer who shared Brownlie's vision was Richard Tighstin, and his sketches showed a car with a narrow front end that got wider toward the rear. Tighstin's side profile showed the car's wedge shape with a built-in rear spoiler. This would be the second-generation Charger.

The new Charger carried many of the same styling cues as the original, including the full-width rectangular grille and large front and rear wheel openings. The body on the new Charger lost its

The roof extension needed to fit the special rear window, which can be seen in the reflection off the driver's side C-pillar. Plymouth installed vinyl tops on all Superbirds to save the enormous amount of expensive metal finishing required to fit the rear window.

High insurance surcharges took their toll on the sales of sleek Charger R/Ts in 1970, when only 10,337 were sold. Of that number, only 112 were equipped with the Hemi engine. Dale Amy

angular lines in favor of a smooth, Coke-bottle shape. The sheet metal at each wheel opening was raised and flared slightly. The black-out grille carried hidden headlights and thin vertical bars similar to the first-generation Charger's grille. The subtle quarter panel scoops on the earlier Charger were moved up to the doors, and an additional set was cut into the hood. Within the scalloped hood

scoops was an optional set of turn indicators. Keeping in sync with the racing theme, Chrysler designers added a large quick-fill gas cap on top of the left quarter panel. The Charger's flat rear window tunneled into the fastback roofline. In the rear, the full-width taillight of the 1966 and 1967 models was dropped in favor of two pairs of circular lights set into an angled panel. The interior of the new

Hidden headlights, formerly standard on the Charger, were now optional. For 1971, the halo-style grille received a center bar. From the angle of this photograph, the Charger's Coke-bottle shape is apparent.

Charger was not as well detailed as the previous model had been. The seats, buckets in front and bench rear, were less supportive, but still attractive. The instrument panel had the efficiency of an aircraft cockpit, with two large dials on the left (clock and 150-mile-per-hour speedometer) and four smaller gauges on the right. An optional tachometer was integrated into the clock.

The chassis and engine combinations for the 1968 Charger were carryovers from 1967. In 1968, a new model was added to the Charger—the R/T

(Road and Track). The R/T was a performance package that offered a standard 375-horsepower 440-ci engine and a host of heavy-duty components. TorqueFlite was the standard transmission, and a four-speed manual was optional. Also standard were rear Bumblebee stripes, but the graphics could be deleted. The Hemi engine was only available with the R/T package, and in 1968 475 were sold.

The 1969 Charger was released with very few changes from the 1968 model, but the most notable change was the addition of a center split in the

Continued on page 51

In 1971 the Dodge Charger and Coronet were merged into one model. Unfortunately, this took away the uniqueness of the Charger, but it didn't diminish its visual appeal. The Charger's new sheet metal had an aggressive rake.

All 1971 Charger R/T models had a distinctive domed hood with flat black graphic and hood pins. All Hemi models had the trapdoor-style Ramcharger hood scoop.

The 1971 Charger interiors were tastefully elegant. All R/Ts came with bucket seats covered in El Paso grained vinyl, and the gauges in front of the driver were nestled into a coved area of the instrument panel. The two larger dials housed the 150-mile-per-hour speedometer and 7,000-rpm tachometer.

Continued from page 47

grille. In the rear, a new pair of rectangular-shaped taillights, reminiscent of those on the 1967 Charger, replaced the circular ones. The Hemi engine was again available only with the R/T option, and 432 were delivered in 1969.

Certain aspects of the new Charger's exterior, while stylish, hindered performance. The deep-set

The Charger R/Ts had special three-segment taillight lenses in an argent silver housing. The rear end treatment featured a contoured rear window that swept down to the deck lid and had a small built-in spoiler on the rear lip. This particular R/T also has an optional rear wing spoiler.

Hemi Crate Motors

Want a Hemi engine for your car? No problem—just call up your local Mopar Performance Parts dealer and ask for a Hemi Crate Motor. Two factory-engineered versions are available. The basic 426-ci engine (part number P5249667) uses a cast-iron block with cross-bolted mains. It has forged 9:1 pistons, cast-iron heads, and a hydraulic cam with 278 degrees of duration. With the recommended 750 cfm carburetor and headers, this engine develops an impressive 465 horsepower and 520 foot-pounds of torque.

If that's not enough power, you can step up and order the 528-ci Hemi (part number P4876690). The 102 extra cubes are available through a bore of 4.50 and a stroke of 4.15. This king of the elephant parade blasts out 610 horsepower and 650 foot-pounds of torque. It uses the same block as the lower horsepower version, but is fitted with 10:25 pistons and aluminum heads. To attain that horsepower, the addition of headers and a single four-barrel carburetor that flows between 850–900 cfm is recommended.

Both engines come equipped with a six-quart oil pan, a dual plane single four-barrel intake manifold, stainless steel valves (2.25-inch diameter intake and 1.94-inch diameter exhaust), and a Mopar Performance electronic distributor.

Legendary power doesn't come cheap. At your local Mopar Performance Parts dealer, the 426-ci version lists for $13,750 and the 528 for $16,975. By shopping around, you can save a few thousand through mail order or specialty suppliers.

Buying a Hemi engine is as easy as stopping by your local Mopar Performance Parts dealer. Two versions are available: a 426-ci version that develops 465 horsepower (pictured), or an aluminum-headed stroker version that pumps out 610 horsepower. Mopar Performance

Bumblebee stripes, which had been common on previous Charger R/Ts, were no longer available in 1971. The new stripes, available only in black, wrapped around the cowl and swept down the belt line, terminating at the end of the quarter panel.

The 1971 Super Bee and Dodge R/T were both performance models, but of the two, the Super Bee was the plain vanilla model, having a more businesslike interior, offering fewer frills. The Super Bee's taillights are standard 1971 Charger units.

grille and tunneled rear window were detrimental to high speed. Late in the 1968 model year, Chrysler designed a modified version it named the Charger 500, which would be released as a 1969 model. The Charger 500 featured a flush-mounted grille and a rear window that followed the sloping shape of the C-pillars. This flush-mounted rear window required a special shortened deck lid. A Bumblebee stripe ran across the back, with the

number 500 on the quarter panel. NASCAR required that a minimum of 500 production-line cars be built in order to qualify for competition. The intent of the rule was to eliminate the building of special race-only cars that weren't available to the general public.

The Charger 500s were equipped with a standard 440 engine at a base price of $3,591 or the optional Hemi at an additional $648.20. A Torque-

In 1971, the Coronet was no longer available, and the Super Bee option was only available on the Charger. The Super Bee shared the R/Ts domed hood (with Super Bee graphics) and body stripes. When equipped with a Hemi engine, the script on the side of the hood declared 426 HEMI.

Flite or a four-speed manual were the only two transmissions available. Records show that only 67 Charger 500s were Hemi powered. *Hot Rod* magazine had three of these Hemi-powered Charger 500s available for road tests for its February 1969 issue. Unfortunately, one of the two four-speed cars was stolen just prior to the test. Of the two Hemi 500s, staffer Steve Kelly favored the Torque-Flite-equipped 500. He wrote, "This is the kind of car you make excuses to drive." One option he

heartily recommended was front disc brakes. Both Charger 500s were run at the drags. The four-speed car was equipped with a 4.10 rear axle and ran the best times at 13.48 seconds and a speed of 109 miles per hour. The TorqueFlite was mated to a 3.23 rear axle on the other Hemi Charger 500, and it ran the quarter in 13.8 seconds at a speed of 105 miles per hour.

The Charger 500, with its revised aerodynamics, faced the Torino Talladega and Mercury Cyclone

The trapdoor Ramcharger hood scoop was opened by flipping a switch under the left side of the instrument panel. This activated a vacuum actuator under the hood, opening the scoop. Fresh air would then be ducted to the engine's air filter.

Spoiler with their modified front ends in NASCAR competition. Whatever the Charger 500 had gained in aerodynamics was now equaled by the Fords and Mercurys. To gain the competitive edge, Chrysler pulled out all the stops with the Charger Daytona.

The 1969 Charger Daytona was the most outrageous and infamous of all the Dodge Chargers. It was Chrysler's throw-down-the-gauntlet approach to building an unbeatable car for NASCAR competition. Costs to Chrysler for the Daytona were rumored to be as high as $1 million. The Charger Daytona picked up where the Charger 500 left off. It retained the 500's flush-mounted rear window, but used a new nose piece and rear wing developed in a wind tunnel. The wedge-shaped nose was constructed of sheet metal and added 18 inches to the front of the car. Rear-facing scoops were added to the tops of the front fenders for tire clearance on the race versions. Engineers added a rear spoiler that was 58 inches wide. It was supported by 23.5-inch-high uprights that grew out of the top of the quarter panels. This wing was adjustable, and it canceled the lift created at the rear of the car. The rear of the Charger Daytona was adorned with a wide Bumblebee stripe that covered the wing. Emblazoned in large letters on the quarter panel was the name DAYTONA. These body modifications reduced the aerodynamic drag by 15 percent over the Charger 500, thus greatly enhancing the Charger Daytona's top speed. Chrysler's adventures into the heady world of aerodynamics paid off with a car that could easily reach and maintain speeds of 200 miles per hour. It was also a public relations success. Other than the race cars, only 503 Charger Daytonas were built in 1969, and only 70 of those had the Hemi engine.

The Charger Daytona proved to be an excellent performer on the high banks. When it made its first appearance at NASCAR's Talladega race in September 1969, it quickly became the fastest stock car in history when Charlie Glotzbach took the pole for the Talladega 500 with a speed of 199.466 miles per hour. The anticipated showdown against the Fords didn't materialize. The Ford drivers withdrew, citing unsafe conditions, and Richard Brickhouse won the race in a Charger Daytona.

Legend has it that because of the success of the Charger Daytona, Richard Petty wanted to switch to a Dodge Charger Daytona, but he was under contract to drive a Plymouth. The people at Plymouth refused to let him compete in a Dodge, so Petty defected and drove a Ford for the 1969 season. In 1970, Petty would return behind the wheel of Plymouth's new winged car, the Superbird.

The 1970 Plymouth Superbird had the assertive good looks of the 1969 Charger Daytona. Like its Dodge Daytona brother, the Superbird was built and sold to the general public to comply with NASCAR rules. At first glance it appears as if the Daytona parts were simply bolted onto a Road Runner to create the Superbird, but they weren't. All Superbird components were unique to that car. The extended nosecone, which housed hidden headlights, had a small rubber strip across the front. Just under the leading edge, there was an opening for air to enter the radiator. To fit the nosecone onto the Road Runner, the leading edges of the front fenders and the hood were extended to match the nosecone's surface. The rearward-facing scoops were placed over the front tires and were the same color as the body work. The Superbird's rear window was also unique. Along with roof and rear deck modifications, the rear window

Dual exhausts were standard on the Super Bee, but the rear wing was optional along with the small vertical bumper guards. Documentation showed that this particular 1971 Super Bee was originally delivered from Grand Spaulding Dodge. The owner has taken the time to add the proper Grand Spaulding license plate frame and decal to the deck lid—both status symbols in their day.

was designed to improve aerodynamics. To facilitate the speedy assembly of the street versions, all Superbirds sold to the general public were equipped with a vinyl top. This precluded expensive metal finishing that would have required extra time and expense. Rising from the top of the quarter panels were the uprights that supported the rear wing. The Superbird's uprights

were much wider at the base than those on the Charger Daytona.

All Superbirds came standard with the 440-ci engine with either a single four-barrel carburetor or the six-barrel configuration of three two-barrel Holleys. The Hemi was also optional and 135 Superbirds were so equipped. All Superbirds came with an all vinyl interior in black, or white with black trim.

A bench seat was standard and front bucket seats were optional. The instrumentation was the same as on the 1970 Road Runner. The exterior colors for the Superbird were limited to Alpine White, Petty Blue, Lemon Twist, TorRed, Burnt Orange Metallic, Vitamin C Orange, Limelight, or Blue Fire Metallic. The Superbird's racing culture was distinctively shown by its graphics. On the quarter panel was a large decal that spelled out the word PLYMOUTH in the same size and font as Richard Petty's race car. On the nose and wing uprights was the rambunctious little bird with a racing helmet tucked under its right wing.

In 1970 the Dodge Charger received only minor tweaks. Most notable were the redesigned grille and front bumper. The doors on the R/T received an added reversed scoop, which was located at the forward edge, covering the stamped depressions. Just as in the previous two years, the Hemi engine was available only in the R/T, and just 112 were sold.

In 1971, Dodge restyled the Charger and combined it with the Coronet. The new Charger/Coronet had to retain the aggressive good looks for the musclecar buyer, but also had to be sedate enough for the buyer of a four-door family car. Many enthusiasts believed that the new Charger had lost its individuality, because it shared a four-door platform.

The new Charger had a forward raked look that was attributed to the raised belt line. Although it had a two-inch-shorter wheelbase, the new Charger looked as long as the original. Many of the original Charger styling cues were still in place on the 1971 model. The grille was still rectangular in shape, surrounded by a halo bumper. Hidden headlights, previously standard on the Charger, were now optional on all but the base Charger. The basic Coke-bottle shape of the body was still there, along with the full wheel openings. The roof didn't have the tunneled rear window, but the deck lid retained a small spoiler.

The R/T and Super Bee were performance models of the 1971 Charger. The R/T featured a domed and louvered hood with flat black accents. When the optional Hemi was ordered, the louvers were dropped in favor of a Ram Charger hood, also optional with the 440 engine. The R/T used unique door outer skins that had two vertical depressions at the door's leading edge. Inside these depressions were tape accents. The R/T also featured a body side stripe that started at the rear edge of the hood and swept along the belt line to the end of the quarter panel. The door accents and body side stripes, which came only in black, could be deleted. Small R/T emblems were added to the sides of the front fenders and to the rear edge of the deck lid. The Charger R/T had a special taillight lens that was divided into three sections per side. In 1971, there were only 63 Dodge Charger R/Ts sold with the Hemi engine.

The Super Bee was the inexpensive hot rod of the Charger lineup, and it came standard with a 300 horsepower 383 with options of a 440 or Hemi. Heavy-duty suspension, wide oval tires, and Rallye wheels were some of the hot standard equipment. Unlike the R/T, the Super Bee was fitted with the standard two-light-per-side Charger taillights. A special Super Bee hood decal was applied to the raised hood dome. The same body stripes ran from the cowl rearward on the R/T. Super Bee emblems were on the side of the front fender and on the back of the deck lid. Only 22 1971 Super Bees were equipped with Hemi engines.

3

Chrysler's Pocket Rockets

Hemi 'Cudas and Challengers

To compete against the Mustang and soon-to-be-introduced Camaro, Chrysler's designers had to offer more than one body style. They also had to make room for larger engines. In the fall of 1966, Plymouth introduced its all-new Barracuda. In addition to the fastback, a coupe and a convertible were added to the lineup. The new Barracuda was longer, wider, and lower than the previous model. It had a muscular look and an engine lineup to match. With the availability of the 383-ci engine, it was the performance equal of Mustangs powered with the 390-ci engine. The 383 was only available with a four-speed manual or TorqueFlite transmission. Even with the two-inch-wider engine compartment, the 383 was a tight fit, and the accessory drive had to be

Performance cars were made to be driven, and driving a Hemi 'Cuda is a definite adrenaline rush. Fat, 60-series tires were standard on the 'Cuda. They complemented the vehicle's overall low and wide design. This 1970 Hemi 'Cuda features the optional Elastomeric bumper and vinyl top.

The 1970 'Cuda was an entirely new vehicle and was designated as an E-body car. It was styled to compete against the hot-selling Mustangs and Camaros. It featured the long-nose short-deck design philosophy of its contemporaries.

redesigned. The new Barracuda sheet metal was fitted over the original platform, limiting the space available for a larger engine. Even when the Barracuda was reskinned in 1968, the engine compartment was limited to the 383. The only exceptions were the purpose-built drag race Hemi Barracudas.

In 1967, the musclecar boom experienced a sharp incline. At that time Chrysler's Advanced Styling Studios began work on what would eventually become the 1970 Barracuda. They worked in concert with the engineering groups to design a car with an engine compartment large enough to accommodate a 440 with air conditioning or a

Hemi. In the musclecar wars, there was no substitute for cubic inches, and Chrysler was determined to build the most potent pony car ever.

To build such a car, an entirely new platform had to be created—the E-body. The larger B-body (Coronet/Charger) cowl was used as the starting point. The front sub frame and rear axle were also borrowed. (It is interesting to note that Camaro was constructed from Nova components in Chevy's parts bins.) The Advanced Styling group packaged the vehicle, determining wheelbase, seating positions, greenhouse, and door sills. With those parameters approved, the package was given to the Plymouth styling group. It was at this time that Chrysler management decided to build a Dodge equivalent—the Challenger. The Challenger would be positioned in the market as the upscale model to compete against the Mercury Cougar and Pontiac Firebird. While appearing similar to the Barracuda, the Challenger would be quite different.

Both cars shared the upper body and the basic design theme of the long, low front end and an aggressive short, kicked-up rear deck. Only two body styles were to be built, a notch-back coupe and a convertible. A fastback wasn't in the

The 1970 Dodge Challenger was built on the same E-body platform as the 'Cuda. While similar in appearance to the 'Cuda, its body was unique and rode on a slightly longer wheelbase.

The sleek new E-bodies carried all the latest design trends, which included flush door handles, streamlined racing style mirrors, and hidden windshield wipers. Protruding through the hood on all Hemi-powered 'Cudas was the Shaker hood scoop.

The 1970 'Cudas and Challengers were only available in two-door hardtop (often called a notch back) and convertible body styles. The new E-bodies were two inches lower and five inches wider than the 1969 models.

Optional on the 1970 'Cuda were "hockey stick" stripes. These stripes accented the rear quarter panel, terminating with the engine's cubic-inch displacement near the taillight. When a 'Cuda was equipped with a Hemi, the stripes simply spelled out HEMI.

cards. The Challenger's wheelbase was 110 inches, 2 inches longer than the Barracuda. The height was just a fraction over 50 inches, 2 inches lower than the previous Barracuda. Both cars, however, were low and wide. The new Barracuda's width was 74.7 inches, an increase of 5 inches over the previous model. The Challenger was even wider, at 76.1 inches. This width gave the E-bodied cars an exceptionally aggressive look from the front or rear. This look was accentuated with the addition of the fat 60-series Polyglas tires. When equipped with narrower standard tires, the E-bodies looked sadly out of proportion. The Challenger was longer at 191.3 inches compared to the Barracuda's 186.7 inches. Both cars offered full wheel openings, with the Challenger's more elliptical in shape than the Barracuda's. The Barracuda carried a soft horizontal character line down the side. The Challenger's body character line was more pronounced and it rose up over the rear wheel opening. It also flared out slightly, which can be attributed to the Challenger's dimensionally wider girth. The sides of both bodies tucked under severely in an area called "tumble home" by body designers. Both cars had flush door handles, hidden wipers, and ventless door glass—all the latest design trends coming out of the Detroit studios. The Challenger, true to its upscale image, had more bright trim, including thin wheel-opening moldings.

The front and rear of the new Challenger and Barracuda were also unique. Both were clean and classy designs. The Barracuda's oval-shaped grille had a single center peak accentuated by a series of deep-set horizontal bars. A pair of headlights was located at the outboard ends. The rolled-under valence panel below the thin horizontal bumper was painted body color, with an elliptical center opening allowing fresh air to the radiator. The Challenger also had a thin horizontal bumper. Below the bumper, the opening in the body color valence panel was more rectangular. The deep-set mesh grille was accentuated with a thin rectangular chrome molding. Two quad headlights were at the outboard ends. The parking lights on the Barracuda were neatly blended into the upper portion of the grill, whereas the Challenger's circular parking lights were tunneled into the valence panel.

The Plymouth designers wanted a full urethane front end for the new Barracuda, similar to the '68 GTO, but unfortunately, the money wasn't available. What they were able to develop was the Elastomeric bumper option. This was an unchromed bumper with high-density urethane foam molded over the surface. It was then painted body color. The Elastomeric was available for both front or rear, giving the designers their body-color bumpers. This option was only available on the Barracuda.

The rear bumpers on the Barracuda and Challenger were thin horizontal bars with an upturn at each end. Small vertical bumper guards were located near the outboard ends and extended down from the bumper onto the rear valence panel. Depending on the engine option, dual exhaust outlets were carved into the rear valence panel on both cars.

The taillight treatment also differed on both E-body cars. The Barracuda had a flat inset panel that housed the license plate in the center and the taillights at the outboard ends. Each rear light fixture incorporated a backup light and had a pair of thin horizontal bars across the lenses. Because of the license plate location, the Barracuda's deck lid lock was offset to the right.

Chrysler's designers were not restricted to adding a new body to an old platform when creating the new E-body 'Cuda. The 'Cuda's body sides carried a smart horizontal character line and a small lip on the full wheel openings. The 'Cuda's tightly integrated design can be seen in the way the rear valence panel was designed to blend smoothly into the vertical bumper guard.

The 'Cuda's interior featured vinyl-covered high-back bucket seats. Leather seats (as pictured) were an option. This 'Cuda's interior also features an optional three-spoke steering wheel, center console, and "Pistol Grip" shifter.

The Challenger's thin recessed taillight fixture carried the full width of the rear panel and featured a backup light in the center. The position of this light required the license plate to be mounted on the lower valence panel.

Both the Barracuda and Challenger could be ordered in three series. The Barracuda was the base model, followed by the Gran Coupe, and then the sporty 'Cuda. The Challenger also had three series: the base Challenger, the optional SE series, and the R/T (Road and Track).

The 'Cuda was easily identified by its special twin-scoop hood, hood pins, driving lights, Rallye wheels, and flat black taillight panel. An optional "hockey stick" body stripe was available. It slashed along the quarter panel, terminating with the engine's displacement figures in prominent letters or, on the cars equipped with the Hemi engine, the word HEMI.

The Dodge R/T came with a standard power bulge hood that featured twin inlets and hood pins. This hood was available with a special blackout paint treatment. Like the 'Cuda, the

R/T also featured white letter tires on Rallye wheels. As part of the R/T package, a rear bumblebee stripe or full-length body stripe was offered at no cost. The body side stripe accented the Challenger's side character line. The Bumblebee stripe had the effect of chopping off the rear of the car.

When ordered with the Hemi engine, the 'Cuda came standard with the Shaker hood scoop (it was optional on 'Cudas equipped with a 340, 383, or 440 engine). This scoop protruded through the hood and, as advertised, shook and shimmied while the engine revved. It had two openings in the front that allowed fresh air to enter the carbs when a lever on the instrument panel opened a valve in the scoop. Interestingly, the Shaker hood scoop was also optional on the Challenger with the Hemi engine. On both the 'Cuda and Challenger, the Shaker hood could be ordered in argent silver, flat black, or body color. The cold air flowing through the scoop enhanced engine performance by a few horsepower. But the visual impact was just as important as the horsepower, especially when everyone was able to see the word HEMI on the side of the scoop.

The catalog of colors for the Barracuda and Challenger was long and kaleidoscopic. Chrysler targeted these cars for the youth market and wanted the colors to be as bright and brazen as the cars themselves. Some of the more catchy colors were TorRed, Lemon Twist, Vitamin C, Sublime, Lime Light, Go-Mango, and of course, Hemi Orange. With the combinations of body styles and series, the addition of body stripes, hood configurations, and tire and wheel combinations, no two cars looked alike.

The interiors of the Barracuda and Challenger were simple but not as well executed as the exterior styling. An excess of plastic tended to make the interior look cheap when compared

The 'Cuda was the performance-oriented model of the 1970 Barracuda line, featuring a standard dual-scooped hood, hood pins, driving lights, and a rear taillight panel painted flat black.

to competitive models, such as the Camaro and Mustang. Typical of the pony cars of the era, the Barracuda and Challenger had front bucket seats and small rear bench seats. The door and quarter trim panels were molded with an integral arm rest. In front of the driver, the padded instrument panel was coved. The three-spoked steering wheel sat high in relation to the driver's seat. This elicited complaints from journalists when first test driving the Barracuda

and Challenger.

When the Mustang was introduced in 1964, it was offered with a wealth of options, so the buyer could build the car of his or her dreams. When the Camaro was released, Chevrolet followed the same philosophy, offering a large number of possible option combinations. Chrysler followed suit with the Barracuda and Challenger. The wide array of interior and exterior options included leather seats, center console, Rallye

The parking lights were integrated into the upper grille opening. The deep-set black grille was accented by a single thin horizontal red stripe. Instead of chrome, body-colored Elastomeric bumpers could be specified for the front and rear of the 1970 'Cuda. The small circular driving light below the bumper was standard as part of the 'Cuda package.

The offset trunk-lock cylinder is partially hidden by the 'Cuda nameplate. The lock was placed there because rear design did not permit a center-mounted lock. All 'Cudas featured dual exhaust with bright rectangular tips that extended through the rear valence panel.

wheels, rear window louvers, vinyl roof, and even a vacuum-operated trunk release.

These options continued under the hood. A host of different engines were offered for the Barracuda and Challenger, culminating with the Hemi. At a cost of $1,227, the Hemi option added considerably to the $2,800 base price for

each car. When adding the Hemi, many heavy-duty components were included, so the car could keep up with the engine. Only two transmissions were offered with the Hemi option, the TorqueFlite automatic and a four-speed manual. Selecting the gears on the four-speed was done with a Hurst shifter. This shifter didn't use a

The big Hemi engine fits snugly into the E-body engine compartment. This Hemi Challenger R/T is equipped with the optional Shaker hood scoop. The Shaker hood scoops were available in flat black, argent silver, or body color. The chrome emblem on the side of the scoop proudly announces that the engine below is a 426 HEMI.

All 1970 Hemi 'Cudas came equipped with the Shaker hood scoop. The opening to the carburetors was controlled by a lever under the instrument panel. A large rubber seal attached to the scoop sealed the hood, preventing water from entering the engine compartment.

Previous page
All 1970 Hemi 'Cudas came with 15x7 Rallye wheels, extra heavy-duty suspension with special front torsion bars, a large front sway bar, unique heavy-duty rear leaf springs, and a Dana 60 rear axle.

The 1970 E-body Dodge Challenger had a pronounced horizontal character line along the side that rose up over the rear wheel opening. The Challenger's R/T option provided the same level of standard performance options as the 'Cuda.

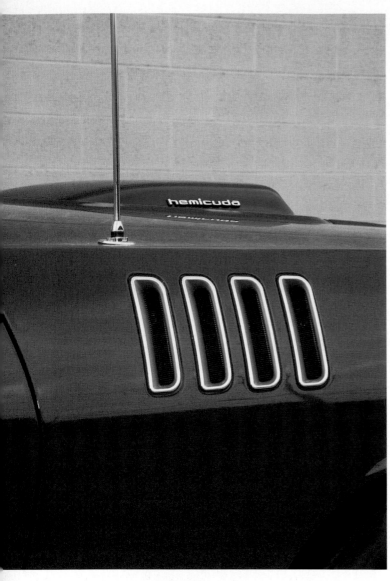

Added to the front fenders of the 1971 'Cudas were "gills," which were four nonfunctional louvers.

ball or T-handle; instead it used a vertical shift handle initially called a "strip-grip" shifter, which later became known as the "pistol grip" shifter. Barracudas and Challengers with a 440 or a Hemi were equipped with extra heavy-duty front torsion bars and a large diameter (0.94) front stabilizer bar. The rear suspension had an unusual combination of leaf springs. The left side had five full leafs with two half leafs and the right side had six full leafs. Hemi cars were not equipped with a rear stabilizer bar. The Hemi-powered Barracudas and Challengers all came with the heavy-duty Dana rear axle that rode on 15x7-inch wheels mounting F60X15 tires.

Motor Trend magazine writer Bill Sanders tested a new 1970 Hemi 'Cuda for the September 1969 issue. In his words, the new Hemi 'Cuda was "quite impressive." He wrote, "With the new Hemi 'Cuda a quarter-mile goes by so fast you hardly know you started. Even though our car had the widest optional F60X15 tires, we still experienced considerable wheel spin, which cut e.t.s. With a 4:10:1 axle ratio, all acceleration figures were out of sight, naturally. Plymouth's own version of the 'Shaker' hood adds to total performance." The Hemi 'Cuda Sanders drove was equipped with a TorqueFlite transmission, power steering, and power brakes, and it tripped the quarter-mile clocks in 13.7 seconds at a speed of 101.2 miles per hour.

Selling 666 units, the 1970 Hemi 'Cudas commanded the second-highest production numbers for any individual model Hemi-powered Chrysler product (the 1968 Road Runner is first). Of that total, 14 were convertibles. In 1970, 356 Hemi Challengers were produced; only

Bold colors were the norm for the early 1970s, and Plymouth pleased its customers with a long list of vivid colors that included Vitamin C, Lemon Twist, and this shade is called TorRed.

Nash Bridges' Hemi 'Cuda

Most of us remember Don Johnson as TV's "Miami Vice" detective who wore white suits over pastel-colored T-shirts, and drove a Ferrari. Today Don Johnson is still playing a cop, but he wears more-mainstream clothes while serving the city of San Francisco. He finally got wise and dumped the Ferrari for a real man's car—a 1971 Hemi 'Cuda. Well, that's what the movie folks would like you to believe. The car, or should I say cars (there are several), that Johnson drives are a taste of Hollywood movieland illusion.

How did Johnson decide on a 1971 Hemi 'Cuda? The story began when Don Johnson called movieland car czar Frank Bennetti into his production office. Bennetti has been supplying cars to the movie industry since 1980. Since then, Bennetti has supplied hundreds of cars to many television and movie projects. Johnson told Bennetti, "This is the car I've got to have." He showed him a photo of a Curious Yellow 1971 Hemi 'Cuda in a book. "The hair stood up on the back of my neck," Bennetti said. "I knew that was the hardest car to find." He explained to Johnson how few 1971 Hemi 'Cuda convertibles had been manufactured. It would cost a king's ransom to obtain one, much less several, for the upcoming television production schedule.

Bennetti offered look-alikes modified to suit their needs. A deal was struck for three 1971 Hemi 'Cuda convertible look-alikes. The Curious Yellow Hemi 'Cuda Johnson saw in the book had been photographed at sunset and took on a much more yellow/orange hue than the original Mopar Curious Yellow paint. As it turns out, Curious Yellow washes out to a pale yellow shade on movie film. All the cars had to be painted a brighter yellow in order to appear the correct color on film. A Sherwin-Williams industrial paint was selected, which Bennetti calls "school bus yellow." Other items demanded by Johnson's production company were a 1970 Parchment interior, working white convertible tops, and nondescript white letter tires on 14-inch Rallye wheels. And all of the cars had to work on the same ignition key.

On a very short schedule, Bennetti, with the help of Mopar restoration specialist Alan Foxx, completed the three cars. Two of the original cars started life as 1970 Barracudas. One of the cars is powered by a modified 360-ci engine backed by a four-speed trzansmission. This is Johnson's favorite car. The other two have 440-ci engines and automatic transmissions. One of the 440-powered cars is equipped with Flowmaster mufflers and it's used for all the show's engine sound recordings. The cars have all been modified with heavy-duty K-members, KYB shocks, heavy-duty torsion bars, and disc brakes.

All four of these cars are in a constant state of change, depending on the needs of the show's production crew. Recently, all of the interiors were replaced with correct 1971 Parchment interiors. Future plans call for safety drive-shaft loops to be installed on all four cars, along with the possibility of adding fuel cells to the three cars with standard tanks. Fiberglass replacements have been offered for the rare 'Cuda front-end sheet metal, but the production crew demands the real thing, even on the jump car. There has been talk of adding a real Hemi car to the group so open hood shots can be filmed.

When all four cars are together, it's nearly impossible to tell them apart. I guess that's part of the movie illusion we all love.

These look-alike 1971 Hemi 'Cudas make up the fleet for the "Nash Bridges" television series. From a few feet away, even the guys who built them can't tell one from the other. None of the cars has a Hemi under the hood.

In 1971, Billboard stripes replaced the hockey sticks. Throughout the era of the street Hemi, this was the most pronounced and extravagant display of engine size.

At a cost of close to $5,000, a new 1971 Hemi 'Cuda was not inexpensive in its day. Today, it would take almost 10 times that amount to buy one of the few produced.

nine were convertibles. The 1970 Challenger also accomplished its mission of outselling the Mercury Cougar. In total, the Challenger sold more than 76,000 units compared to the Cougar's 72,000.

For 1971, only minor but distinctive changes were made to the Barracudas and Challengers. The Barracuda's grille was restyled by adding four additional vertical bars. This new grille is commonly called a "cheese grater" by collectors because of its similarity to the kitchen appliance. The two large headlights were replaced with a quad headlight arrangement similar to the Challenger's. The grille was either painted argent silver or body color. Barracudas with chrome bumpers received the argent grille, and those equipped with the Elastomeric bumpers received a body color grille. Four nonfunctional louvers were added to the sides of the front fenders. These louvers are commonly called "gills" for obvious reasons. Thin chrome wheel opening moldings were added, and the taillights were slightly revised. If you had a high-performance engine in your 1971 'Cuda, why not advertise it to the world with Billboard stripes? These stripes replaced the hockey stick stripes. They were enormous, covering most of the quarter panel and half of the door. In foot-high letters on the leading edge, the billboard announced to the world the cubic-inch displacement of the high-performance V-8 under the hood or, in the case of the Hemi, displayed those four famous letters HEMI.

The 1971 Challenger grille also received a minor change. The full-width inset chrome rectangle was split in the center into two smaller rectangles. In the rear, the full-width taillight was split into two and the center backup light was integrated into the lens on each side. The

All 1971 Hemi 'Cudas came standard with F60x15 tires on 15x7 steel rims. Rallye rims, standard on all 1970 'Cudas, were optional in 1971.

R/T hardtop received a new set of wider body side stripes that terminated at the C-pillar. For 1971 the R/T convertible was discontinued.

Production numbers for both the Barracuda and Challenger declined drastically in 1971. The total production for the Barracuda and 'Cuda was only 16,159, compared to 50,627 in 1970. Hemi 'Cuda production for 1971 broke down to 108 hardtops and only seven convertibles. The Challenger's sales were down to just under 23,000 units. Of that number, only 71 were equipped with the Hemi engine.

4

Defining a Decade of Drag Racing

Hemi Drag Race Cars

In motor racing history, 1964 was a watershed year. The previous year, General Motors had pulled the plug on factory support of any type of racing, leaving Ford and Chrysler to battle in the heavyweight classes. Ford was refining the 427 for both drag racing and the oval tracks, and at Chrysler, the engineers reached back to a proven performer—the Hemi.

Development work on the new generation Hemi engine began in 1962 when a request was made to the Chrysler engineering staff to develop an engine suitable for both oval tracks and drag strips. The Hemi design was the obvious choice for many reasons. The positioning of the valve allows the intake charge flows straight into the chamber and straight out through the exhaust valve, which makes the design a natural choice. The combustion

The Plymouth and Dodge A-990s were Chrysler's front-line offense in the 1965 Super Stock battles. Bill Jenkins, driving a white Plymouth similar to this one, emerged victorious at the 1965 NHRA Winternationals.

271

The A-990's TorqueFlite transmission was modified for manual operation only. The shift pattern was reversed from that of a standard passenger car to prevent accidental shifting into reverse.

chamber's spherical design provides maximum volume with a minimum surface area. The spark plug is placed near the center of the combustion chamber for optimal fuel burn. The design of the cylinder head allows the use of large valves. The 1964 competition Hemi engine was similar only in basic design to the previous version last seen in 1958.

When the race Hemi first appeared in 1964, it was equipped with two Carter AFB carburetors. These were soon replaced with a pair of Holleys. The air horns on top of these Holley carburetors seal against a rubber boot on the bottom side of the hood's scoop opening.

The new blocks were extremely sturdy with cross-bolted main bearings.

The new Hemi made an auspicious debut at the 1964 Daytona 500 by taking the first three spots. Although the Hemi was introduced too late for the 1964 NHRA Winternationals, soon after many Hemi-powered Plymouths and Dodges were breaking track records across the nation. These specially prepared cars were available to the general public on a limited basis. Race teams with proven records in competition were the favored recipients.

The first 1964 Hemi cars built for drag racing were built in the lightest two-door sedan bodies available, the Plymouth Savoy and the Dodge 330. A liberal use of aluminum body panels and the crafty removal of unnecessary extras (rear seat, sun visors, arm rests, etc.) reduced the car's overall weight. The battery was placed on the right side of the trunk for increased traction and weight distribution. The new Hemi cars were easily identifiable by their large hood scoop and by the absence of the inboard upper beams from the standard quad headlights.

The Hemi engines that powered these drag cars were similar to the Hemi that powered the winner at Daytona. Instead of the single four-barrel carburetor dictated by NASCAR, drag racers were given multiple carbs. Chrysler engineers used the short cross-ram design from the successful max-wedge engines and adapted it to the Hemi. On top of the new aluminum manifold was a pair of Carter AFB carburetors. Only the early 1964 Hemi cars were equipped with the dual Carters. They were soon replaced with twin Holley carburetors. Two compression ratios were available: 11.0:1, which produced 415 horsepower, and 12.5:1, rated at 425 horsepower. Only two transmissions were available in 1964, a four-speed manual and the TorqueFlite, and it was the last year for the push-button shift.

At the two biggest drag racing events in the

When the Hemi-powered Dodges and Plymouths first appeared at the drag strip, each was equipped with a large hood scoop that had a rectangular opening. With no additional power accessories, the engine compartment of this former race car seems vast, even with the large Hemi engine in place.

The A-990s interior was merely functional. The seats were from a Dodge van and weighed only 22 pounds each. There was no insulation under the carpet, no radio, and no heater. The fire extinguisher and gauges have been added by the owner.

summer of 1964, the Hemi-powered Dodges of Roger Lindamood and the Ramchargers were dominant. The AHRA (American Hot Rod Association) held its Summernationals in Gary, Indiana, and there the Ramchargers were victorious against Lindamood. One week later at the NHRA Nationals in Indianapolis, Lindamood returned the favor, beating the Ramchargers with an elapsed time of 11.31 seconds and a speed of 127.84 miles per hour. Later at the Super Stock invitational in Cecil County, Maryland, a large fleet of Hemi-powered cars competed

against the factory Fords and Mercuries in a 30-car field. The rules were relaxed, allowing cars that normally competed in the Factory Experimental classes to run against Super Stock entries. Here, the Hemi cars were running elapsed times in the high 10-second range at 130 miles per hour. At the end of the night, the final run pitted Bud Faubel's Hemi Dodge against "Dyno" Don Nicholson's Comet. At the time, Nicholson was one of the best drivers and tuners around, and his Comet was running times comparable to the fastest Hemi cars. Nicholson won and

Hemi Clone Cars

It looks like a Hemi car. It sounds like a Hemi car. It runs like a Hemi car. It must be a Hemi car! Today, that's only partially true, since many of the Hemi-powered cars being driven are clone cars or replicas—a slick combination of the correct components and a few aftermarket pieces designed for the street.

A few years ago, clone cars were the scourge of the car collecting hobby. Unscrupulous car builders found that they could realize larger profits by installing a rare engine option in their restoration. Many made the conversions adroitly, fooling the experts. This easy money led to a tide of fake GTOs, big block Corvettes, and Hemi cars. Today, a clone car is an acceptable way for the enthusiast to get behind the wheel of the car of his dreams for a much lower price than the rare original. A case in point is Mel Wojtynek's A-990 clone.

Wojtynek loves big-block high-performance cars and he knew that the Hemi-powered 1965 Plymouth A-990 was one of the baddest of the breed. Wojtynek, who lives in southern California, also loves to drive his cars. A real A-990, in today's

market, is worth approximately $80,000. That kind of value plus an engine with 12.5:1 compression takes all the fun out of a daily driver. Wojtynek contacted Bob Mosher, at Mosher's Musclecars. Mosher restores and builds replicas of 1962 through 1965 Mopars. He has two "factory demo" clones in the form of a black 1964 Max Wedge Plymouth Savoy and a Hemi-powered 1965 Belvedere A-990. One ride in Mosher's 1965 Hemi car and Wojtynek was convinced: He ordered a 1965 A-990 Hemi.

The cars Bob Mosher builds are works of art. They faithfully hold to the look of the originals with certain allowances for current technology. Wojtynek wanted a more powerful engine and had a 526-ci stroker engine built. The crankshaft is a Keith Black billet steel with a 5/8 stroke. A special Crower roller cam was ground. The heads are Stage V aluminum with 10.5:1 pistons. Backing an engine estimated to develop 700 horsepower is a heavy-duty TorqueFlite transmission and a 3:73 Dana rear end.

Wojtynek took his A-990 look-alike—with just 175 miles on the odometer—to Carlsbad Raceway in Carlsbad, California. He opened the headers, spiked his tank that was full of pump gas with a few gallons of racing gas, and bolted on a set of slicks. Wojtynek did a short burnout to heat the slicks, staged, and when the tree counted down, he punched it. On his first pass he turned an 11.58 elapsed time and 119 miles per hour. Later that day he ran an 11.40 elapsed time and a speed of 120 miles per hour. One week later, Wojtynek drove his A-990 imitator from San Diego to Bakersfield for the NHRA Hot Rod Reunion. The big Hemi never missed a beat during the 400-mile round trip, while registering 10 miles to the gallon.

As a sidebar to this sidebar, I recently had a chance to drive Wojtynek's Hemi Plymouth. When I got out of that car my knees were weak and my hands were shaking. I've driven quite a few high-performance cars in my life, but never one with such throttle response. What a car!

As Mel Wojtynek drops the hammer on his 1965 Hemi, the rear tires instantly turn into embers. Wojtynek's 1965 Plymouth is not an original A-990, but a carefully crafted clone capable of 120-miles-per-hour drag strip passes and casual trips to the local cruise-in.

ironically took home a Hemi engine as part of the prize package.

In 1964, some of the competitors found that if they altered the wheelbase of their cars, they could get more traction and thereby quicker elapsed times. These chassis alterations took the form of moving the front and rear wheels forward, while keeping the engine in the same relative location within the body. This change redistributed more weight to the rear wheels. In 1965, the alterations became more radical, and cars with totally changed proportions were not unusual. Due to the rule structure, classes that allowed chassis modifications also allowed engine changes. Soon the Hemi's dual four-barrel carburetors and large hood scoop gave way to Hilborn fuel injection units with 14-inch-long tuned stacks.

While fun to watch in competition, these cars could not be bought at the local Dodge or Plymouth dealership. In some cases, they lost most of their product identity due to the radical changes that were implemented in the search for speed. But there would be a Hemi-powered alternative available in 1965—the A-990.

In the November 1964 issue of *Plymouth Views*, Chrysler Corporation's Lynch Road Assembly Plant employee newsletter, it was announced that the new 1965 Super Stock Plymouth Belvedere and Dodge Coronet had gone into production that month in an article entitled "Plymouth, Dodge Dragsters With 426 Engines Built Here." The article covered the features of the special cars, and the fact that they were being built to meet the specifications of the major drag racing sanctioning bodies. The photo accompanying the article showed a veteran Lynch Road employee looking under the hood of one of the new Belvederes.

These specially built Dodges and Plymouths, all two-door sedans, came to be known by their engineering code—A-990. The A-990s were understated and audacious and built strictly for drag racing. For

Dick Landy made a career out of racing Hemi-powered Dodges. In 1968, he teamed up with his brother Mike (on the right), who raced the Dodge R/T, for a two-car assault on the nation's drag strips. In addition to racing, the Landy brothers held performance clinics at Dodge dealerships. Dick Landy

1965, the NHRA dictated that cars designed for Super Stock competition could no longer substitute standard body panels with those of fiberglass or aluminum. In 1964, NHRA required Ford to remove the fiberglass front bumpers on the Thunderbolts. It was the NHRA's plan to stop the proliferation of exotic lightweight parts in the stock classes. In 1965, factory experimental classes allowed competitors to exercise their creativity in weight reduction. Chrysler's engineers came up with their plan to comply with the rules, but still lighten the car as much as possible. They removed everything from the car that was not required by federal or state law and made the exterior sheet metal as thin as possible. Special body panels were built that were approximately half the thickness of a standard steel panel. This sheet metal abatement plan also included bumpers. The windshield was the only piece of real glass. All other windows were acrylic and the door hinges were made of aluminum.

The body was devoid of any sound-deadening material or seam filler, and certain small body

For the 1968 drag racing season, Chrysler engineers were given the green light to develop the ultimate factory door slammer. Dodge Darts and Plymouth Barracudas were chosen as the starting point for development. These cars were thoroughly lightened, and the big Hemi engine was added.

splash shields were deleted. The only modification needed to fit the Hemi into the engine compartment was a rework of the passenger side shock tower. This modification was also performed on the 1964 Hemi cars. There was no external badge denoting the engine size. The only giveaway that this wasn't an ordinary sedan was the oversize hood scoop.

All A-990 cars had a tan vinyl interior; there were no other choices. In the front were a pair of small bucket seats from an A-100 van. These seats lacked adjusters and were mounted to the floor with lightened brackets. The carpets had no backing or insulation. The quarter windows were fixed in place

and there was no rear seat. A large piece of thin cardboard covered the area where the seat back should have been. The front door panels did not have even the smallest arm rest. They too were deleted in the interest of saving weight. The instrument panel had plates blocking off the opening where the radio and heater controls would have been on any standard Belvedere or Coronet. To even further reduce weight, the sun visors, coat hooks, and dome light were deleted, and only a driver side windshield wiper was installed.

The engine was the Race Hemi, which had proved itself so well in the drag races in 1964. Now

The Little Red Wagon (left) and the Hemi Under Glass were initially built for drag racing competition. Because the weight distribution was heavily biased toward the rear wheels, both cars were easily able to do crowd-thrilling wheelstands. Soon they became an attraction because they could carry the front wheels for the entire quartermile. Chrysler Historical/Bob Riggle collection

fitted with aluminum heads, it was only available with a 12.5:1 compression ratio. The intake manifold for the A-990s was the same basic design as the one used on the drag cars in 1964, except now the material of choice was magnesium.

Other than the exterior color, the only other option was the transmission. The buyer had the choice of a heavy-duty four-speed manual with a Hurst shifter or a TorqueFlite that had a modified valve body, requiring manual shifting. In 1965, Chrysler abandoned the push-button control of the automatic transmission for a more conventional column shift. To facilitate trouble-free shifting during a drag race, all TorqueFlite equipped A-990s had their shift pattern reversed. The lever would be moved down one detent for the one-two shift and then down again for the final shift into third.

The exhaust system on the A-990s was also unique. The tubular headers swept underneath into 3-inch collec-

tors where 2 1/2-inch pipes joined together and ran rearward to a single muffler, which mounted transversely under the rear bumper. The reason for a full system was a new NHRA rule for 1965. But the muffler was located to concentrate as much weight as possible over the rear wheels. The exceptionally large battery was mounted in the trunk for the same reason. All of the A-990 cars came with a Sure Grip rear axle with 4:56 gears. The rear springs were heavy-duty and were configured to locate the rear axle 1 inch forward of the standard mounting location. This shortened the wheelbase on the Plymouth from 116 inches to 115 and on the Dodge from 117 inches to 116. Pulling the rear wheels forward changed the balance of the car, adding more weight on the rear wheels. These A-990 cars were eligible to run in the Super Stock class. At the 1965 NHRA Winternationals, the Super Stock field was composed entirely of A-990 Plymouths. Bill Jenkins, who ran an elapsed time of 11.39 seconds at a speed of 126.05 miles per hour

Mick Weise has been racing this Hemi Dart for over 30 years. Here at Bakersfield's Famoso Drag Strip, he lifts the left front wheel off the ground on hard acceleration. This car continually proves the unbeatable power of the Hemi by running elapsed times as low as 10.13 seconds at speeds as high as 139 miles per hour.

in the final run, came out on top. Fast and durable, many A-990s were rebuilt into altered wheelbase cars. The few that survived are stunning examples of mid-sixties Super Stock technology.

In the mid-1960s, a peculiar show evolved from the competition in the Super Stock and Factory Experimental cars classes. A few smart competitors came to realize that there were other ways to make money at the drag strip. They saw the reaction of the crowd when one of the cars would pull the wheels off the ground at the start. If the reaction was good for a small wheelie, it would probably be fantastic for a big wheelstand. Before long, two Hemi-powered wheelstanding cars—*The Little Red Wagon* and the *Hemi Under Glass*—were thrilling crowds across the country. What's really amazing is that both of these cars were initially designed to be competitive race cars—not wheelstanders.

The Little Red Wagon started life as a docile Dodge A-100 compact pickup truck. Dick Branster and Roger Lindamood—the brain trust of the Color Me Gone Super Stock—took over a project started by two fellow Detroiters, Jim Collier and Jim Schaeffer. The concept was simple—put a big Hemi engine in the back of a light pickup. A small sub-frame held the engine, transmission, and rear axle. The truck's front suspension was the stock beam axle.

The other famous wheelstander, the *Hemi Under Glass*, was also conceived of in Detroit at the Hurst Performance Products engineering lab. The goal was to build an exhibition car that would display Hurst components. A 1965 Barracuda was selected. Only major surgery would have allowed the big Hemi engine to be installed in the Barracuda's minuscule engine compartment. Therefore, it was installed in the rear, fitted into a sub-frame similar to *The Little Red Wagon*'s. Unlike *The Little Red Wagon*, the *Hemi Under Glass* was initially built with a four-speed manual transmission. What else would the premier builder of four-speed shift linkage install? Many of the components in the independent rear suspension were borrowed from the Corvette, as was the trunk-mounted aluminum radiator. In a fit of overkill, the Hurst engineers sent the front sheet metal out for an acid bath. They also replaced the large rear window with one fashioned of Plexiglas. It was designed to be easily removed to service the engine.

Because the short wheelbase placed most of the weight over the rear wheels, traction was phenomenal. From the starting line, both of these cars could snap the wheels off the ground and carry them clear through the traps. *The Little Red Wagon* and the *Hemi Under Glass* toured the nation, amazing drag racing fans with their aerial acts.

In 1967 Chrysler once again experimented with

lightweight cars for the drag strip, but rather than using a race Hemi, these cars were powered by a modified street Hemi. Special lightweight versions of the Plymouth GTX and Dodge R/T were assembled. These cars assaulted the Super Stock B class, with Mopar drivers Ronnie Sox and Dick Landy leading the charge. Documentation confirms that 55 Dodges and 55 Plymouths were made, all of them white with black interiors. To run as light as possible, the heater, hub caps, sway bar, body sealer, or sound deadener were deleted. Customers buying one of these special cars were required to sign an agreement acknowledging that the car was not warrantied.

In 1968, Chrysler again went all out for the Super Stock ranks with specially built Hemi-powered Darts and Barracudas. These cars were the invention of Chrysler's Dick Maxwell. Maxwell, a Chrysler engineer and Ramcharger Club member, felt that putting the powerful Hemi engine in the smaller A-body Darts and Barracudas would create unbeatable drag racing cars. Within Chrysler there was a considerable amount of discussion about whether these cars should be built or not. Getting the approval to produce these special drag-race-only vehicles was a tough sell to management. The current musclecar boom and Chrysler's dedication to racing contributed heavily to the project's approval.

Chrysler engineer Bob Tarrozi developed the specifications and built a prototype on a Barracuda platform. Because both the Barracuda and Dart were built on the same platform, the modifications made to shoehorn the big Hemi into the Barracuda would be identical for the Dart. Reworking of the front spring towers and the special brake master cylinder (necessary because of the width of the engine) were the two most difficult modifications. The balance of the modifications lightened the car.

Other than the large scoop on the hood, the only other visible modification made to the 1968 A-body race cars was the enlarged rear wheel openings. This was done to accommodate the large slicks necessary to get the Hemi's power to the ground.

The front fenders and hood, with its oversize scoop, were made of fiberglass. The body panels and bumpers were acid-dipped to reduce the thickness of the metal. The heater, radio, rear seat, all body insulation, and sound-deadening material were deleted to save as much weight as possible. The two lightweight bucket seats were added from a Dodge van. The windows were made from a lightweight polymer, and all the window mechanisms were removed. The door windows were raised and lowered with a strap.

Once the prototype was approved, Chrysler contracted with the Hurst Corporation to build 50 Dodge Darts and 50 Plymouth Barracudas in the initial production run. Later, it produced an additional 25 of each car. Some sources claim Hemi Dart production totaled 83. All of these cars were shipped to the dealers with primer covering the metal body panels and the fiberglass front clip components in unpainted gel coat. None of these

Mr. Norm's High-Performance Dealership

When buying a high-performance Dodge in the 1960s, there was only one place to go to get the car, the parts, and the service—Mr. Norm's Grand-Spaulding Dodge. In the 1960s, many Dodge dealers sold high-performance cars, but only one specialized in them—Mr. Norm.

In the late 1950s, Norm Kraus (a.k.a. Mr. Norm) and his brother Lenny had been running a successful used-car lot in the Chicago area. Their specialty was high-performance cars. They went out of their way to fill their lot with tri-power and four-speed-equipped cars. Their success in the used-

car field attracted the notice of the Chrysler Corporation. When a Chrysler representative approached them in 1962 with an offer for a Dodge dealership franchise, the Kraus brothers were very interested. What sealed the deal was the exciting new Ramcharger engine and Chrysler's commitment to performance cars. Ground was soon broken on the corner of Grand and Spaulding for the Kraus brothers' new dealership—Grand-Spaulding Dodge. In the fall of 1962, when the first 1963 Dodge cars were being delivered, the showroom was not complete, and the cars were stored outside in a hastily built corral.

As soon as the small Grand-Spaulding Dodge showroom was completed, it was filled with musclecars. Lots adjoining the dealership were crammed with as many as 350 high-performance Dodges. Customers could usually find what they wanted in dealer stock. A majority of the salesmen were former customers hired by Kraus because of their knowledge and passion for high-performance Mopars. The same was true for the parts and service department staff. Kraus also created a Mr. Norm's Sport Club for his customers. Members received a monthly newsletter and a discount on parts and service. Because of the special performance packages and the gearheads working in the service department, the Grand-Spaulding Dodges were always the fastest Mopars in the city. The best benefit of membership was the new car discount. Club members paid only a low,

In the Midwest, Mr. Norm's Grand-Spaulding Dodge was the place to go for high-performance Dodges. The dealership not only sold and raced them, but it also offered an abundance of performance packages from mild to wild.

no-haggle $200 over invoice for a new car, a figure that other dealers wouldn't match. Sport Club members were also treated to large open-house parties held in the service department of the dealership. Entertainment was provided by a live band, and plenty of food and soft drinks were served. When buying a new high-performance Dodge, customers found that the Grand-Spaulding trade-ins were always better than those of any other dealer. Norm loved to see the used-car lot filled with GTOs, Mustangs, and Camaros—all converts to the Mopar camp.

Three-quarters of the cars delivered at Grand-Spaulding Dodge were high-performance cars. In 1969 Mr. Norm's sales figures were $8.6 million, and in 1970 he took in a whopping $9.1 million. He regularly advertised on Chicago's powerful WLS radio station, whose signal reached far and wide, attracting new customers. Norm even offered to fly (one way) new car customers in from anywhere. The farthest someone came in to buy one of his cars was from Alaska.

When the insurance industry and government regulations killed the musclecar magic in 1971, Mr. Norm quickly shifted gears to van conversions. He offered the van customers the same level of customer service and value as his former high-performance clientele. Norm Kraus has retired from the car business, but hasn't lost his passion for the performance Dodges of the 1960s and 1970s. Today, Mr. Norm can be found at automotive events across the country, signing autographs and reminiscing about the halcyon days of Grand-Spaulding Dodge.

Between 1964 and 1971 there were two different shades of Hemi Orange. The race engines, like this one, were a slightly brighter shade. When the street Hemis were released in 1966, the engine color was changed to a more red-orange hue. This shade was used on all the street Hemis through 1971 and is the one commonly known as "Hemi Orange."

cars met the federal emission laws, and they could not be legally licensed for the street.

Chrysler's famous race Hemi engine, which featured 12.5:1 pistons, dual Holley carburetors on a magnesium cross-ram intake manifold, an aluminum water pump, and Hooker exhaust headers powered these purpose-built drag cars. The Hemi Darts and Hemi Barracudas were built with either a TorqueFlite automatic or a four-speed manual transmission. These specially built Barracudas and Darts were the last purpose-built drag racing cars to come out of Chrysler. Many of these cars have survived and are still racing today because of the excellent overall package and the powerful Hemi engine.

Hemi musclecars continue to do battle on the drag strips, nearly 30 years after their creation. In addition to regular competition on the NHRA Super Stock circuit, many Hemi owners enjoy a little grudge racing at a local track. Every year since 1995, the Pure Stock Musclecar Drags have been held at the Mid-Michigan Motorplex in Stanton, Michigan. The cars participating are limited to

The race Hemi engine was shoehorned into the small Dart and Barracuda chassis. One of the modifications that was necessary for engine clearance was a special master cylinder mount.

Each year a few hearty souls bring their Hemi cars to the Pure Stock Musclecar Drag Race. Anatol Vasiliev in his 1971 Hemi 'Cuda turned consistent 13.7-second quarter-mile elapsed times.

musclecars built between 1961 and 1974, and the cars must carry the factory-correct components for their year of manufacture. This precludes the use of headers, special ignitions, and slicks. This event is designed to put cars on the track that are representative of a well-tuned showroom stock musclecar—the kind of car you might face off against at a stoplight.

As you can imagine, the competition is hot and heavy, with a respectable showing from all musclecar manufacturers. Reigning as some of the fastest cars on the track are the Hemi-powered Mopars. Each year a few courageous owners bring out their elephant-engined cars to compete. With stock tires and tons of torque, getting a good bite off the starting line is the biggest challenge. Too much throttle can turn the rear tires into a barbecue in a matter of seconds. With a light touch, the driver of a Hemi car can get a respectable start with stock belted tires. Once the tires have taken a set, the throttle can be eased down. Upshifts can also break the tires loose, even with a TorqueFlite. It's a balancing act all the way down the strip.

In 1998, two Hemi 'Cudas ran at the event. Both of these cars were equipped with a Torque-Flite and 4:10 gears. They both ran consistently in the high 13-second range with speeds as high as 105 miles per hour. Hats off to the brave Hemi owners who won the admiration of musclecar enthusiasts for wringing out one of the baddest musclecars of all time.

Appendix

Street Hemi Specs

Type	90° OHV V8
Engine code	H, 1966; J 1967–1969; R, 1970–1971
Block	Cast iron with cross-bolted mains
Heads	Cast iron
Combustion chamber volume	168 cc min/174 cc max
Bore x stroke	4.25x3.75
Displacement	426 cubic inches
Horsepower	425@ 5,000 rpm
Torque (foot/pounds)	490@ 4,000 rpm
Compression ratio	10.25:1
Crankshaft	Forged steel
Pistons	Forged aluminum
Connecting rods	Forged steel
Intake manifold	Dual plane, cast aluminum
Carburetors	Dual Carter AFB (AFB-4139S front, AFB-4140S rear)
Camshaft	Mechanical (1966–1969) hydraulic (1970–1971)
Duration	276° (1966–1967) 284° (1968–1971)
Valve diameter	2.25 intake, 1.94 exhaust
Ignition	Dual point distributor with vacuum advance
Spark plugs	N-10Y Champion
Firing order	1-8-4-3-6-5-7-2
Exhaust	Cast-iron manifolds, 2.5 outlet

PONTIAC
MUSCLE CARS

Mike Mueller

Acknowledgments

I would like to extend my gratitude to Terry Spear of Terry's GTOs in Orlando, Florida, for his help and support in putting this project together. The efforts and enthusiasm of GTO fanatic Rob Lamarr of Cocoa Beach, Florida, were also appreciated. Appreciated as well were the cooperation and patience of the people who allowed their fine Pontiacs to be photographed for this book. In basic order of appearance, they are:

Bob and Mary McVeigh, Lake Park, Florida, 1959 Catalina convertible; Ronald Brauer, Crystal River, Florida, 1960 Ventura; Allan and Louise Gartzman, Skokie, Illinois, 1962 421 Super Duty Grand Prix; Henry Hart, Lakeland, Florida, 1962 421 Super Duty Catalina; Robert Gaito, Palm Harbor, Florida, 1963 Grand Prix; Allan Peranio, Coral Springs, Florida, 1965 2+2 convertible; Joe and Evelyn Alterizio, Brandon, Florida, 1967 Grand Prix convertible; Krieg Pruett, Altamonte Springs, Florida, 1964 GTO; Terry Spear, Orlando, Florida, 1966 GTO convertible; Rob and Renee Lamarr, Cocoa Beach, Florida, 1967 GTO; Linda Rutt, Palm Bay, Florida, 1967 GTO convertible; Steve Maysonet, Sunrise, Florida, 1968 GTO; Dan Andrews, Lakeland, Florida, 1971 GTO Judge; Don Maney, Orlando, Florida, 1972 GTO; Mike Webb, 1967 Firebird 400, Longwood, Florida; Jerry Ellis, Longwood, Florida, 1968 Firebird 400 convertible; Morris Otto, Satellite Beach, Florida, 1969 Trans Am; Dick Goodell, Lake Worth, Florida, 1969 Firebird 400 convertible; Terry Spear, Orlando, Florida, 1970 Firebird Formula 400; Jeff Jolley, Champaign, Illinois, 1970 Trans Am; Ed and Cindy Verner, Plant City, Florida, 1972 Trans Am.

Chapter 1

Power and Pizzazz
Pontiac's Performance Legacy

For more than thirty years, General Motors' Pontiac Motor Division truly has been the home of excitement. Once the builder of mundane cars grandpa was proud to drive, Pontiac pulled an about-face in the late 1950s, thanks mostly to the arrival of General Manager Semon E. "Bunkie" Knudsen in 1956.

General Motors had launched the Pontiac division in January 1926. The division's purpose was to fill the price gap between affordable Chevrolet and middle-class Oldsmobile. Named after the revered Ottawa Indian chief who had once ruled over all of the Midwest tribes of the Great Lakes region, Pontiac automobiles displayed their Native American imagery with pride. They ably filled the Chevy/Olds gap, using durability and dependability as main selling points.

By the mid-1950s, however, winning over car buyers was no longer the same game it had been in the 1930s and 1940s—suddenly power and pizzazz became major attractions.

In 1955, Chevrolet proved that putting affordable performance into the hands of young, excitable buyers could boost sales, both today's and tomorrow's. Somewhat ironically, the ball-stud rocker arm arrangement, which had helped make Chevy's first overhead-valve V-8 so hot, had been borrowed from Pontiac's design for its first OHV V-8, a modern power-

When Roger Huntington took his seat next to Jim Wangers behind the wheel of a 1962 Super Duty in January 1962, he didn't know quite what to expect. As he told it in *Motor Trend*, "Boom . . . Wangers got into that big Poncho, and we *went*. Low gear was a rubber-burning fishtail. A snap shift to second at 5000rpm, and 60mph came up in a bit over five seconds. The bellowing open exhausts rattled the whole countryside. Second and third gears almost tore my head off. Then across the finish line in high at 5300—stopping the watch at 13.9 [seconds] and 107mph!" In conclusion, Huntington called the Super Duty "a terrific piece of automobile. I'm still shaking."

Like the surgeon general's warning on a pack of Marlboro's, this badge foretold bad things for unwary stoplight challengers in the early 1960s. Powering Pontiac's full-sized boulevard bruisers, the 421 big-block first appeared in awesome Super Duty form in late 1961.

plant that also debuted in 1955. Pontiac would not lose the jump on the young crowd again. In 1956, Knudsen was promoted to Pontiac General Manager and stated his guiding philosophy: "You can sell a young man's car to an old man, but you'll never sell an old man's car to a young man."

With that precept, Knudsen began to build a young man's car company by surrounding himself with young car guys. In September 1956, just two months after he took Pontiac's general manager position, Knudsen hired Oldsmobile's Elliot "Pete" Estes as his chief engineer and Packard's John DeLorean as director of advanced engineering. At the same time, Knudsen opened PMD's "backdoor" to legendary Daytona Beach speed merchant

Smokey Yunick, whose race-proven practices greatly benefited Knudsen both at Pontiac and later at Chevrolet.

One of Knudsen's first moves towards changing PMD's image was to delete the traditional Silver Streaks from 1957 Pontiac hoods. Knudsen also eliminated much of the Native American imagery that had been a Pontiac trademark for three decades. The new general manager succeeded in cutting most of the ties with the division's stoic past; 1959's debut of the Wide Track Pontiacs severed any remaining ties. These models not only helped establish all-new industry trends, but also kicked off a fresh, exciting image that carried Pontiac to prominence in the 1960s.

While the somewhat sexy, certainly sleek Wide Tracks were basking in the glory of *Motor Trend*'s Car of the Year honors, Pontiac's hot-blooded engineers were hard at work developing their Super Duty performance parts program. Initially, the Super Duty project was an underground, covert operation thanks to 1957's infamous Automobile Manufacturers Association ban on factory racing activities. Pontiac's project quickly escalated into a full-fledged competition program with intimidating results, including total domination of NASCAR's Grand National stock car circuit in 1961 and 1962.

Poised to rise head and shoulders above the other manufacturers in Detroit's performance arena, Pontiac's power brokers suddenly found themselves chopped off at the knees. In January 1963, GM chiefs sent down an edict from corporate headquarter's fourteenth floor ordering all factory-supported racing efforts to cease immediately. Perhaps that edict was a blessing in disguise, however, for it helped redirect Pontiac's focus from the racetrack to the street.

Despite heavy disapproval from the fourteenth floor, Pontiac rolled out its iconoclastic GTO in 1964. The GTO was a groundbreaking performance machine that set the tempo for what would become Detroit's muscle car era. Far from being high-tech, PMD's "GeeTO Tiger" was simply a big engine in a light car. It was also readily available, relatively affordable, and really fast.

As *Car and Driver's* David E. Davis wrote in

Following in the fabled footsteps of Pontiac's 389 and 421 big-blocks, 1967's 428 V-8 emerged at a time when full-sized performance was on the wane across Detroit. Best suited for running power steering pumps and air conditioners under Grand Prix hoods, the torquey 428 was still a force to be reckoned with in 376 horsepower HO form.

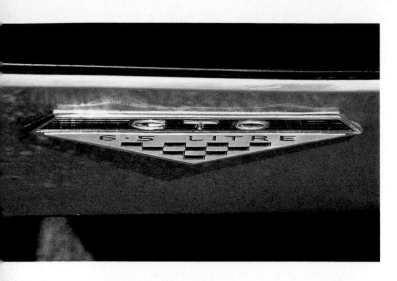

Although early 1960s street racers undoubtedly couldn't have cared less about the metric system, gearheads who couldn't translate this badge to Yankee terms ended up eating dust in a hurry. From 1964 through 1967, Pontiac's front-running GTO relied on PMD's 6.5 liter, 389 cubic inch big-block V-8 to do all the talking

a January 1975 testimonial to the Goat's honored contribution to American performance history:

The real difference between the GTO and everything else of its type at the time was muscle. Back in 1964, Ford was pumping millions of dollars into a vast promotion called "Total Performance," and all the racing entrepreneurs in the country were benefiting hugely from massive transfusions of Ford money. But Ford couldn't make it happen on the street. Not so, GTO. The basic GTO with the basic hot set-up just let you climb inside and then asked you, "How far, how soon,

daddy?" [NASCAR driver] Fred Lorenzen might run like hell in his Holman-Moody Ford, but somehow the [Fords] you could buy never made your eyes bug out. Pontiac, on the other hand, put it right out there on the street; and the seekers of truth along Woodward Avenue and Ventura Boulevard understood.

Of course, performance phenomena like the GTO would have never made the scene had PMD not been led by a succession of gearheads in the 1960s. As engineers first and corporate executives second, Estes and DeLorean followed in Knudsen's footsteps as PMD's general managers. Estes became general manager in November 1961 once Knudsen moved over to Chevrolet; DeLorean in July 1965 after Estes also joined Chevrolet. If Estes had not stuck his neck out over an unproven concept, corporate killjoys would have never allowed the GTO to upset their entrenched apple cart. DeLorean's insistence that Pontiac build a true sports car would prove just as important to the later Fire-

Right
Pontiac chief John DeLorean always wanted a true PMD sports car—what he got in 1967 was the sporty Firebird, a Pontiac pony car that did its Camaro cousin one better in both looks and handling. Fitted with the optional 400 cubic inch big-block, the Firebird was a cinch to put Ford's Mustang out to pasture. In 1968, the 400 also replaced the veteran 389 as the GTO's heart and soul.

bird's existence and help differentiate that car from the rest of Detroit's pony car herd.

Although Estes and DeLorean's supporting cast was full of great names, two stand out: Jim Wangers and Ace Wilson. Full-time ad exec, part-time hell-bent-for-leather drag racer, Wangers joined McManus, John and Adams (Pontiac's advertising agency) in June 1958 after having helped promote Chevy's "Hot One" image as a Campbell-Ewald adman in 1955. A firm believer in the powers of performance in selling cars, Wangers' work on the marketing end may have meant as much to Pontiac's muscle car legacy as the actual design and production of the cars themselves.

One of the first feathers in Wangers' cap came in 1959 when he hooked up with Ace Wilson's Royal Pontiac dealership in Royal Oak, Michigan; that relationship served as a research and development avenue of sorts for Pontiac's performance projects. Chevrolet had

Don Yenko, Ford had Carroll Shelby, and PMD had Ace Wilson and his Royal Bobcat Pontiacs, winners on both road and track. The Royal Bobcat label first appeared in 1961 on a hot Catalina super stocker and later graced a host of equally hot GTOs.

As for the Firebird, its 1967 debut kicked off an exciting performance bloodline that remains pumping strong today. Whether in Euro-style six-cylinder Sprint, muscular Formula 400, or legendary Trans Am forms, Pontiac's pony car has always ranked among Detroit's greatest movers and shakers. The famed Trans Am is the only model from any auto maker to have run nonstop from its beginnings in the classic muscle car era up to the present, retaining its high-profile performance image all the way.

Led by an all-new Trans Am in 1994, Pontiac clearly hasn't lost a step when it comes to building excitement.

Pontiac's 455 cubic inch HO big-block was indicative of just how wild Detroit's horsepower race got before the axe fell in 1971. The evaporation of GM's 400 cubic inch displacement limit for its 1970 intermediates meant that the 455 could be ordered as a GTO option. Pontiac's torque monster also became the sole powerplant for the Trans Am in both 1971 and 1972.

Chapter 2

Warriors
Wide Track Style, Super Duty Might, and Grand Prix Class

Pontiac Motor Division had already been making moves, though slowly, towards a modern image before Bunkie Knudsen—GM's youngest-ever divisional general manager—came on board on July 1, 1956. Like Chevrolet, Pontiac had introduced its first overhead-valve V-8 in 1955, a powerplant nearly ten years in the making. Although Pontiacs in 1955 and 1956 suddenly had modern power, they still lacked pizzazz; much of PMD's image still relied on old-fashioned practices. While Knudsen couldn't transform that image overnight, he could update it a piece at a time.

His first targets were the twin chrome trim strips applied to Pontiac hoods. Knudsen's father, William Knudsen, had first applied the strips in 1935 when *he* was Pontiac's general manager. The elder Knudsen's goal had been merely to turn a few customers' heads, but the "Silver Streaks" soon became a Pontiac trademark, along with its Native American imagery. By 1956, however, father no longer knew best

and son was convinced he had to cut ties to the past.

"We had to get rid of that 'Indian concept,' " claimed Knudsen in an interview some years later. "No reflection on the American Indian, but old chief Pontiac had been associated in the public mind with a prosaic, family-toting sedan from the time Pontiacs were first built." Even as the new 1957 models were nearing production, Bunkie Knudsen made the decision to do away with the Silver Streaks.

He also decided to offer an alarming new Pontiac for 1957, a car young Bunkie hoped would turn a head or two. Introduced in Febru-

The eye-catching 1963 Grand Prix featured clean sheet metal stripped of the long trim common to the base Catalina and longer Bonneville models; "Completely naked of chrome," in the words of *Motor Trend*'s Bob McVay. Pontiac's second-edition Grand Prix found 72,959 buyers, more than twice as many as the previous year.

Coined by Milt Colson, of McManus, John and Adams, Pontiac's advertising agency, the Wide Track label was a natural for the all-new 1959 Pontiacs. At 64in, the Wide Track cars were 5in wider at the wheels compared to their 1958 predecessors. The modern, skinny-whitewall tires are incorrect owner-installed equipment.

ary, the exclusive 1957 Bonneville convertible was a high-profile, high-priced performance showboat powered by a 310 horsepower 347 cubic inch V-8 fed by a Rochester fuel-injection system. The fully loaded Bonneville kicked off a new PMD tradition of conjuring up established, race-bred imagery when naming new models. The Bonneville also established Ponti-

ac as a force to be reckoned with in Detroit's horsepower race. Few customers, however, got the chance to launch one out of the blocks, as only 630 were built.

Window dressing or not, Knudsen's fuel-injected Bonneville was just one step in a rapidly escalating progression of power. Pontiac's first true performance engine, a NASCAR-

Introduced in 287 cubic inch form in 1955, Pontiac's versatile OHV V-8 offered ample room for future growth. Enlarged to 317 cubic inches in 1956, 347 cubic inches in 1957, and 370 cubic inches in 1958, PMD's V-8 was enlarged again to 389 cubic inches for Wide Track duty in 1959. Pictured is the Bonneville 389, which, when

backed by the optional Hydra-Matic automatic transmission, used 10:1 pistons and a Carter four-barrel carburetor to pump out 300 horsepower. When mated to the standard three-speed manual trans, the Bonneville 389's compression dropped to 8.6:1, with a corresponding output decrease to 260 horsepower.

inspired 285 horsepower 317 cubic inch V-8 with dual four-barrel carburetors, had appeared in January 1956 as a limited-edition option.

When Knudsen brought former Olds engineer Pete Estes aboard in September, he also received Estes' knowledge of Oldsmobile's soon-to-arrive J2 triple-carb setup. In 1957, Pontiac debuted its optional Tri-Power atop an enlarged 347 cubic inch V-8. Top output for the Tri-Power 347 was 317 horsepower. In 1958, both displacement and maximum output increased to 370 cubic inches and 330 horsepower, respectively.

With the engineering groundwork laid, it was left to the design crew to hold up their end, which they did in award-winning fashion. As the first totally new Pontiac to follow hot on the heels of another totally new Pontiac, the 1959 Wide Tracks were longer, lower, and, naturally, wider than their predecessors. They established a trend all GM divisions would adopt. Underpinning Joe Schemansky's Strato-Star styling were a reported forty-seven new mechanical features. That was enough to convince *Motor*

Right
Offered as a trim package on the Catalina four-door Vista sedan and two-door hardtop, the Ventura option was introduced in 1960, further endearing buyers who preferred a little pizzazz in their daily transportation. Included in the deal was exterior identification, deluxe wheel covers, a sport steering wheel, and distinctive tri-tone seats done in Morrokide (Pontiac's imitation leather). In this case, the wheel covers were superseded by Pontiac's attractive eight-lug aluminum wheels. Pontiac built 27,577 Ventura hardtops in 1960.

Beneath that large, black air cleaner are three Rochester two-barrel carburetors, the mixers that made up Pontiac's famed Tri-Power option, first offered in 1957. This 1960 Tri-Power 389 V-8 was rated at 333 horsepower.

Trend to honor Pontiac with its coveted "Car of the Year" award. When introducing his Wide Tracks, Knudsen bragged that "Pontiac had broken all bonds of traditional styling and engineering with the most progressive changes in our division's history." Those changes resulted in an amazing 77 percent sales increase over 1958's recession-racked results.

According to some Pontiac performance experts, 1959 was also the year the fabled Super Duty legacy was born. No one is sure who first used the Super Duty moniker or exactly when it was first used. Most PMD followers point to the December 1959 release of numerous high-performance parts, which were intended for 1960 NASCAR competition, as the Super Duty debut. Fireball Roberts' 1960 Pontiac—armed with a 348 horsepower 389 Super Duty V-8 (a 363 horsepower Tri-Power variety was also built)—announced that debut in February with a then-incredible 155mph lap around Daytona's high banks. Pontiac's racing dominance continued into the fall as Jim Wangers piloted a Super Duty "Poncho" to

Super Stock and Top Stock Eliminator victories at drag racing's Labor Day weekend NHRA Nationals in Detroit.

Maximum Super Duty 389 output jumped to 368 horsepower early in 1961, a year when Pontiacs would win thirty of fifty-two NASCAR races. Then, just before the NHRA Nationals in Indianapolis, PMD engineers introduced a grossly underrated 373 horsepower 421 cubic inch Super Duty V-8. Only about a dozen were delivered to professional drag racers, inspiring NHRA rule-makers to step in. In the interest of fairness, NHRA officials specified that a performance package had to be offered to the public as a regular production option to remain legal for stock-class competition on the drag strip.

Pontiac's answer in 1962 was a special run of even more powerful 421 SD V-8s offered as factory options for Catalina sedans and hard-tops, as well as Grand Prix sport coupes. A certified super stock screamer, the 1962 421 Super Duty was based on a beefy four-bolt block stuffed full of 11.1:1 Mickey Thompson forged aluminum pistons, a forged steel crank and a radical "#10 McKellar" solid-lifter cam, the latter feature named for its designer, engineer Malcolm McKellar.

Also included were twin Carter four-barrels, an eight-quart oil pan, and a pair of free-flowing cast-iron headers incorporating convenient cutouts for wide-open running. Output was quoted as 405 horsepower, although veteran road tester Roger Huntington claimed in his famous May 1962 *Motor Trend* review that actual power production was closer to 465 horsepower.

To top off the Super Duty package, Pontiac also offered various lightweight parts, including a hood, front bumper, fenders, inner fenders, and radiator brackets, all stamped out of alu-

If it wasn't clear Pontiac was aiming its products at the youth market, the 1960 Ventura trim package's tri-tone interior was quick evidence. The steering wheel and an electric clock were also included with the Ventura option.

Like the GTO to follow, Pontiac's first Grand Prix was set apart from the standard 1962 Catalina model it was based on by the addition of an exclusive blacked-out grille. Five 389 Trophy V-8 engine options were available ranging from a 230 horsepower economy version to a 348 horsepower Tri-Power bully. Little known, and even less understood, were the sixteen 421 Super Duty Grand Prix hardtops, cars offering race-ready brute force dressed in a classy package suited for a night on the town. This burgundy 1962 Super Duty Grand Prix is the only documented survivor. All sixteen 421 SD Grand Prix models were equipped with steel front clips.

minum. Also keeping the weight down were optional aluminum exhaust manifolds and a special frame. The frame was modified by cutting out sections of the perimeter rails, transforming rectangular tubes into channel. At the track, all this Super Duty equipment translated into a 13.9-second quarter-mile pass at 107mph. "Acceleration figures like these are not uncommon in Super/Stock classes on our drag strips," wrote Huntington. "But when you can turn them with a car just the way you buy it, you have something to scream about."

If Huntington thought the 1962 Super Duty was something to shout about, the 1963 rendi-

A special, finned, blacked-out rear cove panel represented the quickest way to identify a 1962 Grand Prix from the rear. Pontiac's popular, optional eight-lug rims were installed on fourteen of the sixteen Super Grand Prix sport coupes. Total 1962 Grand Prix production was 30,195.

Pontiac's vaunted 405 horsepower 421 Super Duty was fed by two Carter AFB four-barrels on an aluminum intake. Total flow for the twin Carters was about 1000cfm. The intake had no provision for exhaust warm-up (keeping the fuel mixture cool provided maximum volumetric efficiency), contributing to the Super Duty's cantankerous nature on the street. According to *Motor Trend*'s Roger Huntington, "you can get there and back [in a Super Duty], but it's like driving a racing car in traffic."

tion would have had him hollering his head off. It was slated to have more power and even less weight, especially if the car was one of the fourteen or fifteen plexiglass-windowed,"Swiss cheese" A/FX Catalinas (frames were drilled for lightening, thus the Swiss cheese reference). NASCAR variants of the 1963 Super Duty

Right
Contributing to the 1962 Grand Prix's sporty image were standard bucket seats and a console. Choosing the optional four-speed stick further heightened that image. Notice the conspicuously absent radio in the dashboard's center, something uncommon for a Grand Prix but typical in a Super Duty's case.

would have surely helped Pontiac continue its NASCAR domination (twenty-two wins in 1962). But another season on the superspeedways was nipped in the bud by GM officials.

In January 1963, GM's top brass had determined that they had seen enough of Pontiac's, as well as Chevrolet's, performance escapades and sent word to all divisions to cease and desist such shenanigans. A curt memo was delivered to "all zone car distributors" at Pontiac explaining that "effective today, January 24, 1963, 389 and 421 Super Duty engines are canceled and no further orders will be accepted. Suggest you advise dealers who normally handle this type of business verbally." And just like that, the Super Duty tale came to an end, although the name would later return as a Firebird badge of honor in 1973.

Radical, not-ready-for-prime-time performers like the 421 Super Duty cars were gone by mid-1963, and Pontiac's more civilized models were left to temporarily carry on as the division's most muscular offerings. This wasn't all bad considering that hot options like Tri-Power and a more street-worthy 421 High Output (HO) V-8 were still available to the average stoplight warrior. Also present was the sporty, classy Grand Prix, which had debuted in 1962 as Pontiac's response to Ford's Thunderbird in the four-place, personal-luxury market.

A relatively quick fix, the 1962 Grand Prix was simply a basic Catalina sport coupe with a few trim tricks applied on the outside and standard bucket seats with a console and tachometer inside. Throw in the wonderfully sporty optional eight-lug aluminum wheels, the 333 horsepower 389 Tri-Power V-8, and perhaps a four-speed transmission and you were ready to fly first class. As far as *Motor Trend*'s critics saw it, "style-wise and price-wise [the Grand Prix]

Heavy-duty 15in steel rims were included with the Super Duty's optional heavy-duty brake package, which featured widened 11in aluminum front drums (rears were cast-iron) with cooling fins.

Left
Notice the missing fender script (normally located just behind the headlights) on this black 1962 Catalina. Not all 421 Super Duty Catalinas had aluminum front ends but this one does, and apparently drilling those fragile fenders for the stock script wasn't always performed—some Super Duty Pontiacs have the trim pieces, some don't.

competes directly with the Thunderbird. Performance-wise, it's in a class by itself."

A complete Bill Mitchell restyle resulted in a truly refined Grand Prix for 1963. Super clean lines combined with equally clean body sides absent of unnecessary chrome baubles convinced *Car Life*'s crew to call PMD's second Grand Prix "one of the most handsome [cars] ever to come out of a Detroit styling studio." Performance was also attractive thanks to the optional 370 horsepower 421 V-8. In a *Motor Trend* test, a 370 horsepower Grand Prix stormed 0–60 in just 6.6 seconds and required only 8.5 seconds more to complete a quarter-mile—exceptional numbers for a big car loaded down with classy luxury. As *Motor Trend*'s Bob McVay concluded, the 1963 Grand Prix was "designed for the man who likes to go places fast in quiet elegance and luxury."

The slightly face-lifted 1964 Grand Prix offered a nearly identical combination of performance and luxury. Later renditions, however, tended more towards the luxury side as horsepower options were played down and the

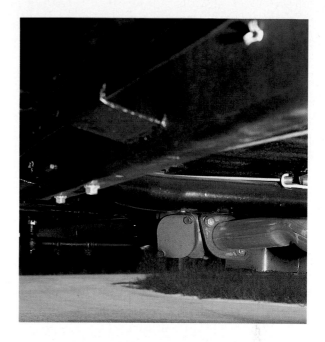

Standard Super Duty exhaust manifolds were large, "long branch" cast-iron headers with individual runners and two openings on the lower end. One typically fed a 2.25in header pipe leading to a low-restriction muffler. The other was this 3in cutout sealed by a bolt-on cover. With the bolts in place, a Super Duty could operate reasonably quietly on the street; unbolting the cover allowed unrestricted wide-open running at the track. Exotic aluminum long branch exhausts were also offered.

**Left
According to Pete McCarthy's fabulous book, *Pontiac Musclecar Performance, 1955-1975*, Pontiac built 213 Super Duty V-8s for 1962, with thirteen being single-carb 385 horsepower 389s. Apparently, 179 Super Duty Pontiacs were built that year: twenty-four Catalina sedans; 139 Catalina hardtops; and, oddly enough, sixteen luxo-cruiser Grand Prix sport coupes. Of the total, 172 were 405 horsepower 421s, seven were 389s. The difference between engines built and cars produced probably involved racing team spares.**

cars grew heavier. It wasn't until the downsized G-body Grand Prix debuted in 1969 that real performance would again become a GP feature. Lighter and easier to handle than previous renditions, the 1969 Grand Prix SJ responded well with either the standard 370 horsepower 428 or optional 390 horsepower big-block under its stretched hood. According to *Car Life*, the 390 SJ was capable of a truly hot 14.10-

second quarter-mile blast—serious traveling for a luxury cruiser. Even more power was available from the Hurst-converted Grand Prix SSJ—which could be equipped with the big 455 V-8—but this gentleman's bomb was a rare beast. Less than 500 were sold in 1970, 1971, and 1972.

In between the original Grand Prix and the redesigned G-body, full-size performance was also offered in the form of 1964 to 1967's big 2+2 models. Initially a $291 optional package for the Catalina hardtop and convertible, 2+2 equipment included a 389 V-8 with as much as 283 horsepower, bucket seats and console, a special Morrokide interior, and exterior badges. Still a Catalina option, the second-edition 2+2 added distinctive exterior fender gills, a 421 V-8 backed by a Hurst-shifted three-speed, heavy-duty springs and shocks, and a 3.42:1 performance axle, all as standard features. Top power choice was the 376 horsepower 421 HO Tri-Power.

A somewhat odd combination, this race-minded 1962 Super Duty was also equipped with the distinctive tri-tone Morrokide upholstery included in Pontiac's Ventura trim package. The T-10 four-speed manual was a $234 Super Duty option and was topped by a Hurst-Campbell shifter.

Pontiac's optional eight-lug sport wheels didn't get by on looks alone; the unique rims were mated to integral hub/aluminum brake drums featuring cooling fins and superior stopping power. As Bob McVay wrote, "We can't say enough good things about the brakes on this big automobile. Although we used them hard, they refused to fade and brought more than two tons to a screeching halt in 30 feet from 30mph and in 156 feet from 60mph."

A 1965 2+2 specially prepared by Ace Wilson and the crew at Royal Pontiac made well beyond the stocker's 376 horsepower and was campaigned by David E. Davis across the pages of *Car and Driver* magazine. Davis posted some incredible numbers with this special: 0–60mph in 3.9 seconds and quarter-mile performance of 13.8 seconds at 108mph. Clearly, the gang at Royal knew how to make a Pontiac—even a 4,400lb Pontiac—move like nobody's business. Closer to reality was *Motor Trend*'s test of a stock 338 horsepower 2+2, a car that ran from rest to 60mph in eight seconds.

For 1966 only, the 2+2 was offered as a unique model. It returned for its final performance as a Catalina option, this time with a standard 428 V-8 rated at 360 horsepower. A 376 horsepower 428 HO was offered, but Tri-Power was no longer available. A tough sell from the beginning, Pontiac only managed to move 1,768 2+2 Catalinas in 1967 before discontinuing the option. Big car performance was a thing of the past by that point, leaving the GTO, Firebird, and later the resized Grand Prix to wave Pontiac's performance banner.

The 7000rpm tachometer was a standard 1963 Grand Prix feature when a four-speed was ordered, optional with an automatic. Checking off the automatic transmission traded the four-speed's flat console for a unit that rose up to meet the dashboard and included a pod-mounted vacuum gauge.

Pontiac's 2+2 equipment was first offered in 1964 as an optional package for the Catalina hardtop and convertible and returned for 1965, priced at $397 in droptop form ($419 for the hardtop). Upper fender pinstriping and the front fender "gills" were part of the package. According to *Motor Trend*, the 1965 2+2 was "one of those rare machines that asks to be driven fast and well."

Following pages

At nearly two-and-a-half tons, the 1965 2+2 convertible wasn't exactly a vehicle you'd use to leave rivals in the dust at the light. Despite its bulk, its performance was surprisingly strong. Production was 7,998 in 1964; 11,521 in 1965; 6,383 in 1966 (the only year the 2+2 was a distinct model and not an optional package); and 1,768 in 1967.

The 2+2 image simply begged to be complemented by Pontiac's optional eight-lug wheels. PMD's 421 cubic inch big-block V-8 replaced the 389 as the 2+2's standard power source in 1965.

Pontiac designers rarely took a back seat to anyone when it came to sporty interiors. Bucket seats and a console were included as part of the 2+2 deal. Adding the optional custom gauge cluster and four-speed with Hurst shifter and tachometer only helped make things inside a 1965 2+2 all that more exciting.

A 338 horsepower 421 V-8 was standard for the 1965 2+2, with this 421 HO Tri-Power available on the options list. Output was 376 horsepower at 5500rpm. Compression was 10.75:1. Chrome engine dress-up was a standard 2+2 feature.

Simulated wire wheel covers were a Grand Prix option in 1967, as was the 428 V-8.

Left
Pontiac offered a Grand Prix convertible in 1967 only. Just 5,856 were built. Hideaway headlights were a standard 1967 Grand Prix feature and a first for Pontiac.

Have new tigers. Need tamer. Apply any Pontiac dealer.
—1964 Pontiac advertisement

A full dose of extra-cost comfort and convenience features could pile up in a hurry on an already luxurious 1967 Grand Prix. Options on this Grand Prix convertible include power steering, brakes, seats, windows, and antenna; AM/FM radio; tilt wheel; air conditioning; and cruise control.

Standard 1967 Grand Prix power came from a 350 horsepower 400 V-8 with a four-barrel carburetor. Next on the list was a no-cost option, the economical 265 horsepower 400 two-barrel. At the top were two 428s, a 360 horsepower version and this 376 horsepower bruiser. Both 428s received chrome dress-up, with the 376 horsepower V-8 getting an exclusive open-element air cleaner. Notice the optional cruise control equipment at the air cleaner's right.

Chapter 3

A Tiger by the Tail
GTO—Detroit's First Muscle Car

If you wanted a fast American car in the early 1960s, your choices were limited. At that time, big cubes in big cars represented the only way to fly for performance-minded drivers, basically because one size fit all; Detroit built full-sized models and nothing else. Almost. Chevrolet's Corvair, Ford's Falcon, and Plymouth's Valiant had emerged in 1960 to help fend off the foreign compact invasion, but their arrival was of no concern to the hot-blooded buyer hunting the biggest bang for his buck. Equally ignored the following year was the introduction of General Motors' senior compacts, Buick's Special, and Oldsmobile's F-85. These cars were comfortably larger than the groundbreaking Corvair, yet still lacked any real performance potential.

Even less enticing was Pontiac's Tempest, a bona fide budget buggy with its unconventional rear transaxle and "rope" driveshaft (which reduced harmonic vibration) tied to an economical four-cylinder powerplant (created, simply enough, by cutting Pontiac's 389 cubic inch V-8 in half). A dozen or so 1963 Tempests powered by 421 Super Duty V-8s were specially built for factory experimental (FX) drag racing competition, but this was before GM clamped down on such outrageous behavior. Standard street-going Tempests, optional 326 cubic inch V-8 power notwithstanding, remained as slow as slugs with none of those Super Duty shenanigans ever intended for anyone but professional drag racers.

All that changed in 1964, the year GM introduced its A-bodies, a new class of automobiles. A-bodies picked up where the senior compacts left off, retaining the existing name-

Wearing the same body shell introduced the previous year with its attractive tunneled rear glass design, Pontiac's 1967 GTO received a slightly revised tail treatment that did away with the flared endcaps and traded the triple-louvered taillights for a double rank arrangement.

Pontiac brochures called the 1964 GTO "a device for shrinking time and distance"—today, most performance fans recognize it as Detroit's first muscle car, a machine that successfully combined big-block V-8 power with a light, manageable, **mid-sized body. This incorrectly painted 1964 GTO convertible is one of 6,644 built. Hardtops numbered 18,422, coupes 7,384. The twin exhaust tips were a popular option.**

plates while they were at it. Soon to be called intermediates, GM's redesigned Special, F-85, and Tempest, along with Chevrolet's all-new Chevelle, were not all that much smaller inside and out than their full-sized brethren, yet they were lighter and more agile. Most important, these mid-sized models could easily handle serious V-8 power, something obviously impossible in the compact Corvair's case and initially a difficult proposition as far as the

slightly larger Chevy II Nova was concerned.

Dropping a powerful V-8 in the 1963 Tempest had proven more trouble that it was worth, even though PMD's big 389 V-8 took up no more space than the 326. Engineers Bill Collins and John DeLorean had experimented with a 389-powered Tempest in 1963, but the unit-body/rear-transaxle layout wasn't exactly designed with high performance in mind. Although beefing up the platform may have worked for the few experimental Super Duty Tempests, the modifications required for a regular-production, street-going super Tempest would have never been approved by the guys on the fourteenth floor. Nearly all headaches were cured, however, once the mid-sized 1964 Tempest came along with its full-perimeter frame and conventional solid rear axle.

Not one to overlook a performance opportunity, PMD's ever-present advertising wizard Jim Wangers was already at work with DeLorean on a trend-setting performance package before the ink even dried on the 1964 Tempest's blueprints. DeLorean had the engineering groundwork laid, while Wangers had his finger on the pulse of a youthful market poised to pounce on his powerful proposition. All that remained was to sell the idea of a big-block intermediate to GM's top brass, a task that wouldn't be easy considering the corporation's anti-performance stance, as well its 330 cubic inch maximum displacement limit for the new mid-sized models.

Well aware of these roadblocks, Wangers and DeLorean made an end run. New models required corporate approval, but option packages could be created without a nod from above, leaving a loophole to at least get the project off the ground. From there, it was basically a matter of running until someone told Wangers and DeLorean to stop. Since receiving permission to supersede the 330 cubic inch limit would clearly never come, the best bet was to build a 389 Tempest first and worry about the consequences later. Of course, none of this plan had a prayer without the support of

PMD General Manager Pete Estes. He loved the 389 Tempest idea and went nose-to-nose with GM's disagreeable ivory tower crew over the plan. Without a doubt, it was Estes' perseverance seemingly against all odds that made the project possible.

This optional custom wheel cover with its three-bladed spinner helped to dress up a 1964 GTO. A simulated wire wheel cover was also offered. Original equipment tires, long since gone in this case, were US Royal Tiger Paw redlines, while a whitewall tire could have replaced the redlines at no extra cost.

Bucket seats and an engine-turned dashboard appliqué were standard on the 1964 GTO. Optional equipment appearing here includes the console, Hurst-shifted four-speed manual transmission, 7000rpm tach (in the right-hand instrument pod), vacuum gauge (on the console), and the popular four-spoke, woodgrain Custom Sport steering wheel.

Left
Standard GTO transmission fare in 1964 was a three-speed manual, with the M20 wide-ratio four-speed, M21 close-ratio four-speed, and Powerglide automatic available at extra cost. Manual transmissions all received Hurst shifters. The optional console and vacuum gauge were available with any transmission.

Credit for naming that project went to DeLorean, who chose GTO, a moniker brashly borrowed from Enzo Ferrari. In Italian, GTO stood for "Gran Turismo Omologato" ("Grand Touring Homologated" for all you Yankees). When Ferrari used the name, he meant it—his legendary 1962 250 GTO was built to homologate (legalize) itself for FIA-sanctioned GT racing competition. Not all among the motoring press approved of Pontiac's somewhat shameless attempt to ride the coattails of Ferrari's fabled image.

Referring to Pontiac's tradition of naming vehicles after competition events—Grand Prix and LeMans had already been snapped up by PMD label-makers—*Road & Track*'s critics let loose with both barrels. A March 1964 *R&T* report said it all:

These thefts were bad enough . . . displaying the intention of the company to trade on an image that was not deserved and had not been earned. Now, however, Pontiac has gone even further, lifting the exact designation of a highly successful GT racing car, the GTO, from Ferrari. There is an unforgivable dishonesty in such a practice as this and the insult should be sufficient to prevent any intelligent person from regarding it with anything except derision.

Car and Driver's David E. Davis disagreed wholeheartedly, even going so far as to bark-up a Ferrari GTO versus Pontiac GTO shoot-out on the cover of his magazine's March 1964 issue. While *Road & Track* was pointing out that Pontiac's GTO was certainly no match for its Ferrari counterpart, Davis was pointing out that such a comparison was akin to squaring off apples and oranges. While the Ferrari would lose in a drag race, the Pontiac was no match on a European road course. "Ferrari never built enough GTOs to earn the name anyway," wrote Davis, "just to be on the safe side though, Pontiac built a faster one."

Officially released on October 1, 1963, Pontiac's GTO debuted, per Wangers' ploy, as an option package for the deluxe Tempest model, the aforementioned LeMans. Initially, it was available for the LeMans sports coupe and convertible and was joined soon after introduction by a hardtop. The GTO options package included a 325 horsepower 389 big-block V-8 featuring a hydraulic cam, a Carter AFB four-barrel, and a pair of high-compression heads borrowed from the 389's big brother, the 421. Stiffer suspension, a three-speed manual with a Hurst shifter, and various dress-up items including a blacked-out grille, GTO identification, and twin dummy scoops on the hood were also part of the deal. Popular options included a Muncie four-speed, a limited-slip Safe-T-Track differential, and an even hotter 348 horsepower 389 topped by three Rochester two-barrel carbs.

Armed with the optional 348 horsepower V-8 and 3.90:1 rear gears, a 1964 GTO could trip the lights at the drag strip's far end in 14.30 seconds according to *Popular Hot Rodding*. As *Car and Driver*'s Davis saw it, the new GTO "does what so many others only talk about—it

The 1966 GTO's louvered taillights, flared rear-quarter endcaps, and Coke bottle body were welcomed styling improvements. Convertible production in 1966 was 12,798; 10,363 coupes and 73,785 hardtops were also built.

really does combine brute, blasting performance with balance and stability of a superior nature."

Inspiration for Davis' raves were two 1964 Royal Bobcat GTOs specially prepared by Roy-

Left
Pontiac reshaped its A-body for 1966, creating a less angular GTO, again offered in coupe, hardtop, and convertible form. This year it was offered as a model series all its own instead of an option package for the LeMans. After selling 75,352 Goats in 1965, Pontiac hit a peak in 1966 as GTO production reached 96,946.

al Pontiac—PMD's backdoor performance dealership—using various hot stock parts, as well as a tuning tweak or two. In *Car and Driver*'s test, a Royal Bobcat GTO screamed from rest to 60mph in 4.6 seconds. Quarter-mile performance was listed as 13.1 seconds at 115mph. Non-stock test subjects aside, it was Davis' GTO review that helped vault both his magazine and Pontiac's new performance machine into the forefront.

Thanks to the boldness of Estes, Wangers, and DeLorean, Pontiac had become the first mainstream manufacturer to combine brute, large-displacement power with a relatively

331

lightweight body, a practice that would soon escalate throughout Detroit. GTO copies quickly followed, cars like Buick's Gran Sport, Oldsmobile's 4-4-2, and Chevrolet's Chevelle SS 396.

Advertisements described PMD's GTO as a tiger; average Joes affectionately called it the "Goat." Popular hit records sang its praises. As for critics and complainers on GM's fourteenth floor, they were silenced once sales started to soar. The GTO would have undoubtedly stood as the star of Detroit's 1964 show had not Ford chosen the same year to introduce its Mustang, a mass-market marvel if there ever was one. But while the wildly successful Mustang became everyone's darling, the GTO, as David

The GTO's fabled Tri-Power setup, its top performance option since the car's 1964 inception, made its last appearance in 1966. Effective for the 1967 model year, GM officials canceled multi-carb equipment for all models except Chevrolet's Corvette. These three Rochester two-barrels helped the GTO's 389 big-block pump out 360 horsepower. Compression was 10.75:1. Tri-Power production in 1966 was 19,045.

E. Davis wrote in 1975, "appeared on the American scene like a Methodist minister leaving a massage parlor."

The GTO's first-year success inspired Pontiac officials to project production of 50,000 for the second-edition version in 1965. They missed their mark, however, as sales eventually surpassed 75,352. A revised front end exchanged 1964's horizontal quad headlights for a stacked arrangement, and a slight power boost came courtesy of an upgraded cam and improved intake. Still an option for the three LeMans models, the 1965 GTO package contained a standard 335 horsepower 389 four-barrel, with the Tri-Power version now rated at 360 horses.

New extra-cost features included "Rally Cluster" instrumentation, Rally wheels (supplied by Kelsey Hayes), and an air scoop package, released on August 17, 1965. The first in a long line of GTO Ram Air equipment, the air scoop package was offered over dealer counters only for Tri-Power models. Ram Air made the restyled 1965 hood's distinctive single scoop fully functional by sealing the three Rochesters' small air cleaners to the hood's underside using a special tub topped by a large foam gasket.

Whether in standard trim or fully loaded, the 1965 GTO continued to impress. "In all, the GTO is a fun-to-drive machine," wrote *Hot Rod*'s Eric Dahlquist. "Success formulas are elusive creatures at best but Pontiac seems to have at least part of the market cornered for the time being." Mincing fewer words after his turn trying to hold Pontiac's tiger, *Car Craft*'s LeRoi

The 1966 dashboard was similar in layout to the 1965 GTO's four-pod panel, but came standard with a woodgrain face. The walnut shift knob, like the Hurst four-speed stick it's threaded on, was an optional piece in 1966.

Smith concluded, "as a total driving impression, handling the GTO is best described as WILD!"

Fueled by even more success, Pontiac's brain trust decided to transform the GTO into a model series all its own for 1966. Revamped A-body sheet metal was also supplied, with a similar split-grille/stacked-headlight nose mated to an updated shell that hinted slightly at a Coke bottle shape. In back was a definitely different tail treatment featuring louvered taillights. Appearing fresh while still looking much like the original, the 1966 model ended up as Pontiac's most popular GTO with sales topping out at 96,946.

Power levels carried over identically from 1965 with one major exception. Quietly released in February 1966, the XS-code Tri-Power 389 featured an even stronger cam, stiffer valve springs and the functional air scoop package introduced in 1965. Ordering the XS 389 also meant adding the M21 close-ratio four-speed, heavy-duty fan, metallic brakes, and 4.33:1 limited-slip differential, all mandatory options. Estimates put production of XS-equipped 1966 GTOs at about 185.

While looking much the same on the outside—save for a slightly restructured tail,

The 14in Rally wheel—introduced in 1965—carried over as an option for the 1966 GTO. Standard 1966 GTO wheels were 14x6in stamped steel rims with wheel covers. Simulated wire wheel covers and deluxe wheel covers were again available on the options list.

enlarged rocker brightwork, and a mesh grille—Pontiac's 1967 GTO differed considerably from its 1966 predecessor underneath. For starters, the venerable 389 was bored out to 400ci and the famed Tri-Power option was dropped as GM vetoed multiple carburetor setups for all models but the Corvette after 1966.

In all, four varieties of the 400 big-block were offered, beginning with a standard four-barrel version rated at 335 horsepower. Buyers who preferred a little less oomph could opt, at no extra cost, for a milder, low-compression 255 horsepower 400 topped by a two-barrel carburetor. On the other side of the coin was the HO 400, an engine that also carried a familiar rating of 360 horsepower. Top of the heap was the Ram Air 400, again conservatively rated at 360 horsepower like its 1966 XS Tri-Power predecessor. Much of the 1966 XS equipment carried over with new additions being the HO's free-flowing exhaust manifolds and a Quadra-Jet four-barrel instead of the three Rochesters. Late in the year, better heads with revised valves and springs were also added. According to *Motor Trend*, this equipment could help propel a 1967 GTO to a 14.21-second quarter-mile pass.

Also of note was a new optional transmission, GM's three-speed Turbo Hydra-Matic,

Right
The distinctive wire mesh grille and large, bright rocker trim set the 1967 GTO apart from its 1966 predecessor as sheet metal carried over in basically identical fashion. Pontiac built 9,517 1967 convertibles.

A slight overbore upped the GTO's displacement ante from 389 to 400 cubic inches for 1967. Standard power came from this 335 horsepower 400 four-barrel V-8, with a low compression (8.6:1) two-barrel "economy" version offered at no extra cost. Compression for the 335 horsepower big-block remained at 10.75:1.

which replaced the aged two-speed Power-glide. And when auto trans GTO buyers also checked off the optional console, they got the innovative Dual Gate shifter, yet another popular Goat feature supplied by Hurst. Known as the His and Hers stick, the Hurst Dual Gate allowed the driver to chose between conventional automatic transmission operation or manual selection of shift points. Demonstrating the merits of both the Turbo Hydra-Matic and the His and Hers shifter, production of auto-

matic-equipped GTOs surpassed their manual trans counterparts for the first time.

GM's killjoys got their way at the end of the 1966 model run and canceled the popular "GeeTO Tiger" ad campaigns that had reportedly incited unacceptable behavior among this country's driving youth, at least according to Ralph Nader and the Federal Trade Commission. Accordingly, in 1967, Pontiac's GTO became "The Great One" as safety consciousness, federally mandated or otherwise, began to take root in the muscle car realm.

Big news for 1968 came in the form of a totally restyled, rounded body featuring hideaway wipers and an innovative energy-absorbing bumper up front. Reportedly, the color-keyed plastic Endura nose could survive minor impacts and spring back to its original form within twenty-four hours. Optional hideaway headlights and an eye-catching hood tach (first offered in 1967) only helped sweeten the appearance. Inside, the 1968 GTO's redesigned three-pod dash layout was, in *Hot Rod* magazine's terms, "the best instrument panel in super-car-land." Overall, the fifth-edition Goat remained at the head of Detroit's muscle car pack—as PMD ads claimed "others have caught on, but they haven't caught up."

Again, four 400 big-blocks were available under the 1968 GTO's hood, which reverted back to the original twin-scoop style. Still at the top, at least early in the model run, was the 360 horsepower 400 Ram Air V-8. In March 1968, the Ram Air 400 was replaced by the Ram Air II, an improved 400 with a beefed-up crank, forged pistons, larger pushrods, and new heads featuring revised combustion chambers, rounder ports, and lighter valves. Output for the Ram Air II remained at 360 horsepower.

Building a better Goat remained basically an underhood affair for 1969 as outward appearances carried over with only minor modifications—but what a job Pontiac engineers did beneath those scoops. While powertrain choices once more numbered four, the 400 HO was dropped in favor of a 366 horsepower Ram Air 400, since labeled the Ram Air

III. Ram Air III features included improved heads with D ports and free-flowing exhausts.

Even more impressive was the new Ram Air IV 400, a radical 370 horsepower big-block with large-port heads, a lumpier cam, low-restriction exhausts and a Rochester Quadra-Jet four-barrel on an aluminum intake. According to *Car Life*, the Ram Air IV was "a very peaky engine. The idle is a rough, rolling bark, music to the driver's ears and a warning to people in

The 1967 GTO's interior again incorporated the woodgrain touch. New for the year was Hurst's innovative "His and Hers" Dual Gate shifter. The His and Hers stick was connected to the equally new three-speed Turbo Hydra-Matic automatic transmission and offered a choice between typical automatic operation or manual shifting. Outnumbered two to one in previous years, automatic-equipped GTOs surpassed manual models by about 3,000 in 1967, a trend that continued with every Goat to follow. The underdash gauges are non-stock owner-installed items.

the next lane." Mandatory Ram Air IV options included a choice between a 3.90:1 or 4.33:1 Safe-T-Track rear end and a heavy-duty radiator.

Along with the Ram Air IV, Pontiac also introduced The Judge for 1969. Initially meant to be a bare-bones GTO comparable to Plymouth's budget-minded Road Runner, PMD's Judge was actually introduced with a few more frills than planned, though as a $332 GTO

This five-spoke Rally II sport wheel, featuring bright trim rings and color-keyed lug nuts, joined the optional Rally wheel in 1967.

option, it would have been tough to find a bigger bang for the buck. Included in The Judge deal was a 366 horsepower Ram Air III 400, a Hurst-shifted three-speed, heavy-duty suspension, Rally II wheels (without trim rings), and various exterior dress-up (rear deck spoiler, body side tape stripe, and The Judge decals). Also available at extra cost was the intimidating Ram Air IV. The first 2,000 Judges off the line were painted Carousel Red, with paint choices expanding to any GTO color after February 1969. Judge production continued through 1971.

GTO advancements for 1970 included a revised nose and tail and an anti-sway bar added to the rear suspension. Under the hood, the low-compression 400 two-barrel V-8 was dropped just in time to make way for Pontiac's 455 cubic inch big-block. Before 1970, 400ci had been the limit for GM's A-bodies, but that barrier came down just as the corporation's intermediates were gaining some serious weight. Joining the Ram Air III and IV on the GTO options list, the torquey 360 horsepower 455 was really no match for its smaller 400 cubic inch running mates, a fact pointed out by *Car and Driver*'s staff, who called Pontiac's biggest big-block a "low-revving device that makes very little ruckus."

With the handwriting on the wall, the 1971 GTO rolled out with yet another new nose and even lower compression under the hood. Like the dinosaurs before them, the Ram Air V-8s were history, superseded by the 335 horsepower 455 HO. Standard power came from a 300 horsepower 400. Clearly indicative of the

A totally new body helped boost GTO production from 81,722 in 1967 to 87,684 in 1968, the second highest total in the eleven-year Goat run. The hideaway headlights were optional, but so many 1968 GTO buyers opted for this trendy feature that most innocent bystanders thought them standard. While the twin-scooped hood was a throwback to the original GTO rendition, the innovative, color-keyed Endura front end was typical of Pontiac's state-of-the-art design tradition.

339

times, GTO production dropped from 40,149 in 1970 to only 10,532 in 1971. That downhill slide continued as emissions controls, safety-conscious legislation, and intimidating insurance rates finally succeeded in bringing the muscle car crowd to its collective knees. In 1972, the GTO again became an optional LeMans package and a coupe reappeared as the convertible was dropped. Total 1972 production was a mere 5,807.

With Pontiac concentrating on its Firebird Trans Am, the GTO was left to flounder in the shadows, first as an almost overlooked option on the totally restyled 1973 LeMans, then as another optional package on the little 1974 Ventura—the first and only time a GTO would rely on small-block power. Although reasonably attractive and somewhat intriguing, the Ventura GTO just didn't fill the bill, and it was only right to bring the once-proud bloodline to an end.

Pontiac's popular Rally II wheels appeared yet again as a GTO option in 1968, as did a choice between standard US Royal redline or whitewall tires. Wider G70 rubber was an option as well.

Standard power for the 1968 GTO was boosted up to 350 horsepower in 1968. The low-compression, two-barrel 400 big-block was again offered at no extra cost, this time rated at 265 horsepower. Discriminating performance buyers could order the optional 360 horsepower 400 HO, shown here equipped with the over-the-counter Ram Air induction setup. Available only as a dealer-installed option (shipped in the trunk) through 1968, the Ram Air induction equipment became a true factory option in 1969.

F errari never built enough GTOs to earn the name anyway, just to be on the safe side though, Pontiac built a faster one.

—Car and Driver,
March 1964

The hood-mounted 8000rpm tach, first offered in 1967, was a popular option that perfectly suited The Judge image.

Previous pages
Introduced in December 1968, with actual production beginning in January 1969, The Judge was initially offered as a budget-minded performance package for the GTO priced at $332. Borrowing a popular image from television's Rowan and Martin comedy team ("Here come da' judge . . . "), Pontiac's brain trust originally envisioned a performance car with few frills. Relatively speaking, the first Judge in 1968 had few frills even with its standard rear spoiler and Judge graphics. The following year, however, PMD's Judge was adorned with even splashier graphics The performance imagery carried over to 1971 as exemplified by this 1971 Judge hardtop.

Rally II wheels without trim rings (to keep costs down) were standard Judge features from the beginning. This 1971 Judge hardtop is one of only 357 built, thanks to the model being discontinued midyear. A mere seventeen 1971 Judge convertibles were built.

Along with all that reflective striping, Judges from 1969 to 1971 also received a standard rear wing. Notice the engine identification on the wing, a relocation required since "The Judge" decal occupied the typical engine decal front fender location. Judge hardtop production was 6,725 in 1969 and 3,629 in 1970. Another 108 convertibles were built in 1969, followed by 168 the following year.

Other than "The Judge" glovebox identification and the Hurst shifter's T-handle, the 1971 Judge interior was identical to the standard 1971 GTO's.

The optional Formula steering wheel, first used as a 1969 Trans Am feature, had become an extra-cost GTO feature in 1970.

Left
All 1971 Judge models were equipped with the 335 horsepower 455 HO V-8 and Ram Air. In 1970, the 455 big-block had become a Judge option late in the year, joining the Ram Air III (standard) and Ram Air IV (optional) 400s.

A UAW strike in 1970 delayed the appearance of GM's totally restyled A-body until 1973, meaning Pontiac ended up breaking its traditional two-year styling cycle in 1972, relying on the same shell for the third straight year. Total 1972 GTO production was only 5,807, counting 134 coupes. For the first time, Pontiac did not produce a GTO convertible.

T he idle is a rough, rolling
bark, music to the driver's
ears and a warning to people in
the next lane.

—Car Life
on the Ram Air IV engine

GTO power choices numbered three in 1972: the standard 250 horsepower 400, the 250 horsepower L78 455, and the 300 horsepower LS5 455 HO. The L78 455 big-block was only offered with the Turbo Hydra-Matic automatic. This Cardinal Red 1972 GTO hardtop, which sports the 1971-style rear valance and twin exhaust outlets, is one of only 325 equipped with the 455 HO V-8 and automatic transmission.

Chapter 4

Pontiac's Pony Cars
High-Flying Firebirds

In General Motors' terms, its newest platform was known as the F-body, a small car with a long hood and short rear deck that was similar to Ford's incredibly popular Mustang. The similarity between Dearborn's pony car progenitor and Chevrolet's impending F-body was no mere coincidence. Roughly four months after the Mustang had kicked off the breed in April 1964, GM chiefs sent the word down from the fourteenth floor to develop direct competition. Chevy designers wasted little time copying Ford's record-setting formula. Per parameters already established by the Mustang, GM's pony car would be sporty, practical, and affordable. And also like its Ford rival, the new F-body would offer its fair share of performance potential.

On September 29, 1966, Chevrolet rolled out a pony car legend of its own: the Camaro. The race-bred Z/28 followed early in 1967, and the rest is history—few American performance machines can brag of careers as long and successful as Chevy's hot little F-body. But in terms of uninterrupted service, one macho machine stands above the Z/28, and again by no coincidence it, too, is a GM F-body.

Introduced February 23, 1967, Pontiac's Firebird hit the streets running and has never stopped. Two years later, PMD rolled out its famed Trans Am variant, a spirited, splashy road warrior that has managed to survive oil embargoes, restrictive emissions standards, and safety legislation to become Detroit's only 1960s muscle car legend offered nonstop every year from its debut to the present. (Chevy's Z/28 took leave after 1974 and returned as a midyear model in 1977.) And to think Pontiac

Essentially identical from 1970 to 1973, Pontiac's Trans Am was only offered with one powerplant, the 455 HO, in 1971 and 1972. This Trans Am is one of only 458 built in 1972 with a manual transmission; another 828 rolled out the door with automatics, a no-cost option.

That distinctive split-grille Pontiac nose, in concert with the Firebird 400's attractive twin-scoop hood, made mistaking PMD's first F-body for its Camaro cousin impossible. Popular Firebird options included the hood tach and 14in Rally II wheels (an $84.26 option for the 1967 Firebird). The Rally IIs on this Firebird are incorrect 15in versions, and the rear traction bars are non-stock owner additions.

people almost had to be dragged kicking and screaming into the pony car corral.

PMD General Manager John DeLorean had liked the idea of a small, sporty Pontiac, but in no way did he want Chevy's F-body leftovers. Having risen to the general manager's post in July 1965 after Pete Estes moved to Chevrolet, DeLorean was still a performance-minded engineer at heart. He harbored visions of a true Pontiac sports car, a dream both he and Estes had been considering since early 1963. DeLorean's ideal involved two seats, fiberglass bodywork, four-wheel independent suspension and Euro-style six-cylinder power—a low-priced Corvette of sorts. A clay model of his XP-833 prototype, later named the Banshee, first saw light in August 1964, about the time GM officials were giving the go-ahead for Chevrolet's F-body Panther project. Rolling XP-833 test beds followed in the fall as DeLorean stood steadfast—to hell with the F-body, his Banshee would be ready for production by 1967.

DeLorean's far-fetched Banshee never really had a prayer of following in the Goat's footprints as a proposal-turned-production-reality-despite-disapproval-from-the-fourteenth floor. Enough smart men at GM knew the GTO would sell in 1964; a few years later, many of those same people recognized the Banshee as a certified lead balloon. Nonetheless, DeLorean continued lobbying for his sports car and designers were sculpting on his ideal as late as February 1966, even as work on Pontiac's version of GM's F-body was progressing.

Fed up with DeLorean's persistence, GM Executive Vice President Ed Cole laid down the

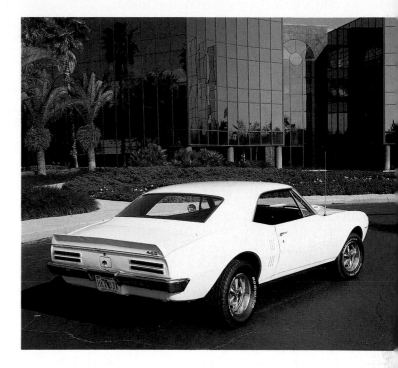

Best quarter-mile performance (14.03 seconds at 103.6mph) for a 1967 Firebird 400 was recorded by *Super Stock & Drag Illustrated*'s testers. Total 1967 Firebird 400 production, coupe and convertible, was 18,632.

law in March 1966, informing PMD's general manager to forget the Banshee and "make a car out of the Camaro." Although time was short and there wasn't all that much PMD's design crew could do to separate their F-body from Chevy's Camaro, they managed to inject enough Pontiac flair into the new pony car to give it its own identity.

Named after GM's experimental turbine cars of 1954, 1956, and 1958, Pontiac's Firebird emerged looking, understandably, much like a Camaro in the middle. Simple modifications in back helped set it apart, but the real

This fully loaded black beauty features the optional Rally II wheels, E70x14in redline tires, "HO" body side stripe, and Pontiac's trademark twin-split exhaust tips.

difference came up front where Pontiac's traditional split-grille theme was applied in particularly attractive fashion. Measuring 5in longer than a Camaro's nose, the Firebird front end offered a much more pleasing facade than the one applied to Chevy's F-body.

After selling 82,560 F-bodies in 1967, Pontiac returned with a basically identical Firebird package for 1968. Total sales grew to 107,112, including 16,960 convertibles. This droptop 1968 Firebird 400 is one of only 2,087 (coupe and convertible) built with the 400 HO V-8.

Even so, many among the automotive press were initially cool to the new Firebird. *Car and Driver* characterized it as a "last-minute Camaro conversion" and went on to report:

It was immediately apparent that a reasonably successful job had been done in giving the Firebird a personality of its own, although in profile it is barely distinguishable from a Camaro. We are confident that next year, with several months to shape the F-body to their own requirements, Pontiac's Firebird has an excellent

357

chance of turning into a wholly distinctive member of the Detroit sporty-car set.

What critics couldn't deny, however, was that the Firebird was initially superior to the Camaro beneath the skin, thanks to an engineering tweak or two developed too late to make Chevy's F-body lineup. The Firebird's engine was located farther back than the Camaro's, improving weight balance, while rear springs were reinforced with radius rod traction bars to combat axle hop under hard

Firebirds were both boulevard cruisers and strong street performers. This 400 HO-powered 1968 carries a wide range of Pontiac options, including the close-ratio four-speed transmission with its Hurst shifter and custom walnut shift knob. Also present are air conditioning, power steering and brakes, and console with Rally clock.

acceleration. Overall, the Firebird was a better handler than its F-body cousin, a plain fact that grew even more noticeable once options started piling on. In *Motor Trend's* words, "a Firebird with heavy-duty components will execute a tight corner like a young Curtis Turner on a moonlight run."

Pontiac's 1967 Firebird debuted as five distinct models delineated by underhood power. PMD ads announced that "The Magnificent Five are here," and bragged that "you'd expect Pontiac to come up with a nifty new sports car like this. But did you expect five?" Reflecting DeLorean's ideals, the lineup began with two Firebirds equipped with Pontiac's innovative overhead-cam six-cylinder, the hottest of the two being the Sprint. Standard Sprint features included the 215 horsepower 230 cubic inch OHV six, a floor shifter, and special "road hugging" suspension.

Next came the V-8s, a mundane 250 horsepower 326, followed by a lively 285 horsepower small-block for the "light heavyweight" Firebird HO. Pontiac's real heavyweight was its Firebird 400, armed with a 325 horsepower punch. An additional $616 added the Ram Air option, which made the Firebird 400's typically Pontiac twin hood scoops fully functional. Although maximum output for the Ram Air 400 remained at 325 horsepower, those horses came on at 5200rpm, 400 higher than the base 400 big-block. According to *Car and Driver*, quarter-mile performance for the Ram Air Firebird 400 was a healthy 14.4 seconds at 100mph.

Basically unchanged from 1967 on the outside, Pontiac's 1968 Firebird was updated

Introduced as both a GTO and Firebird option in 1967, this 8000rpm hood tach was a $63.19 option in 1968.

underneath with multi-leaf rear springs (replacing the 1967's single-leaf units) and staggered rear shocks to further combat axle hop. Underhood revamps included upgrading the base 326 V-8 to a 265 horsepower 350 cubic inch small-block. The 350 HO version was rated at 320 horsepower. Meanwhile, increased compression helped boost the base 400 up five horsepower and the Ram Air V-8 up ten. Also rated at 335 horsepower was a new big-block, the 400 HO. In March 1968, the existing Ram Air 400 was replaced by the 340 horsepower Ram Air II featuring revised heads, forged crank and pistons, and a more aggressive cam.

Firebird styling updates for 1969 included Mercedes 300SL-like fender scoops and an innovative, color-keyed Lexan nose. Underhood affairs for the Firebird 400 basically carried over from 1968 with the exception of the

The 400 High Output (HO) was a new power option introduced for the 1968 Firebird and priced at $350.72. Horsepower was listed at 335, **five more than the standard 400 thanks to a more aggressive cam. Compression was 10.75:1.**

even stronger Ram Air IV big-block, an $832 option that featured an aluminum intake, better-flowing heads, and 1.65:1 rocker arms.

But of course the really big news for 1969 was the somewhat quiet March introduction of Pontiac's first Trans Am, a potentially high-profile performer that, unlike its prominently promoted GTO Judge sibling, was rolled out with

next to no fanfare. Priced at $1,100, the WS4 "Trans Am Performance and Appearance" package went basically overlooked in its debut year. In all, only 697 first-year Trans Ams were built, including eight highly-prized convertibles.

Included in the WS4 package was the 335 horsepower 400 HO (or Ram Air III) backed by a three-speed manual, heavy-duty suspension, 3.55:1 Safe-T-Track differential, power front discs, variable-ratio power steering, F70x14in fiberglass-belted tires, and an exclusive, functional scooped hood (per Ram Air specs). The distinctive front fender scoops were also functional as engine compartment air extractors, as was the large rear airfoil. Polar White paint with blue racing stripes and unobtrusive "Trans Am" identification on the fenders and rear wing topped things off. Optional equipment included, among other things, the 345 horsepower Ram Air IV 400, the M20 or M21 four-speeds, and the Turbo Hydra-Matic automatic. Although few apparently noticed, the package represented an exceptionally attractive send-off for the long-running first-generation design.

As was the case with Chevrolet's Camaro, delays getting the totally new F-body to market for 1970 meant some remaining 1969 Firebirds, including Trans Ams, were sold as 1970 models. When the all-new 1970-1/2 models were finally introduced at the Chicago Auto Show in February 1970, most agreed that the wait was well worth it. Sleek, sexy, and modern, the 1970-1/2 Firebird design was suited only for one bodystyle, a quasi-fastback, leaving a convertible model in the past.

New for 1970 was the Formula 400 with its beefy suspension, rear sway bar, 330 horsepower 400 big-block, and that distinctive "dual-snorkel" fiberglass hood. Per Pontiac tradition, adding the optional 345 horsepower Ram Air III 400 made those two imposing scoops fully functional.

A step above the Formula was the second-generation Trans Am, which, unlike its predecessor, left little doubt about its presence. Featuring a fully functional body package incorporating a rear ducktail spoiler, a new set of front fender air extractors, wheelhouse air deflectors, a rear-facing "shaker" hood scoop, and a front air dam (an item strongly suggested by *Sports Car Graphic's* testers in 1969), the new Trans Am looked every bit as hot as it ran. Standard power came from the 345 horsepower Ram Air III, with the 370 horsepower Ram Air IV available at extra cost.

From 1971 to 1973, Pontiac's Trans Am rolled on in almost identical fashion on the outside, with a few changes coming beneath that vibrating scoop. Only one big-block, a 455 cubic inch V-8, was offered for the 1971 and 1972 Trans Ams, and it was also included as a Formula option. In 1971, the 455 HO was pegged at 335 horsepower. When net ratings became vogue the following year, HO output dropped to 300 horses. The net-rated 455 HO dropped again in 1973, to 250 horsepower, but a hot, new option appeared to at least partially stem the power drain.

Reaching back to Pontiac performance's outrageous heydays in the early 1960s, PMD engineers dusted off the Super Duty designa-

Following pages
Unlike the redesigned 1968 GTO with its Endura front end, the slightly restyled 1969 Firebird relied on a Lexan nose. Facing increased competition in the pony car field, Pontiac officials watched as 1969 Firebird sales dipped slightly to 87,708. Convertibles numbered 11,649.

tion for a specially prepared 455 introduced early in 1973. Available for both the Trans Am and the Formula, the 455 Super Duty initially pumped out 310 net horses, although an emissions-mandated cam change quickly dropped that figure to 290 horsepower. Included in the 455 SD lineup was a beefy block with four-bolt main bearing caps, a forged-steel crank, and excellent heads with large, round ports.

At a time when the days of the great American muscle car were numbered, Pontiac's 455 SD Trans Am served as a final performance salute, rolling out one last time in 1974 before Pontiac discontinued the 455 under F-body hoods. Called "the last of the fast cars" by *Car and Driver*, the 1973 455 SD Trans Am came "standard with the sort of acceleration that hasn't been seen in years." Quarter-mile performance was listed as 13.8 seconds at 108mph. "Just when we had fast cars relegated to the museum sections," continued *Car and*

Driver's report, "Pontiac has surprised everyone and opened a whole new exhibit." Reportedly, 252 455 SD Trans Ams were built for 1973, followed by 943 in 1974. Forty-three 1973 and fifty-eight 1974 Super Duty Formulas were also produced.

It was only right that Pontiac engineers saved the best of the big-block Trans Ams for last. Although both the Formula and Trans Am carried on into the lukewarm 1980s, it was just never the same after the Super Duty 455 came and went. But at least Pontiac had been among the last of Detroit's auto makers to give up on brute-force performance.

The Trans Am was a little-known Firebird option when introduced in March 1969. Only 697 were built, 634 with the standard L74 400 HO and 55 with the optional L67 Ram Air IV 400. Eight convertibles, all with the L74, were also produced. Loaded with functional body parts—air extractors on the fenders, scoops on the hood, an airfoil in back—the 1969 Trans Am still left *Sports Car Graphic*'s test drivers slightly disappointed. Their report complained of front end lift at highway speeds, and they wished for a front air dam. At the strip, they drove Pontiac's first Trans Am through the quarter-mile lights in 14.3 seconds.

Although steel rims and small hubcaps were standard, almost all of the rarely seen 1969 Trans Am Firebirds have the optional Rally II wheels.

Available in only one color, Polar White, the 1969 Trans Am exterior was complemented by twin blue racing stripes and a matching rear cove panel. Pontiac borrowed the Trans Am name from the Sports Car Club of America racing class , but when SCCA officials threatened to sue over the usage, Pontiac agreed to pay a royalty of $5 per car sold.

Pontiac's second-edition Trans Am featured a truly sporty interior as standard equipment. Included were bucket seats, an engine-turned dash insert, Rally gauges, an 8000rpm tachometer, and the distinctive Formula steering wheel. Choosing the M20 or M21 four-speeds typically added a Hurst shifter. Only 1,339 Trans Ams were ordered with the Turbo Hydra-Matic automatic in 1970.

According to Pontiac's promotional people, the new Trans Am nose with its front air dam and fender-mounted air extractors created 50lb of down force at highway speeds. In *Car & Driver's* words, the machine was "a hard-muscled, lightning-reflexed commando of a car, the likes of which doesn't exist anywhere in the world, even for twice the price." The ever-present Rally II wheels, without trim rings, were standard features. Only 3,196 1970-1/2 Trans Ams were built, including eighty-eight with the optional Ram Air IV 400.

The all-out Ram Air V 400 began life in 1969 as a destroked 303 cubic inch big-block intended for SCCA Trans Am competition. Rules at the time placed a 305 cubic inch limit on race-legal stock engines. The Ram Air V was never included in a regular production Pontiac for sale to the public. After Pontiac failed to build the 1,000 planned Ram Air V Firebirds in 1969, SCCA officials did away with the limit, allowing PMD engineers to continue work on a 400 cubic inch tunnel-port Ram Air V that reportedly dynoed in the 475 to 525 horsepower range. Again, regular production was planned but fell victim to changing attitudes. Offered only over dealers' counters for a brief time, the Ram Air V 400 made it into public hands as a "crate" motor to be installed by the owner.

Right
The distinctive, twin-scooped Formula 400 joined the Trans Am in Pontiac's pony car performance ranks for 1970. Total 1970 Formula production was 7,708, with this model being one of only 293 built with the 340 horsepower Ram Air III 400 backed by the Turbo Hydra-Matic automatic transmission. Testing a base 330 horsepower Formula 400 with automatic trans and 3.08:1 rear gears, *Car Life*'s hotfoots managed a 14.86-second/95.5mph quarter-mile pass.

Choosing either the Ram Air III or Ram Air IV 400 made the Formula's large, twin scoops functional. Beneath these scoops is the Ram Air III big-block, which produced 345 horsepower at 5000rpm; the Ram Air IV pumped out 370 horses at 5500rpm.

Right
In exchange for $94.79, a Formula 400 buyer in 1970 could add the same Rally Gauge Cluster tach/clock combination offered as standard equipment to Trans Am customers.

B ack when the Chisholm Trail was considered an express way, you needed 355 horses to haul the mail. We figure you still do.

—1969 Pontiac advertisement

Previous page
From 1970 to 1972, Trans Ams were only offered in two colors: Cameo White (Polar White for 1970) and Lucerne Blue. In 1973, Lucerne Blue was dropped, and Buccaneer Red and Brewster Green were added.

When first offered in 1971, Pontiac's honeycomb wheel was listed as being available for all Firebirds except the Trans Ams. The 15in Rally II wheel (without trim rings at this point) was the TA standard. Later in 1971, however, the honeycombs were listed as a $36.86 Trans Am option.

The standard 1972 Trans Am interior carried over basically unchanged from 1970. Optional equipment appearing here includes power door locks, power windows, AM/FM stereo, and air conditioning.

Were Pontiac designers optimistic or what? Detroit's speedometers didn't read much faster than the Trans Am's 160mph unit.

Right
Using Detroit's new SAE net rating system, Pontiac engineers advertised the 1972 Trans Am's 455 HO as producing 300 maximum net horsepower at 4000rpm. Basically the same 8.4:1 compression big-block offered at 335 gross horsepower the year before, the 1972 455 HO also produced 415lb of torque at 3200rpm.

INDEX